D1547948

The Accountable Corporation

The Accountable Corporation

BUSINESS-GOVERNMENT RELATIONS

VOLUME 4

Edited by
Marc J. Epstein
and
Kirk O. Hanson

Praeger Perspectives

Westport, Connecticut
London

Library of Congress Cataloging-in-Publication Data

The accountable corporation / edited by Marc J. Epstein and Kirk O. Hanson.
    p. cm.
  Includes bibliographical references and index.
  ISBN 0-275-98491-5 ((set) : alk. paper)—ISBN 0-275-98492-3 ((vol. I) :
alk. paper)—ISBN 0-275-98493-1 ((vol. II) : alk. paper)—ISBN 0-275-98494-X
((vol. III) : alk. paper)—ISBN 0-275-98495-8 ((vol. IV) : alk. paper)
1. Corporate governance. 2. Business ethics. 3. Social responsibility
of business. I. Epstein, Marc J. II. Hanson, Kirk O.
  HD2741.A282 2006 v. 4
  174'.4—dc22   2005025486

British Library Cataloguing in Publication Data is available.

Library of Congress Catalog Card Number: 2005025486
ISBN: 0-275-98491-5 (set)
        0-275-98492-3 (vol. 1)
        0-275-98493-1 (vol. 2)
        0-275-98494-X (vol. 3)
        0-275-98495-8 (vol. 4)

First published in 2006

Praeger Publishers, 88 Post Road West, Westport, CT 06881
An imprint of Greenwood Publishing Group, Inc.
www.praeger.com

Printed in the United States of America

The paper used in this book complies with the
Permanent Paper Standard issued by the National
Information Standards Organization (Z39.48-1984).

10 9 8 7 6 5 4 3 2 1

Contents

Introduction

MARC J. EPSTEIN and KIRK O. HANSON

The complex relationship between the modern business corporation and the society in which it operates has evolved continually since the modern corporation emerged in the United States during the last third of the nineteenth century. The corporation initially enjoyed significant autonomy. Gradually, in the Progressive Era, in the New Deal, and in the 1970s rush of consumerism and environmentalism, the corporation became subject to an increasing set of laws and expectations that changed its character and its behavior. But we believe that the first years of the twenty-first century represent the most intense change in the corporation's relationship to its environment ever experienced.

This set of volumes is designed to explore the new and changed state of this relationship. We believe the most important change in the role of the corporation is that, to a degree never before achieved, the corporation is subject to new controls on its behavior. The recent months and years have seen the rise of the Accountable Corporation.

Whereas one might have simply cataloged legislation and counted regulations to evaluate whether the corporation had been made more accountable, today one must examine a much wider range of social and economic controls. Traditional regulation represents only one form of making the corporation accountable. Advances in communications and information technology have made information about the behavior of corporations much more available than ever before in history. Reporters and producers are using investigative reporting and lightweight video cameras to "get" stories they never would have gotten before. The modern press and media can track the behavior of corporations as they never have before.

At the same time, the outlets for media stories have exploded. The coming of cable television has greatly expanded the space and demand for programming. Mass access to the Internet as well as the ability to use e-mail to gather more information have revolutionized the "always on" availability of information about corporations. And, New York attorney general Eliot Spitzer has shown how forensic examination of past e-mails can document corporate behaviors that before would never have come to light.

The capabilities of the Internet have also mobilized the growing cadre of citizen activists who have followed Ralph Nader's footsteps in examining and publicizing corporations' misbehavior. Today, on very short notice, activists by the thousands can be mobilized to march in the streets of Seattle against the actions of global corporations. But activism itself has changed. Whereas activism has been associated more with the longhaired Vietnam War protester, social activism today is more frequently embodied in the rise of the "social entrepreneur." A substantial new cadre of individuals has embraced a personal vocation to produce significant social change by pressuring—or starting—businesses. These social entrepreneurs, some of whom are being trained in business schools such as Stanford and Oxford, want to make corporations more responsive to the needs of society, or want to create new types of businesses that are more responsive.

We believe the modern corporation has entered a decidedly different era, one in which it must dedicate substantially more resources to being accountable, and to demonstrating to a skeptical society that it is actually more accountable. This series documents many aspects of this transition to the Accountable Corporation, presenting the state of the art of Corporate Governance (Volume 1), Business Ethics (Volume 2), Corporate Social Responsibility (Volume 3), and Business-Government Relations (Volume 4).

We hope the portrait presented in these volumes helps those leading the modern corporation to guide their institutions to become more accountable. We believe the success of the corporation in the twenty-first century depends upon how the corporation can satisfy this new reality.

We also hope this portrait can aid scholars of the modern corporation to understand how significant this disjuncture in corporate history is, and to identify avenues of research that will aid the corporate executives and citizen activists of the twenty-first century to shape the Accountable Corporation.

THE IMPACT OF GLOBALIZATION

During the last two decades of the twentieth century, American-style capitalism and democracy made great strides around the world. With the collapse of Eastern European communism in the late 1980s, free market capitalism and its vanguard—the modern global corporation—have become ubiquitous around the world. McDonald's, KFC, and now Starbucks have achieved a global presence. As if to illustrate how far things have come, Starbucks even opened a store inside Beijing's Forbidden City in 2001, only to have the Chinese Communist Party expel it after a month.

The globalization of business has helped set the stage for the intense debate over the accountability of the corporation. World Trade Organization riots in Seattle and Genoa demonstrated a pent-up frustration with the behavior of corporations and the dark side of free markets. Is globalization removing the tenuous ties corporations have had to the welfare of even their own home nations and local communities? Are global corporations now accountable only to themselves? The workings of global capitalism are seen as broadening, not narrowing, the substantial gap between the developed and less-developed world.

It is in the midst of this unease that the financial manipulations and frauds perpetrated by Enron executives and those at so many other large corporations shocked American citizens. The scandals in the United States were sadly mirrored by corporate meltdowns in Italy and France, and even in Sweden and Switzerland, where corporations were thought by many to operate with a greater rectitude.

The scandals of 2002–2005 set off a debate in the United States over how to rein in corporate malfeasance and make the corporation accountable. The Sarbanes-Oxley Act of 2002 was adopted by the United States Congress and led to extensive changes in corporate procedures, controls, and reporting. The collapse of Arthur Andersen as well as enactment of the Sarbanes-Oxley Act stiffened the backbone of the remaining large accounting firms in the United States, perhaps making them more like the watchdogs they were meant to be. In the European Parliament and in legislatures around the world, politicians are seeking the right levers to control the increasingly powerful local and global corporations.

But what are the most effective levers of accountability? Many politicians and critics of business are convinced that only draconian legislation can keep corporations in line. Others are shaping voluntary codes of behavior—on an industry, national, or global basis. Corporations themselves are creating policies and programs that express a new commitment to ethical behavior and corporate responsibility. New internal mechanisms and strategies of responsibility and accountability are being forged for the corporations themselves. But the balance between internal and voluntary standards on the one hand and compulsory legislated standards on the other is yet to be determined. And should standards be national, regional, or global, undoubtedly the balance will be struck somewhat differently from country to country and from company to company.

VOLUME 1: CORPORATE GOVERNANCE

Though we have seen accounting scandals and other violations of trust throughout corporate history, only recently have these scandals begun to impact larger sectors of the population. With increased individual stock ownership and the increased ownership of pensions and retirement funds, many more people are affected when companies fail. It is not just the wealthy, but an increasingly broad spectrum of the society that is harmed. Among these are large and small investors, employees, customers, governments, and communities.

The recent flurry of very public failures including Enron, WorldCom, Global Crossing, Adelphia, Arthur Andersen, and others have caused intense activity by government regulators, industry associations, and individual firms to correct deficiencies in corporate governance and accountability.

Given the severe reaction to recent scandals, there is no longer any choice for companies. Increased external transparency and improved internal governance are required. The Sarbanes-Oxley Act along with new regulations at the stock exchanges have mandated that. Further, increased enforcement of existing regulations and more frequent investigations of corporate behavior have caused corporations and their directors to focus far more on the responsibilities they have both to the corporation and its stakeholders. The chapters in Volume 1 address all of these issues in depth. They address how boards should evaluate their responsibilities in this new environment. The history and development of the roles and responsibilities is examined in both the United States and internationally, and current activities and trends in enforcement are discussed. Further, eminent researchers and practitioners in corporate governance both from a legal and management perspective describe the challenges for corporate directors and prescribe ways to improve corporate governance, transparency, and accountability.

Generally, we think of boards of directors as having three primary responsibilities: a) strategic oversight and guidance, b) accountability to corporate stakeholders, and c) evaluation, selection, and succession of senior management. But, how corporations can better meet those responsibilities is often the challenge. Though some have criticized various new regulations and enforcement as being more burdensome than necessary to correct deficiencies, it is clear that this has encouraged some very positive changes. For some companies, the regulations only caused a formalization of existing practices, but for many others they caused a new reexamination and dramatic changes in governance and internal controls. Recent developments have also caused corporate directors to carefully reexamine their roles and responsibilities and the processes in place in the corporations to protect the company from crises and to provide better corporate oversight and accountability.

At Enron, for example, we saw that an overreliance on trust caused cataclysmic governance problems. The board was, in our view, guilty of lax oversight of both corporate activities and the CEO. Excessive trust also caused the board of directors to relax their scrutiny of the company's operations and its financial statements. The directors were seduced by a rising stock price and impressive financial performance that they believed validated their trust. In other cases there is additional evidence that just complying with regulations may not be enough. Ticking boxes on issues of board composition or process is not enough. Corporate boards must follow the rules but must also have underlying principles of accountability guiding their actions. They must put processes in place to more effectively implement and evaluate better board performance. And, they must provide increased transparency to both corporate actions and the actions of the board. Good corporate governance improves both the reality of better corporate performance as well as the market's perception of better performance.

Though regulation may provide the outline of a solution, there is much more that needs to be done. This will require a careful reexamination of these inputs and processes that will drive improved governance. Companies need to be focused on improving accountability including both internal corporate governance and external transparency. This volume provides the latest thinking of corporate governance leaders in industry, law, and academia as to the way forward to improve the performance of both corporations and their boards.

VOLUME 2: BUSINESS ETHICS

The ethics of business has been debated since the first railroad corporation in the 1870s engaged in questionable practices. But the debate over business ethics in the United States and the deliberate management of ethics in the corporation dates from the late 1970s. Two major corporate scandals dominated the decade's attention: illegal corporate contributions to the Nixon reelection campaign in 1972, and bribery by American corporations seeking business around the world. Over 100 large American corporations confessed to making illegal political contributions, many of them "laundered" through accounts in Mexico. Over 200 large American corporations that investigated their own marketing practices abroad in the late 1970s disclosed patterns of bribery. In the wake of these two scandals, American businesses began to think deliberately about managing ethical behavior, and American business schools began to introduce the formal study of business ethics.

Throughout the 1980s, despite major insider trading, savings and loan, and defense scandals, most companies continued to believe the problem of ethics was one of insuring that lower-level employees toed the line and followed legal and other compliance standards. Rarely was it thought that the executive suite faced ethical problems. A few companies, however, notably Johnson & Johnson, reached back in their histories for statements of values, and ethical standards, and promulgated them for all employees to follow—from the executive suite to the shop floor to follow.

In the defense industry, congressional and public pressure led to the creation of the Defense Industry Initiative on Business Ethics and Conduct in 1986, which in turn led to the hiring of the first generation of "ethics officers" in many American companies. Their learning informed the work of newly appointed ethics officers and staff in other industries. Throughout the 1990s, corporate ethics programs and the ranks of ethics officers grew, but the debate between compliance programs and values programs remained unresolved.

The scandals of 2002–2005 changed the shape of the debate over business ethics in significant ways. There was no doubt in the cases of Enron, World-Com, and Tyco that it was the ethics of the executive suite and not the shop floor that was the problem. In the Sarbanes-Oxley Act and in other standards promulgated by the SEC and the stock exchanges, efforts were made to make the individual CEO, CFO, and corporate director personally responsible for the integrity of the company's accounts and behavior. The Federal Sentencing Guidelines, the rules by which judges determine fines for corporations and jail sentences for individuals, were revised in 2004 to give credit for ethics programs and for companies that did such things as assess the ethical risk in their systems and organizations. In business schools, a second wave of curriculum development on ethics and management more firmly established these topics in the required curriculum.

Business ethics was less easily embraced in cultures beyond the United States. In Western Europe, academics and a small number of corporate executives in the 1980s established the European Business Ethics Network and several national business ethics organizations, but the continent-wide debate focused more on corporate responsibility and such concepts as the "triple bottom line." In Asia, business ethics had a particularly hard time gaining a foothold in Confucian cultures or in the economic giant Japan. A few individual executives and academics there promoted business ethics based on particular religious or spiritual values.

The future of business ethics is clearly being driven by globalization and the global reach of giant corporations. There is a realization that national regulation must be aided by the corporations' own internal values and management of their behavior. The second force is the growing understanding of the debilitating effects of corruption. In the mid-1990s, World Bank studies demonstrated clearly that business and governmental corruption held up development. This led the World Bank, the world's largest lender for economic development, to establish an office and program to fight corruption. In particular countries, the problem of corruption has led to national government and business ethics reform efforts. Even in China, the problem of corruption has led the Communist Party to sanction the establishment of the first national center on business ethics and "eastern wisdom" in Beijing.

VOLUME 3: CORPORATE SOCIAL RESPONSIBILITY

The concept of corporate social responsibility (CSR) has gone through several major transitions in the past fifty years. Though the discussion over what the appropriate nature and level of corporate involvement with its community continues, the discussion about whether companies have a responsibility and whether they should be engaged with their stakeholders is reasonably settled for most senior managers and researchers. The question is no longer should companies include stakeholder concerns in their decision-making processes. The question is how to do it.

Companies question the appropriate level of engagement, how to integrate issues of corporate social responsibility into capital investment and operational management decisions. They are challenged by the real difficulties of integrating societal issues into their organizational systems and structures. They are looking for ways to better institutionalize it in both the internal and external reporting platforms and to find ways to better identify and measure the impacts of the company on society. This then leads to questions about whether social responsibility expenditures should be examined based on societal impacts or on long-term profitability, or on both. That is, when there are win-win situations, the answers and the decisions are easy. We have learned, for example, that there remain many win-win situations in business where companies can reduce environmental waste, thereby both reducing societal costs and increasing corporate profits. But what happens when companies are faced with products, services, processes, or other activities where the benefit to the company is high and there is significant cost to society? Can these externalities be voluntarily internalized? Will this occur in the short term or long term? What will be the impact on corporate reputation, and will that impact corporate profitability? How should companies measure the payoffs to both the company and the community?

Thus the discussions on CSR included in this series focus primarily on the nature of the engagement, and how to implement CSR in the corporation. The chapters provide an overview of the arguments and the development of CSR. They describe the dimensions of CSR. But, they also look forward at the future of the concept, the challenges to implementation, and the opportunities for corporate involvement in solving societal challenges.

Though there have been various starts and stops in the development of CSR, companies have recently recognized that they have no choice regarding whether to integrate stakeholder concerns into the management decision-making process. The consequences of ignoring these concerns are just too great.

As companies move forward to better integrate CSR into the fabric of the organization, the focus has become how to improve the formulation of a social responsibility strategy and how to develop the plans, programs, structures, systems, performance evaluations, rewards, and culture necessary to implement the strategy effectively. There is increased focus on how companies must more effectively engage their stakeholders and identify, measure, monitor, and report the impacts of the company's products, services, processes, and other activities on society. Both the definition of stakeholders and the analysis of the impacts must be broadly defined. To effectively implement CSR, companies must find ways to help managers better evaluate, integrate, and make the trade-offs necessary for making improved corporate decisions. Understanding how various stakeholder reactions will likely impact corporate performance and anticipating these reactions when designing and committing to corporate investment is critical.

Senior corporate managers have the opportunity to make important advances in improving the long-term welfare of both society and the corporation. They can be forward-looking and anticipate factors in the external environment that will likely affect corporate success. They can also anticipate how corporate activities will affect their various stakeholders. Through more effective management of the impacts of corporate activities on society, both social welfare and corporate performance can be enhanced.

VOLUME 4: BUSINESS-GOVERNMENT RELATIONS

The relationship between business and government in the United States has always had distinct characteristics. Put simply, most business executives have never trusted, perhaps because they have never understood, their government and its workings. Big business and the modern corporation grew up in the United States before the emergence of big government in the New Deal. A sizable segment of business executives has argued that they should be free of any government regulation and even of any taxation. Small businesses, represented in Washington by such groups as the United States Chamber of Commerce and the National Association of Manufacturers, has had a distinctly conservative tone, opposing almost all regulation and business taxation, and much of the social legislation of the last half of the twentieth century.

There are signs that American business is emerging from this dark naysaying period. Corporations are more frequently involved in collaborative efforts to find solutions to social and business issues rather than stonewalling as before. In 1954, President Dwight D. Eisenhower called a group of business executives to the White House and urged them to create an organization to educate businesses about government and about the opportunities to be involved in influencing government decisions. As the turn of the century approached, corporations more frequently supported regulatory or tax legislation, even proposing more effective ways to achieve the social goals behind the regulation. Companies partnered with traditional enemies, including unions and activists, to support or oppose particular legislation. In industries where regulation played a major role in shaping business opportunities, CEOs were hired who had a more sophisticated understanding of government and had the skills to operate in Washington.

Following the scandal over illegal political contributions by corporations in 1972, new legislation made it unambiguously legal for corporations to sponsor "political action committees," entities that could solicit funds from company executives and other employees and then contribute them to election campaigns. The result was that corporations dramatically increased their legal political and campaign activities, and corporate staffs in Washington grew apace. During the 1990s a backlash against the large amounts of corporate contributions flowing to candidates and political organizations emerged, and many different forms of legislation were proposed to reduce corporate influence. Efforts to substitute public funding for corporate and individual contributions to campaigns foundered, but pressure on corporate influence continued.

In the twenty-first century, the debate over business-government relations will address such questions as limits on corporate lobbying and contributions, and detailed disclosure of these. One of the most difficult questions concerns the impact of conflicts of interest on the ability of individuals and corporations to function as a legislator or regulator, or as a business executive.

The chapters in Volume 4 explore both the present and future shape of business-government relations in the United States.

CONCLUSION

It is our hope that the reader of these volumes will discover new insights into the future of the corporation. We are grateful to the authors of the many chapters in these volumes for their wisdom and for these contributions to all of our learning. We also have trust that the wisdom and resourcefulness of regulators, activists, and above all, corporate management itself, will shape a healthy future for the modern *accountable* corporation.

I
BUSINESS-GOVERNMENT RELATIONS IN THE UNITED STATES

———— 1 ————

The Purposes and History of Business Regulation

KAREN E. SCHNIETZ

M any managers believe the best regulation of business consists of no regulation. After all, as soon as the government gets involved in private markets, it messes things up—or so the thinking goes, especially in the United States, where business hostility to regulation is generally stronger than in many other industrialized nations (McCraw, 1984a). But this attitude is shortsighted. While there are many dysfunctional and counterproductive regulations, to be sure (Howard, 1994), there also would be no private markets in the absence of public policy. In short, markets do not exist in some ideal state of nature. They are human inventions that rely on underlying rules and enforcement mechanisms that specify property rights, correct market failures, address social goals, and provide structure to the economic game.

This chapter provides a broad overview of the main types of U.S. business regulation and their history. It also attempts to draw connections between some of the earlier regulations in the U.S. and the goals of the post-Enron reforms, particularly corporate governance and accounting measures like the 2002 Sarbanes-Oxley legislation.

CREATING MARKETS

Without a system for creating and protecting property rights, individuals would have little, or even no, incentive to invest time and resources into the production of goods and services. Imagine the disincentive a farmer would face in growing corn, or raising cattle, if the farmer's hulking neighbor simply helped himself to the ripening corn or fattening cattle whenever they were hungry, and the farmer had no legal recourse to prevent the theft. In the absence of property rights, and a relatively fair and speedy court system through which to adjudicate property and contract disputes, the farmer is out of luck, unless he is significantly larger than his thieving neighbor (and willing to fight him for the corn or cattle). Or, perhaps more germane to contemporary U.S. business, imagine the incentives of an entrepreneur to build a better widget, or write innovative software, or create the next *Star Wars* or *Lord of the Rings* movie trilogy, if the entrepreneur's less talented or lazier competitor could simply copy the entrepreneur's invention. Indeed, intellectual property rights regulations (patents, and trademark and copyright laws) are attempts to allow innovators or artists to reap the economic rewards of their discoveries or creations. Despite the goal of stimulating innovation, intellectual property protection regulations correct problems of piracy only imperfectly (Teece, 1986), as is amply demonstrated by the music, movie, software, and pharmaceutical industries, where losses to pirates are estimated to be anywhere from a quarter to almost half of annual industry revenues.

The state facilitates exchange with a set of contractual rights and a system for enforcing those rights, thus providing the foundation upon which a market economy develops. For example, contract law assures parties to private agreements that promises will be enforced and diminishes the reneging that would occur in the absence of the threat of enforcement. Indeed, the legal definition of a contract is simply an agreement that can be enforced in a court of law. Similarly, property consists of the legally protected rights and interests a person has in anything with value that is subject to ownership. Property would have little value if the law did not define the right to use it, sell it, or prevent trespassing upon it. Without a legal framework of reasonably assured expectations within which to plan (that contract and property rights provide), businesspeople would be able to rely only on the good faith of others when making investment decisions. The way in which property and contract rights are defined (and how well they are enforced) has enormous consequences for the actions of market agents and the outcomes of market transactions (Casper, 2001). Thus, the specification of property rights and contract laws are actually the most fundamental regulation of business—they facilitate and structure the very essence of commercial activity.

Even Milton Friedman, arguably the most persuasive and influential proponent of free markets and minimal government intervention into markets, grants the creation of property rights and contract law, and their enforcement, as legitimate and necessary functions of the state:

> And just as a good game requires acceptance by the players both of the rules and of the umpire to interpret and enforce them, so a good society requires that its members agree on the general conditions that will govern relations among them,

on some means of arbitrating different interpretations of these conditions, and on some device for enforcing compliance with the generally accepted rules . . . on the part of those few who would not otherwise play the game. (1962, p. 25)

Given the crucial economic infrastructure role of property rights and an efficient, noncorrupt judicial system, it is not a surprise that the first country to industrialize, Great Britain, was also the first nation to establish courts and property rights independent of the royal or ruling class. Moreover, like Great Britain, the United States possessed an early, strong common law system, a sound judiciary, and thus also the status of an early industrializing nation (Gerschenkron, 1940; Horowitz, 1977; Lazonick, 1991; North, 1990). Interestingly, the field of developmental economics recently has placed significantly greater emphasis on the importance of sound legal institutions to a nation's economic development than on foreign financial or technical assistance (de Soto, 2000; Lewis, 2004). Similarly, one of the most vibrant streams of research in the international business field focus on the assessment and management of political risks when multinational corporations enter newly industrializing or democratizing nations (Delios and Henisz, 2003; Henisz, 2000). This area of research has arisen both because of increased globalization, but also because newly industrializing nations typically have underdeveloped property rights and judiciaries, particularly relative to those found in highly industrialized nations. For example, China has been seeking to establish market-based rules for state-run and privately held companies to declare insolvency since 1994. Existing law addresses only public sector bankruptcies and puts the interests of labor ahead of those of creditors and investors (*Wall Street Journal*, 2004b). Indeed, students of international business agree strongly that the public policy environment is often even more important to the competitive environment of U.S. firms when they operate internationally than it is domestically, because there is so much variation in other nations' rules for economic activity (Murtha and Lenway, 1994; Rugman and Verbeke, 1998).

ADDRESSING EXTERNALITIES

The earliest regulations in the United States addressed two goals: attempting to constrain anticompetitive industrial behaviors, such as the development of huge conglomerates in the oil, steel, and railroad industries, and officially sanctioning so-called "natural" monopolies. The latter are addressed in this section (the former in the next section).

Until the late 1970s and early 1980s, many industries were state-sanctioned monopolies. For example, from 1938–1978, the federal Civil Aeronautics Board (CAB) controlled the commercial airline industry's routes, schedules, and prices. Similarly, most public utilities (gas, electricity, water, and phone service) were legally protected monopolies with rate regulation. The primary rationale for permitting these industries to operate as monopolies was an economic one: The fixed costs of the infrastructure for the provision of these services is so large (for example, the costs of laying electric transmission lines or telephone cables to all U.S. residences and businesses), that they could be recouped profitably by only one service provider. In industries characterized by such negative externalities, a free market would undersupply the service since multiple competitors would be unable to recover fixed costs and thus would not enter that market.

The secondary rationale for allowing monopolies in the utility industries was a social one: to price their services so that all Americans could afford them. Thus, rate regulation of utilities was driven in part by the policy goal of "universal service" in which services to people living in less densely populated parts of the country, where service provision was relatively more expensive, were cross-subsidized by the artificially inflated prices charged to people living in more densely populated parts of the country, where service provision was relatively less expensive. Thus, with the deregulation of rate regulation came significantly lower airfares, for example, on heavily trafficked routes such as New York to Los Angeles, and significantly higher airfares on thinly trafficked routes such as New York to Omaha (Bailey, 2002), and greater efficiency and thus lower prices in telecommunications (Krouse et al., 1999).

Deregulation of the former natural monopolies was spawned both by political pressures (Kroszner and Strahan, 1999), and also by new technologies that undermined some of the fundamental economics for the original monopolies. For instance, in telecommunications, new technologies such as microwaves allowed the transmission of phone calls by means other than AT&T's landlines, thus allowing a viable substitute to telephony (Faulhaber, 1987). The same occurred in electricity, where advances in electric power storage and transmission made multiple providers within a region economically feasible (Hirsch, 2002; Thompson et al., 2004). Moreover, the deregulation that swept the United States throughout the 1980s also spread internationally, particularly among nations in Europe and Latin America, where privatization and deregulation was pervasive in the 1980s and 1990s (Emmons, 2000).

Despite the trend toward deregulation in formerly monopoly industries, a great deal of regulation in those industries still exists, of course. The primary difference is that deregulation relaxed many line-of-business restrictions (such as whether local phone companies may provide long-distance service) and largely eliminated most rate regulations. Nonetheless, as legislation such as the 1996 Telecommunications Reform Act and ongoing wrangling between long-distance and local phone providers before the Federal Communications Commission in the past decade illustrates, public policy still impacts the private competitive environment of many of these former monopolies quite directly. And in some industries, such as cable, regulation still defines the boundaries of the competitive environment and which firms may compete inside those boundaries. Finally, in the commercial airline industry post–September 11, while direct economic regulation of the industry (in the form of rate and route regulation) will not return, heightened security fears appear to have expanded the future of financial stabilization programs (bailouts and loan guarantees) and security-related regulations for the industry (Transportation Safety Authority).

STRENGTHENING COMPETITION

Much business regulation is aimed at strengthening or enhancing market competition. The three most important broad forms of regulation in this area are international trade laws, antitrust statutes, and regulations aimed at correcting problems of asymmetric information, such as the Food and Drug Administration (FDA) and the Securities and Exchange Commission (SEC) are intended to do. Notably, many of the recent corporate accounting scandals stemmed in large part from a failure of accounting regulations and standards to keep pace with the changing nature of U.S. businesses, making it easier for opportunistic companies to hide unfavorable financial conditions and more difficult for investors to detect them. The bulk of post-Enron regulations, particularly the 2002 Sarbanes-Oxley legislation, falls within this broad category of regulation.

International Trade Regulation

Just as the basic rules of exchange must be established to facilitate trade and transactions *within* a country, rules must also be established to facilitate trade and investment *between* countries. Thus, multilateral trade organizations such as the World Trade Organization (WTO) are designed to enforce tariff and trade agreements among member countries and to serve as a moderator between firms and countries in trade disputes. Without such institutions, very little international trade and investment would occur. Countries would be free to raise tariff rates whenever they wanted (and most countries have strong domestic political pressure from uncompetitive industries to do so), potentially rendering a firm's location-specific investment in additional capacity for export goods worthless (Williamson, 1985; Yarbrough and Yarbrough, 1992).

One of the fundamental assumptions of microeconomic theory is that markets consist of many buyers and sellers. When this condition is met, prices are driven downward and innovation upward by the many sellers competing for customer sales. The number of sellers is expanded—sometimes greatly so—in the presence of free trade among nations. Foreign trade allows the consumers of a country to purchase products from sellers outside their domestic market who may have a comparative advantage in the production of a certain good, and thus the ability to make (or grow) that good cheaper than domestic producers can. Moreover, when competition among sellers is increased, so too is the pressure to innovate as, for example, was seen by the U.S. auto manufacturers' response to Japanese import competition from the late 1970s on

(Womack et al., 1990). Indeed, one of the fundamental conclusions of the neoclassical welfare analysis of trade is that a nation and its consumers are always made better off under free international trade (Bhagwati, 2004; Stolper and Samuelson, 1942). Perhaps unsurprisingly then, the main goal of the multilateral trade organizations of the post–World War II period (the 1934 Reciprocal Trade Agreements Act, the General Agreement on Trade and Tariffs, and its successor, the WTO) is not simply to facilitate trade, but rather to expand trade among nations (Destler, 1992; Schnietz, 2000). U.S. trade regulations are deliberate attempts to maximize consumer welfare by increasing the number of sellers available to U.S. consumers.[1]

Moreover, as many U.S. firms and the U.S. economy become increasingly dependent on export markets for profits, growth, and job creation, the importance of other countries' business regulations to the United States also increases. For example, in 1960 the United States exported only 4 percent of its GDP; by 2000 that amount had quadrupled (see Figure 1.1). As foreign sales and operations continue to generate an ever-increasing portion of U.S. firms' revenues and profits (indeed, fully one-third of *Fortune* 500 firms derived a quarter *or more* of their 2000 revenues from foreign sales),[2] and thus become more important to the economic health of the nation, international trade regulations will affect an increasing portion of U.S. business operations and jobs. Moreover, the rising opposition to continued trade and investment liberalization that began in earnest with the 1994 North American Free Trade Agreement and reached its popular zenith with the massive antiglobalization protests in Seattle in 1999, helping to scuttle a WTO ministerial meeting for the first time since 1947, also suggests that international trade regulations will continue to be a focus of great change, controversy, and importance in the near

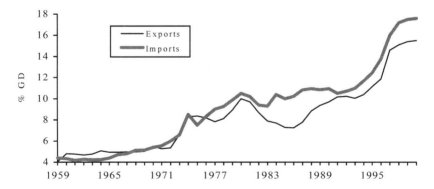

FIGURE 1.1. Imports and Exports of Goods and Services as a Percentage of U.S. Gross Domestic Product, 1959–2000
Source: Economic Report of the President, various issues.

future (Oxley and Schnietz, 2001; Nieman and Schnietz, 1999). This trend was illustrated in fall 2004 by the WTO ruling that the Byrd Amendment—whereby American firms petitioning the United States trade bureaucracy for tariffs on foreign firms "dumping" in the United States (that is, selling below the domestic firms' cost of production) would henceforth receive the antidumping duties assessed on foreign firms, not the U.S. government—was an illegal violation of international trade rules.

In the international business realm, not only do multilateral trade regulations matter to firms, but increasingly, the laws and regulations of a host country affect the decisions and profits of foreign investors. This is particularly so because countries with poorly defined or enforced property rights pose large risks for foreign investors. Contracts can be reneged upon in the foreign country with little recourse for the foreign investor. Indeed, the possibility of shifting investment terms and other regulations, and of poor property and contracts rights specification and adjudication mechanisms, are frequent difficulties encountered by firms making investments in newly industrializing nations. Broadly, political risk is any foreign government or policy-related change that diminishes the profitability or viability of a business venture. It includes nationalization of assets, refusal to enforce laws such as those protecting intellectual property, shifting contractual terms and regulations, or having an incomplete property rights and judicial system.

Many people equate political risk with a massive, dramatic event, such as nationalization of a foreign firm's assets, which fully eradicates the value of firm's foreign investment. For instance, in 1979 the assets of U.S. firms in Iran were nationalized during that country's revolution. Similarly, Conoco was forced to flee Somalia in the early 1990s in the face of that country's civil war. While episodes such as these are very dramatic, they are also very infrequent. For the most part, country leaders want to remain on good terms with the multilateral, global lending institutions and the rest of the international investment community, and rarely nationalize the assets of foreign firms. Moreover, insurance generally can be obtained to cover losses due to war expropriation and nationalization.

Although far less dramatic than nationalization of assets, shifting regulations and corruption are forms of political risk that have more serious consequences for most firms. These less dramatic forms of political risk are far more frequent, and there is no insurance a firm can purchase to protect itself from these risks. Although lower-level risks do not eliminate the entire value of a project at once they way nationalization generally does, shifting regulations or lack of access to proper adjudication of contractual disputes can increase a project's cost, lengthen its payoff period, or even slowly bleed it to death (Elliot, 1997). What all types of political risk have in common is a reduced level of profitability, which affects investors' incentives to invest.

In short, the fundamental regulations upon which markets are built matters to business in the United States, but especially abroad. And thus asserting that the only good regulation of business is no regulation is to miss a fundamental reality of all firms' domestic and international competitive environments.

Antitrust Regulation

When firms collude (on prices, product features, or market territory), the critical economic assumption of many sellers is violated, since the firms are acting in concert rather than competing against one another. The practical consequences of collusion first became highly visible in the United States at the end of the nineteenth century, when the so-called "robber barons" in industries such as steel, railroads, oil, and food processing amassed industrial behemoths with disproportionate market and pricing power (Beatty, 2001; Chandler, 1962). Legislators responded to the growing popular political pressure at the turn of the twentieth century by enacting the foundational U.S. antitrust legislation, the 1890 Sherman and the 1914 Clayton Acts, and establishing the Interstate Commerce and the Federal Trade Commissions in 1887 and 1914 respectively (McCraw, 1984b). Antitrust regulations and the agencies charged with the enforcing the law have been regularly revised with both legislation and incase law since then. While the definitions of anticompetitive behavior and the technical means for measuring and preventing such behavior have changed over the past century (largely in response to changed industrial conditions stemming from technological innovations or foreign competition), the broad, underlying goal has not: U.S. antitrust regulations promote competition and discourage monopolization. In short, they seek to enhance market competition.

Correction of Asymmetric Information

Some regulations are intended to correct the market imperfection of asymmetric information, or the imbalance between a buyer and seller when the seller has both more information than a buyer and an incentive to behave opportunistically by minimizing the risks of the product or overstating its benefits. When this imbalance is corrected, consumers generally have greater confidence in the product they are purchasing, and thus this type of regulation expands the size of the market by reducing risk and inducing more consumers to participate in an industry characterized by this market imperfection. Regulations governing the sale of pharmaceuticals and the manner in which firms report their financial status are the two most prominent examples of this kind of regulation in the United States. However, there are a myriad of state and federal regulations that correct this fundamental imbalance, such as labeling requirements and standards on weights and measures, which are not discussed in this chapter.

The Food and Drug Act of 1906 was the first attempt by the federal government to respond to the false marketing claims and shoddy (and often dangerous) product quality of the many unregulated patent medicines available in the nineteenth century (see Figure 1.2). It was also an example of business lobbying *for* regulation, in stark contrast to the accepted wisdom that no businesses actually invite regulation. However, in the case of patent medicines at the turn of the twentieth century, "honest" drugmakers—the ones who made realistic claims of what ails their medications addressed and used nonharmful components in their patent medicines—knew that the overall level of demand for medicine was being adversely affected by the many opportunistic drugmakers, whose products carried inflated claims and/or actually harmed customers more than helping them (Wood, 1985). The modern Food and Drug Administration has advanced this goal with lengthy regulations for testing and certifying pharmaceuticals for efficacy (to ensure that the drug acts in the way claimed by the seller) and safety. Clearly, few consumers have the technical skill to conduct tests of efficacy or safety themselves on the drugs and medical devices marketed by the pharmaceutical and biotech industries. The FDA approval process thus provides the correction to consumers' information asymmetry in this industry.

When the stock market speculation of the 1920s ended in the Great Depression of the 1930s, the centerpiece regulations that were intended to prevent future speculative excess were the 1933 Securities Act and the 1934 Securities Exchange Act (McCraw, 1984; Tyler, 1965). These mandated the disclosure of detailed information pertaining to the issue of new and existing securities so that investors could fully and accurately evaluate financial risks of equity investments in firms, and have been implemented ever since by the Securities and Exchange Commission in conjunction with the accounting industry's private standards–setting organization, the Federal Accounting Standards Board (FASB) (Hawkins, 1963; Loss, 1951).

SEC regulations do two things that greatly enhance the size of the market for equity capital. First, the information required for SEC filings largely filled the gap in accurate knowledge about a firm's financial health that had previously existed for most investors. Consider, for example, the incentive of an entrepreneur to keep hidden information about pending lawsuits, or prior failed enterprises, all of which will raise her cost of capital, from potential investors who would see this firm as a risky investment if they were fully informed of both the negative as well as the positive circumstances of the firm. Most firms wanting to raise equity capital prefer to downplay the risks of their operations, and maximize the likely benefits, to potential investors. Moreover, the well-documented agency problem (Berle and Means, 1932) between management and investors further illustrates the information asymmetry between firms and potential investors: Only firm insiders know if the firm is being honest in its disclosures or is shirking its efforts to put investors' interests above their own.[3] Second, the new regulations on SEC filings imposed uniformity on the disclosure of corporate financial statements that had not existed previously and thus made it easier for investors to compare the economic prospects of firms. With greater confidence that an individual firm's financial condition was being fully disclosed, and with greater comparability of financial data between firms, investors returned to the equity markets. Indeed, the U.S. capital markets are among the most innovative and vibrant in the world, and this is in large part because the U.S. corrected fundamental market imperfections in the industry early and well.

While SEC regulations largely corrected the problem of information asymmetry between firms wanting to raise equity capital and potential investors for most of the post–World War II period, one way to view the Enron-like accounting scandals is as a failure of the regulations to keep pace with the changing nature of U.S. business. Thus, most of the current standards for firm financial statements evolved during a period when the majority of U.S. business revenues were derived from manufacturing activities. However, since the 1980s, services have comprised an increasing, and now dominant, portion of firm activities, and many of these transactions are difficult to capture transparently in financial reports that were devised in another era. For example, the use of stock options to motivate employees (particularly in service-oriented, high-tech, and start-up industries) is relatively recent and, in the absence of a mandate from the SEC to treat options as expenses, their existence and cost has largely been treated as a footnote in most firms' financials, thus obscuring the true costs of compensation to potential investors. Similarly, the off–balance sheet partnerships that Enron made infamous were possible in part because of outdated methods for accounting for innovative new revenue streams. There were no well-established accounting rules for many transactions in the New Economy, creating large "gray areas" for how to account (on the part of both firms and their outside auditors) for such transactions that opportunistic managers and increasingly revenue-driven outside accounts could, and did, exploit. And, when it became apparent to investors in 2002 that the many checks and balances intended to correct information asymmetries (the "independence" of outside auditors) had failed or become outdated (many financial disclosure rules), the size of the market for equity capital invariably shrank, as all but the most risk-tolerant investors fled from the stock markets. Clearly, the recent accounting scandals illustrate well the impact of regulation on market robustness.

Unlike earlier securities regulations, the 2002 Sarbanes-Oxley Act targets not just managers and outside accountants in attempting to correct agency and information asymmetry problems, but also imposes new requirements on boards of directors. The main features of the bill are an expanded role for directors on board audit committees, a requirement that firms establish tight controls over financial reporting, new "whistle-blower" rules making it easier for employees to report questionable practices, the creation of a five-member Public Company Accounting Oversight Board to investigate and discipline outside auditing firms, and new funding for the SEC. Sarbanes-Oxley departs from prior securities regulation in its emphasis on improving governance practices and oversight, and relative de-emphasis on addressing some of the specific accounting practices that are believed to have contributed to the accounting scandals, such as treatment of stock options, disclosure of related-party transactions, and executive pensions. It is likely that these more narrow issues will be addressed by individual legislation or rule-making within the SEC. Moreover, as firms in an ever-widening array of industries are found to have misled investors on crucial dimensions of their business—such as the *Chicago Sun-Times* overstating its circulation numbers or Shell overstating its oil reserves—regulatory actions that attempt to correct the asymmetric information between investors and firms is only likely to continue. Indeed, the very recent investigations of the SEC into how the cable and telecommunications industries count subscribers (*Wall Street Journal*, 2004b), or New York attorney general Eliot Spitzer's investigations of investor-abusing practices in the mutual fund industry or bid-rigging among insurance brokers, demonstrate the ongoing regulatory vigilance that the Enron-like accounting frauds sparked.

ADVANCING NONMARKET (SOCIAL) GOALS

Finally, a large amount of business regulation is aimed at advancing nonmarket, or social, goals. Probably most well known among the federal regulations of this type are environmental laws. Pollution, of course, is the classic negative externality, where the benefits to a firm from pollution-creating manufacturing (firm-specific profits), for instance, are concentrated on that firm, while the costs of pollution are widely distributed across society as whole in the absence of environmental controls. Thus, environmental regulations, administered primarily in the United States through the Environmental Protection Agency (EPA) since 1970, have historically set limits on the pollutants facilities can discharge, and imposed fines on firms not in compliance with regulations. More recently, and in response to the increasing sense among business and policy leaders that the "command-and-control" style of environmental regulation administered by the EPA is overly costly and ineffective, environmental policy is turning toward creating markets for trading pollution allowances. For example, the EPA has recently begun allowing firms to trade the right to emit sulphur dioxide, creating incentives for interested firms to invest in sulphur-reducing technologies with which they can reduce their annual output to less than their allotment, allowing them to sell their any of their "unused" emissions to more-polluting firms (*Fortune*, 2002). This approach, like many of the fundamental property rights specifications discussed earlier, is creating markets and incentives for innovation where none previously existed and, so far, has been very successful in both spurring new environmental technologies and reducing the targeted pollutants. U.S. businesses thus should expect to see the markets for tradable pollution allowances to expand significantly in future years.

Another well-known area of federal regulation that promotes social goals concerns labor conditions, wages, and standards. Since the 1930s, the United States has imposed federal maximum hour and minimum age requirements on employers, and since the 1970s, largely through regulations established by the Occupational Safety & Health Administration, it has also imposed work condition regulations on places of employment. These regulations constrain the behaviors of employers in ways the U.S. public has demanded, such as by not allowing child labor, or enacting limits to the length of a standard work-week. Similarly, but on state and local levels, zoning laws and building codes impose regional and local communities' desires on developers by preventing such things as commercial areas from being allowed to penetrate into residential areas or by requiring minimum construction standards to prevent structural failures.

Lastly, there are many products in which free markets are simply prohibited. In the United States, the sale of recreational drugs, most body parts, and human beings is illegal. These prohibitions advance deeply held social and cultural values. What regulations of this sort share is a constraint on market boundaries (in the case of prohibiting the sale of certain items) or constraints on how business is conducted (in the cases of labor and zoning laws). They also tend to impose costs on firms that would not exist in the absence of the regulation, or at least they would be lower. Perhaps because most regulations advancing nonmarket social goals constrain economic actors, these kinds of regulations tend to be the most frequent target of criticism and political appeals for reform, at least by business. Nonetheless, the trend has been in favor of stronger controls in these areas. Politically active Americans have demanded, and received, increasing levels of environmental protection, and workplace and housing safety. There is no reason to expect this trend to reverse, especially not if U.S. per capita wealth continues to increase, and thus too Americans' ability to "afford" these social goods.

FUTURE TRENDS

With respect to future regulatory trends in the near term, strengthening the fundamental economic infrastructure of markets will remain a strong trend both domestically and internationally. However, the type of regulatory reform being sought tends to differ based on a nation's level of industrialization.

Intellectual Property Protection

Highly developed nations, such as the United States, the European Union, and Japan are increasingly proposing strengthened intellectual property protection and enforcement, both within their borders as well as internationally. This is being driven by two sources of piracy: international piracy, where commercial interests counterfeit many of the products of the music, movie, software, and pharmaceutical industries, and private piracy, which has been witnessed most prominently in the music industry by music listeners bypassing the purchase of music for illegal music file-sharing. The powerful industries that have been losing billions in revenues for years due to both kinds of piracy are pressing for stronger enforcement of copyright and patent protection at home and for expanded protection and enforcement in most developing nations, through the next multilateral trade round of the WTO (the agenda of which has not yet been formalized).

Property Rights and Agricultural Subsidies

Meanwhile, relatively economically underdeveloped countries are pursuing two kinds of regulation. First, many countries are attempting to enhance international investor confidence and thus attract investment to their economies by attempting to strengthen the property rights and courts in their countries. Until the recent scandal with Yukos oil, Russia's Putin government was widely viewed as having greatly improved the rule of law, thus creating an increasingly stable economy into which foreign and domestic investors were pouring money. Similarly, China has been making many changes to strengthen its market, from allowing the convertibility of the yuan to attempting to rein in government corruption at all levels. Second, many developing nations are seeking, primarily through the WTO, to lower trade barriers to agricultural goods in developing nations. Since many newly industrializing nations often have few globally competitive products to export outside of agricultural goods in the early years of their industrialization, the subsidies that protect the politically powerful farm interests in the United States and the European Union are particularly vexing regulations for developing nations. Indeed, much of the tension in the past half decade over the agenda of the next WTO trade round, has been fueled by disagreements between the developed and the developing nations over when and by how much developed nations' agricultural trade barriers will come down. This will continue to be an important issue in the future.

Monopoly Deregulation

In the area of regulation of formerly state-sanctioned monopolies, the trend toward deregulation, particularly outside of the United States, will continue. Indeed, a key component in the successful adjustment from socialist to market economies of the former Soviet satellite states lies in differing styles of privatizing former state-owned (and generally monopoly) industries. The countries that privatized relatively completely and early after the fall of the Soviet Union, such as Poland, now have the strongest economies in Eastern Europe. Similarly, in South America, Chile was a leader in deregulation of its industries (including even its Social Security system) and now has one of the strongest economies on that continent. Other developing countries looking for ways to spark their domestic economies often turn to the examples of countries like Chile and Poland. Moreover, this trend does not apply to developing nations alone. Japan is perhaps the most visible example of a highly developed country that has allowed substantially more competition in many of its formerly near-monopoly industries (such as telecommunications and finance) in the past decade, primarily as a way to shake off a decade-long period of economic decline and stagnation. Finally, technology is spurring the pace of deregulation and privatization. It is increasingly difficult—if not impossible—to allow monopoly providers in when technological innovations provide compelling substitutes. For instance, in the United States, the cable industry is losing its monopoly status in many areas, not so much because of statutory deregulation but because of increasing competition from satellite television and broadband services through telephone providers. Eventually, the regulations in industries like this will catch up to what the market already knows: Cable is no longer a monopoly industry.

In the regulatory arena of strengthening market competition, the United States is likely to continue adopting regulations aimed at increasing corporate financial and ethical transparency, particularly as revelations of corporate misdeeds continue to make national headlines, such as Eliot Spitzer's apparent uncovering of bid-rigging among the largest U.S. and international insurance brokers. The U.S. accounting scandals are largely seen as being the result of two related issues: SEC and FASB regulations for the disclosure of financial information that were largely crafted during a very different industrial and social era, but nevertheless defined recent U.S. public accounting procedures, and relatively weak governance and oversight mechanisms for publicly traded U.S. firms that should have brought many of the corporate abuses to public light much sooner. Expect changes, in addition to Sarbanes-Oxley, related both to increasing financial disclosure (such as the expensing of stock options) and to strengthening corporate governance by minimizing conflicts of interest (such as perhaps mandating the rotation of outside auditors every few years). Relatedly, activist district attorneys, such as Eliot Spitzer, who have strong public backing and approval, will continue to root out practices that disadvantage insiders (largely firms) at the expense of outsiders (largely consumers and clients) in a post-Enron era of heightened suspicion over corporate malfeasance. The more such scandals are brought to public attention, the more public pressure there will be to counteract the political advantage that the offending firms and industries often have over a rationally ignorant public not to change the status quo. Most future regulations in this area will emphasize heightened corporate transparency in an attempt to correct the information asymmetries between investors and firms, or firms and their clients.

Social and Safety Regulations

Finally, in the area of regulations advancing social goals, there are likely to be two trends. First, the 2004 U.S. presidential election has been interpreted as being driven primarily by social issues, that are claimed to have divided the nation into the so-called "red" (Republican) versus "blue" (Democratic) states. One such issue, with critical impact on business, is stem-cell research. On the one hand, the Bush presidential victory was seen as a strong confirmation of President Bush's abolition of federal funding for future, additional lines of stem cells. On the other hand, California voters funded $3 billion for stem cell research in a ballot initiative. Technological advances almost certainly guarantee that the United States is likely to face continued conflicting issues as the country squares off on social and value-laden issues such as bioethics and privacy rights. Second, the United States' continued vulnerability to terrorism makes continued regulation of travel-related industries (such as airlines) and many other industries (such as private flight schools), for safety purposes, almost certain.

Environmental Regulations

Second, environmental concerns will continue to dominate the agenda of many developed and developing nations. The United States' refusal to sign the Kyoto Protocol notwithstanding, the political pressure on governments the world over to constrain pollutants will only continue as the people of industrializing countries, such as China and India, become increasingly able to "afford" to agitate for cleaner air and water. Corporations from developed nations that have long looked to developing nations with laxer environmental standards and enforcement as a place to export environmentally damaging production practices will find increasing regulatory barriers abroad in the future (such as bans on manufacturing certain chemicals or products, such as plastic bags). Thus, it is likely that the firms that are now already preparing for heightened environmental standards—that are already operating above legal requirements—will face lower compliance costs than firms operating only just at the level of the law. Concurrent with rising global pressure for firms to reduce pollution will likely be the expansion of international markets for pollution trading, since this has been seen as a highly effective way to both stimulate innovations in pollution abatement as well as reduce pollution levels. Again, this may place environmentally responsible or forward-thinking firms at an advantage—firms that have made investments in environmental technologies above what is legally required may have expertise that can generate substantial revenues and profits in markets for pollution.

NOTES

1. Of course, many trade regulations are protectionist and serve to restrict the free access of foreign products into the United States. Chief among these are antidumping and countervailing duty regulations (Bovard, 1991; Mastel, 1998). Nonetheless, many political economists believe that U.S. protectionist trade laws are the short-term trade-off made to politically powerful domestic producer groups, who must be "bought off"

in order to facilitate the longer-term expansion of relatively free international trade (Rothgeb, 2001).

  2. Figures compiled from 2000 data on the *Fortune* 500 in *Research Insight*.

  3. Of course, the SEC has many other kinds of regulations intended to "level the field" between firm insiders and customers or investors, such as insider trading laws. Like accounting disclosure regulations, what these have in common is the attempt to prevent firms and insiders from capitalizing on their superior knowledge in ways that disadvantage outsiders. See also Calomiris, 2002, on changing regulations in U.S. financial services.

REFERENCES

Bailey, E. (2002). Aviation policy: Past and present. *Southern Economic Journal, 69,* 12–21.

Beatty, J., ed. (2001). *Colossus: How the corporation changed America.* New York: Random House.

Berle, A., and Means, G. C. (1932). *The modern corporation and private property.* New York: Macmillan.

Bhagwati, J. (2004). *In defense of globalization.* London: Oxford University Press.

Bovard, J. (1991). *The fair trade fraud.* New York: St. Martin's Press.

Breyer, S. (1982). *Regulation and its reform.* Boston: Harvard University Press.

Calomiris, C. (2002). *U.S. bank deregulation in historical perspective.* New York: Cambridge University Press.

Casper, S. (2001). The legal framework for corporate governance: The influence of contract law on company strategies in Germany and the United States. In *Varieties of capitalism: The institutional foundations of comparative advantage,* ed. Peter Hall, 387–416. United Kingdom: Oxford University Press.

Chandler, A. (1962). *Strategy and structure.* Cambridge: MIT Press.

de Soto, Hernando. (2000). *Mystery of capital: Why capitalism triumphs in the West and fails everywhere else.* New York: Basic Books.

Delios, A., and Henisz, IV. (2003). Political hazards and the sequence of entry by Japanese firms. *Journal of International Business Studies, 34.*

Destler, I. M. (1992). *American trade politics.* Washington, DC: Institute for International Economics.

Elliot, K.A., ed. (1997). *Corruption and the global economy.* Washington, DC: Institute for International Economics.

Emmons, W. (2000). *The evolving bargain: Strategic implications of deregulation and privatization.* Boston: Harvard University Press.

Faulhaber, G. (1987). *Telecommunications in turmoil.* Cambridge, MA: Ballinger.

Fortune. (2002, September 2). Hog wild for pollution trading, 137–140.

Friedman, M. (1962). *Capitalism and freedom.* Chicago: University of Chicago Press.

Gerschenkron, A. (1940). *Economic backwardness in historical perspective.* Cambridge: Harvard University Press.

Hawkins, D. (1963). The development of modern financial reporting practices among American manufacturing corporations. *Business History Review, 37,* 145.

Henisz, W. (2000). The institutional environment for multinational investment. *Journal of Law Economics and Organization, 16.*

Hirsch, R. (2002). *Power loss: The origins of deregulation and restructuring in the American electric utility system.* Cambridge: MIT Press.

Horowitz, M. (1977). *The transformation of American law, 1780–1860.* Cambridge: Harvard University Press.

Howard, P. (1994). *The death of common sense.* New York: Random House.

Kroszner, R. (1999). What drives deregulation? Economics and politics in relaxing bank branching restrictions. *Quarterly Journal of Economics, 114,* 1437–1468.

Krouse, C., Danger, K., Christos, C. and Carter, T. (1999). The bell system divestiture: Deregulation and the efficiency of the operating companies." *Journal of Law and Economics, 42,* 61–84.

Lazonick, W. (1991). *Business organization and the myth of the market economy.* New York: Cambridge University Press.

Lewis, W. (2004). *The power of productivity.* Chicago: University of Chicago Press.

Loss, L. (1951). *Securities regulation.* New York: Little, Brown.

Mastel, G. (1998). *Antidumping laws and the U.S. economy.* New York: M. E. Sharpe.

McCraw, T. (1984a). Business and government: The origins of the adversary relationship. *California Management Review, 26,* 33–53.

McCraw, T. (1984b). *Prophets of regulation.* Boston: Harvard University Press.

Nieman, T., and Schnietz, K. (1999). Politics matter: The 1997 derailment of fast-track negotiating authority. *Business and Politics, 1,* 233–251.

North, D. (1990). *Institutions, institutional change, and economic performance.* Cambridge: Cambridge University Press.

Oxley, J., and Schnietz, K. (2001). Globalization derailed? Multinational investors' response to the 1997 demise of fast-track trade authority. *Journal of International Business Studies, 32,* 479–496.

Rothgeb, J. (2001). *U.S. trade policy: Balancing economic dreams and political realities.* Washington, DC: CQ Press.

Rugman, A., and Verbeke, A. (1998). Multinational enterprises and public policy. *Journal of International Business Studies, 29,* 115–137.

Schnietz, K. (2000). The institutional foundations of U.S. trade policy: Revisiting explanations for the 1934 Reciprocal Trade Agreements Act. *Journal of Policy History, 12,* 417–444.

Stolper, W., and Samuelson, P. (1941). Protection and real wages. *Review of Economic Studies, 9,* 58–73.

Teece, D. (1986). Profiting from technological innovation: Implications for integration, collaboration, licensing, and public policy. *Research Policy, 15,* 285–305.

Thompson, E., Scott, F and Berger, M. (2004). Deregulation in the electric utility market: Excess capacity and the transition to a long-run competitive market. *Growth and Change, 35,* 1–20.

Tyler, P., ed. (1965). *Securities, exchanges and the SEC.* New York: H. W. Wilson.

Wall Street Journal. (2004a; June 22). Beijing to update bankruptcy law, A17.

Wall Street Journal. (2004b; July 1). SEC dials 411 on telecom math, C1.

William, O. (1985). *The economic institutions of capitalism.* New York: Free Press.

Womack, J., and Jones, D., Roos, D. (1990). *The machine that changed the world.* New York: HarperCollins.

Wood, D. (1985). The strategic use of public policy: Business support for the 1906 Food and Drug Act. *Business History Review:* ___-401.

Yarbrough, B., and Yarbrough, R. (1992). *Cooperation and governance in international trade.* New Jersey: Princeton University Press.

II
PERSPECTIVES ON BUSINESS-GOVERNMENT RELATIONS

2

Business and Government:
Friends and Foes

DOUGLAS G. PINKHAM

Business and government have had a long, tortuous relationship. Since the early years of the nation the government has regulated commerce and business practices to serve the public interest. Sometimes these efforts have succeeded and society has benefited. Other times the government has been misguided or its ideas have been poorly implemented—and the results have not been so positive.

But still the relationship endures. That's because these two institutions have enormous influence over the economic well-being, security, and personal happiness of 300 million people. And, like an ill-tempered, old, married couple, they need each other more than they are willing to admit.

For corporations, government provides stability in the marketplace. Laws and regulations are the rules for the business game; without them there can be no prosperity. For government, corporations are the ones who provide jobs, grow the economy, and, in short, give the nation the financial means to provide social services.

Yet, based on some of the antigovernment rhetoric coming from the business community and the antibusiness talk emanating from politicians, you'd think either party had the ability to walk away from the game. But nothing could be further from the truth.

As tension between government and business has increased over the years, it has become increasingly difficult to influence public policy or, for that matter, to even have one's voice heard in Washington, DC. The practice of public affairs has always been challenging. But here are some additional adjectives to describe the world of business-government relations:

• *High-stakes:* Over the last decade Congress has debated (and sometimes approved) major shifts in health care, energy, welfare, defense, homeland security, and Social Security funding policy. It has restructured the telecommunications industry. It has embraced free trade—to a point. All of these changes have created new business opportunities for some companies while damaging the financial prospects of others.

• *Unpredictable:* As the nation becomes more divided, public policies can shift dramatically when a new administration comes into office. And as presidents and governors pay more attention to opinion polls, they can reverse field faster than O. J. Simpson in his prime. In addition, the Law of Unintended Consequences says that legislation often doesn't accomplish what it sets out to do. (For an excellent look at the unintended consequences of political reform, read *That's Not What We Meant to Do* by Steven M. Gillon.)

• *Never-ending:* A legislative proposal is typically amended all the way up to the House and Senate floors and then again in conference committees. And at the end of the day, the measure may be tabled until the next congressional session—where it will be amended all over again. If eternal vigilance is the price of freedom, then eternal patience is the defining quality of the lobbyist.

• *Complex:* Since the early 1990s, state and local governments have been known to dabble in foreign policy and the federal government has—alternately—devolved issues to the states and then taken them back again. And it's just as confusing in the other branches of government; jurisdictional battles between courts and between regulatory agencies are now commonplace.

• *Chaotic:* The First Amendment gives Americans the right "to petition the government for a redress of grievances." In 2003, says the Congressional Management Foundation, the U.S. House of Representatives received 90 million e-mails from constituents who decided to exercise that right. Some congressional offices sorted them by zip code, bill number, and topic. Others read a handful and then pressed "delete." Meanwhile, more than seventy thousand trade associations, representing every conceivable industry and cause, exist in the United States to promote a common business interest. When these are added to the thousands of activist groups, unions, and corporations engaged in the political process, it's no wonder Congress has a difficult time getting anything done.

Faced with this environment, some companies have tried to stay out of the political fray, keep a low profile, and let others engage with government. They understand that government keeps the playing field level and balances various interests. But they think it's possible to run a profitable enterprise, be successful in a competitive market, and not face major public policy challenges.

To this argument I say, "Microsoft."

THE VALUE OF PUBLIC AFFAIRS

Needless to say, the pre-1998 Microsoft Corporation has become a poster child for how not to engage government and greater society in positive ways. Until the late 1990s, the company had a Washington office consisting of one overworked lobbyist and only a small public affairs staff at headquarters. It certainly wasn't proactive about building alliances and boosting its reputation among policy-makers. In the words of *Fortune* magazine, Microsoft was "famous for its disdain of government."

One of the first steps in creating an effective public affairs program is to find common ground with others who might help your cause. What was remarkable about Microsoft's approach—and the treatment it received from the federal government, the states, the media, and a lot of average consumers—was that this company had "common ground" with just about everyone in America. All of us used its software, either at home or at work or both.

Yet the company was not able to capitalize on these relationships. As a result, its legal troubles with the Justice Department and twenty state attorneys general has dragged on for years, and its senior management has spent much of its time trying to avoid controversy and make amends for past misjudgments.

Now Microsoft has, in the words of *Fortune,* "one of the most dominating, multifaceted, and sophisticated influence machines around." It has a large Washington office staff and a well-organized state government affairs operation. It also operates the Freedom to Innovate network—a nonpartisan, grassroots network of citizens and businesses that have a stake in the success of Microsoft and the high-tech industry. Microsoft and its employees also have become major contributors in federal elections in recent years.

What lessons can be learned from the experience of Microsoft and other companies that thought they could ignore government? Here are four:

1. **Big government is here to stay.** The government decides many things, including how business is conducted, who owns information, who merges or acquires another firm, and who pays what taxes. Trade wars, homeland security laws, governance rules, and other public policy directives have actually expanded the role of government. At the state level, rising deficits have caused legislatures and governors to consider corporate tax increases, user fees, and other means that would force the business community to close the budget gap. In Europe and throughout the rest of the world, international bodies such as the World Trade Organization have a growing influence on commerce. Despite what Ronald Regan and Bill Clinton said, the era of big government is not over.

2. **Brands are valuable, but fragile.** Studies show that some major brands are worth as much as $60 billion, yet antibrand activism has put many global brands at risk. A company such as McDonald's or Coca-Cola can become a target simply because it is big, successful, and familiar. Politicians, like activists, have been known to make an example out of an industry leader in order to advance a broader public policy issue.

3. **Public distrust is growing.** A 2004 poll by Harris Interactive indicates that 74 percent of respondents say corporate america's reputation is either "not good" or "terrible." But the fact that people don't trust corporations is not news. What's different now is that people are beginning to act on this opinion. Both political parties are finding it useful to accuse the other of being beholden to corporate interests. And advocacy groups that often oppose corporations carry much greater credibility with the public.

4. **You can't go it alone.** Companies that try to stay isolated from policy-makers and influencers generally find themselves without friends when they need them. They don't know legislators or their staff, they don't understand their priorities, and they have not become a trusted source of information on the impact of laws on business practices. Leading companies work to build rapport with regulators, legislators, shareholders, employees, customers, and local communities. "[The] central game of strategic management is moving from managing oneself to leading a community of allies," wrote James F. Moore in his best-seller *The Death of Competition*. "Having a business model for your own firm is not enough."

THE CORPORATE POLITICAL TOOLBOX

When most people think of corporate involvement in politics, they think of direct lobbying. Indeed, many large companies spend millions of dollars a year on efforts to influence state and federal legislation. Some of them maintain well-staffed Washington offices as well as a slew of state government relations specialists spread throughout the country.

Other companies make extensive use of contract lobbyists at both the federal and state levels. Using contract lobbyists can be a cost-effective option when legislative issues are short-term, highly technical, or involve specialized areas of expertise. However, contract lobbyists can't build long-term relationships for a company and can't capitalize on the positive reputation of a brand when calling on legislators.

But lobbying is only one way for corporations to try to manage their political environment.

A 2002 study by the Foundation for Pubic Affairs examined all of the ways in which companies participate in politics. The four most often-mentioned strategies were making federal Political Action Committee (PAC) contributions, hosting visits by public officials or candidates at company locations, participating in coalitions, and lobbying and "relationship-building" by senior executives. Other popular strategies included attending candidate fund-raisers, engaging in grassroots activism, making state PAC contributions, and relationship-building by non–public affairs employees.

These are not the only options open to businesses, however. More than half of the surveyed companies noted that they hosted get-out-the-vote drives during election years, and many firms published political newsletters, trained employees on political involvement, hosted candidate debates, or supported issue-oriented advertising. It also goes without saying that many companies get involved in politics indirectly through their regional and national trade association memberships.

Less than half of the respondents also said they made soft money contributions to national political parties—an option that has now been eliminated by passage of the Bipartisan Campaign Reform Act (BCRA) of 2002. While so-called Section 527 groups have sought to serve as a substitute depository for these large contributions, they haven't met with the same level of success with the business community.

Contributions to federal PACs, meanwhile, increased by 19 percent in 2003. This marked a return to prominence of the nation's most enduring and heavily regulated form of campaign finance.

Most PACs represent business, labor, or ideological interests, according to the Center for Responsive Politics (CRP). PACs can give $5,000 to a candidate committee per election, up to $15,000 annually to any national party committee, and up to $5,000 annually to any other PAC. PACs may receive up to $5,000 from any one individual, PAC, or party committee per calendar year.

The first PAC was created sixty years ago by a major labor union, but this method of financing elections didn't become popular until the Federal Election Campaign Act of 1974 set strict limits on both individuals and PACs. Once the rules were clarified, the number of PACs grew rapidly in the 1980s and '90s.

Because PAC contribution amounts are strictly limited and in the public record, one can argue that they provide an open window on our democratic process. By searching the Federal Election Commission (FEC) website or independent sites such as the CRP's www.opensecrets.org, you can find out a PAC's total receipts, expenditures, recipients of contributions, and major donors.

Nevertheless, the amount and extent of campaign finance contributions made by companies and their employees is an ongoing source of controversy—despite the fact that only two out of the top ten PACs operating in the 2003–2004 political cycle were sponsored by corporations. (Four were sponsored by labor unions and four were sponsored by associations.) Companies engaged in government relations need to understand this controversy and be willing and able to explain their level of political involvement to employees, the news media, and other parties.

TRENDS IN BUSINESS-GOVERNMENT RELATIONS

We've already talked about the complex and chaotic pace of public affairs, but there are other trends at work as well.

Within companies, there is an increased pressure to document the *return on investment* in public affairs. Managers and executives are being asked to show quantitatively how their efforts have minimized risk, reduced costs, or opened up new business opportunities for the corporation. Some firms—notably Eastman Kodak, International Paper, and Coors Brewing, to name a few—have formal evaluation systems in place. They "score" legislative/regulatory victories, examine costs and benefits, and/or survey stakeholders to evaluate both their corporate reputation and the effectiveness of their staff.

Companies are also struggling with managing *global public affairs* operations. While more and more corporations claim that the majority of future profits will come from overseas, most have severely underresourced their public affairs functions around the world. According to a Foundation for Public Affairs survey, nearly two-thirds of respondents rated their international public affairs capability as a two or lower on a scale of one to five.

At the same time, more and more resources are being devoted to *state government affairs*. That's because many companies are regulated substantially at the state level and all businesses are at risk for changes in state tax policies. State politicians—especially attorneys general—have also become more activist in taking on national issues (and national companies) within their own states. It's not surprising that a separate Foundation for Public Affairs study reports that many companies expect to increase resources devoted to all forms of state government affairs.

The last major trend affects all areas of business-government relations. *Internet technology* is revolutionizing all forms of politics and political discourse. It is global in its reach but personal in its touch. It is the most effective tool ever created for organizing people.

The Internet has fundamentally altered the "marketplace of ideas" in four major ways:

1. **It favors information networks over traditional information channels.** In the Internet Age, information spreads horizontally—from PC to PC—across-the political landscape. The good news is that this characteristic can harness the power of an entire online community to solve societal problems and hold people and institutions accountable. The bad news is that the Internet is full of rumor, gossip, and hoaxes that are difficult to dispel once they've been widely distributed.

2. **It increases expectations for transparency.** Journalists and watchdog groups have always wanted businesses to be more transparent, but technology placed limits on how quickly or thoroughly companies could release information. Now those companies have no such barrier. Pressure for more openness has also increased because of corporate scandals and the fact that government agencies have made great strides in their efforts to become transparent. Citizens and shareholders expect other large institutions—like corporations—to do the same.

3. **It transforms the news media.** Corporate leaders and politicians used to be able to manage the timing of news releases. Now there is no so-called "news cycle." The pace of coverage is unrelenting, with media websites updating stories twenty-four hours a day and more sites cropping up each week.

As a result, companies and government need to move quickly to get their side of the story out in front of the public. Many find themselves constantly playing defense in an effort to counter attacks from opponents.

4. **It facilitates activism.** The Internet is especially effective at helping like-minded people mobilize others to push for changes in public policy or corporate behavior. The customization and linkages possible through the Net provide tremendous tools for advocacy—especially if an individual or group wants to spread the word about social injustice. But activist groups aren't the only ones who have taken advantage of the power of the Internet to further their causes. Corporations, associations, and other business organizations have adopted many of the same tactics in their efforts to influence government policy, forge alliances, protect their reputations, or build brand loyalty.

WINNING FRIENDS AND INFLUENCING POLICY

Success in business-government relations demands a new set of skills—skills that go beyond being knowledgeable and persuasive.

Managers and executives need to know how their efforts support business goals. They need to understand how to measure and evaluate their programs—but not in terms of "congressional offices visited" and "bills lobbied." Can you prove through stakeholder surveys that you have improved the reputation of your company? Can you demonstrate that this improvement is translating into positive action? In public policy activities, can you count up your legislative wins and losses and explain—with a straight face—how much you contributed to those wins and losses?

They must have a knack for discerning which opponents to take seriously. In the Internet Age, it's easy to be an activist. (A search on Google will reveal over 1.3 million hits for the word "boycott.") But just like big corporations, some of these activist groups are credible and some are not. You can't have a constructive dialogue with a group that has a reputation for telling half truths and attacking corporate brands in order to support its fund-raising. In fact, when your company is under attack, one of the toughest calls is deciding whether to respond at all. Many corporations have exacerbated problems by calling a press conference to refute charges that few people took seriously in the first place.

They must integrate all communications functions. Fewer than 60 percent of large companies have integrated public relations and government affairs departments, yet a crisis rarely affects one constituency and not the others. Even if your organization still operates in management silos, it is possible to coordinate all communications and relationship-building activities. Many companies have integrated issues management programs that bring together staff to prioritize issues, set clear objectives, and develop complementary tactics. These tactics include media outreach, direct lobbying, grassroots activism, PAC contributions, executive speeches, investor communications, and community outreach.

They must understand how to control key messages. In a global company, it is especially difficult to ensure that all business units are coordinating their communications to the outside world. One of the negative impacts of the reengineering of the early 1990s was that many corporate staff jobs were eliminated or moved to decentralized locations. But now many of the same consulting firms that brought us decentralization are recommending that companies bring the message-development process back to headquarters. The fact is, consumers and other important stakeholders don't distinguish between the behaviors of different businesses in the same corporate family. And if one of those companies is operating unethically or sending mixed messages, it reflects on the whole enterprise.

They must develop political influence without being too partisan. Politicians often complain about company PACs and individual executives that support both political parties. But when you think about it, how much do you gain by choosing one party exclusively over the other? Yes, a lot depends on who is in leadership positions at the state and federal levels and what specific issues your company faces, but most organizations can pursue their legislative goals while keeping their political options open.

They must have a talent for synthesizing, filtering, and validating information. We are overwhelmed with information—and it's coming at us from all directions. We have plenty of access to intelligence; we simply lack the capacity to pull out the nuggets of knowledge from the stream of data. You need to position your department as the ones who can make some sense out of all the noise.

They must have an aptitude for information technology. Elections, legislative battles—and even reputations—are now being won and lost because of the Internet. Virtually every public policy or public relations campaign has an online strategy, and you can bet that all of your opponents are at least as web-savvy as you are. You need technology to build a network of supporters, communicate with thought-leaders, keep employees informed, and get your message out to key audiences. But once again, you need to take an integrated approach to technology management.

They must have a global perspective. American companies—in particular—need to learn more about the far-off countries where they manufacture or market their products and services. The concept of global corporate citizenship is not about giving away assets in order to reduce the cost of doing business. It is about creating win-win relationships with local communities and entire nations so that everyone benefits from economic growth. And that takes specific knowledge of a country's specific issues. Companies also need to understand multilateral organizations and the differences among various political and social systems.

Most of all, business-government relations professionals need to remember that no amount of technology or management expertise will take the place of the ability to sustain strong personal relationships. If you want to be taken seriously in a public policy debate, you need a reputation for intelligence and credibility. In fact, the more political leaders and other stakeholders are deluged with news and opinion, the more they come to trust those whom they respect on a personal level.

The job of the business-government relations professional is to earn that trust. If you succeed, you will be much better equipped to manage crises, get your message across, and improve your company's political environment. If you fail, then you have put yourself—and your company—at a distinct disadvantage.

3

Government's Role in Regulating Business Ethics

A SPEECH BY ELIOT SPITZER

Eliot Spitzer, New York State attorney general from 1999, has sought to make New York a national leader in investor protection, environmental stewardship, labor rights, personal privacy, public safety, and criminal law enforcement. Several of his most significant investigations have sought reform of the nation's financial services industry. He has forced companies in several industries to pay huge fines.

A candidate for New York governor in 2006, Spitzer is running on his understanding of the need for integrity in business and the need for regulation and enforcement by government. In this speech to the National Press Club on January 31, 2005, Spitzer makes the case for government regulation of corporate behavior. In doing so, he provides an analysis of the specific corporate scandals he prosecuted during the 2002–2005 period. He is highly critical of both businesses and of federal regulators whom he believes failed the public.

What I want to do today is begin by sort of throwing out a few facts that I think I can then tie together and try to frame a political debate that we are in the midst of. And it's an enormously important political debate, and it relates to a critical issue, which is the government's role in regulating and controlling and defining the parameters of appropriate business behavior. And the facts that I want to begin with are, I think, beyond dispute.

The first is that the business leadership in the nation right now is pushing back against the effort to ensure codes of conduct, ethical behavior; objecting to Sarbanes-Oxley, objecting to the SEC's effort to mandate disclosure and certain behavior patterns. The business leadership is saying, "Enough. We got the lesson. Back off."

Second, the Chamber of Commerce, which is the U.S. Chamber, which is perhaps the preeminent [voice], or styles itself as the preeminent voice for business leadership, is going to court to challenge the SEC's capacity to issue the regulations relating to mutual funds, board behavior, accounting rules, and other like series of rules that the SEC believes are essential to ensure integrity in the capital markets.

Third, the president of the Chamber of Congress, in a rather direct attack on the cases that my office has made, said recently that he felt that we were targeting individuals for honest mistakes. . . .

And fourth, there has been an enormous effort, sponsored by some of the business leadership, to preempt states, and my office in particular, preempt us from our capacity to bring the types of cases that we have been bringing over the past number of years.

Now, what is this all about? Really, this is a debate about the role government should play in defining the boundaries of appropriate business ethics; defining what it means to participate in our economy and what the expectations are for our business leadership, and who is supposed to enforce those boundary lines.

Now, the interesting thing about this debate is that everybody invokes the same heroes. Everybody these days, and for good reason—maybe it's because of the biographies that have just been written—harkens back to Alexander Hamilton, everybody harkens back to Teddy Roosevelt. These are the two icons, the two individuals whom we all embrace and say they understood what government should do, they understood how the economy should function, they understood how to make the marvel of the private sector generate the wealth that we so desperately want.

Now, the interesting thing is that a hundred years ago is when Teddy Roosevelt was running and was elected president, of course, and he assumed the presidency after the assassination of McKinley, so he didn't run for the presidency in 1900. But in 1904 . . . , when he ran for the presidency, he had just had a term, or a first couple of years, where he had become the scourge of business. Teddy Roosevelt had attacked the cartels, attacked illegal behavior, and he was reviled by business leadership.

So the irony is that those who now invoke him, if they actually looked back at what he did and what their predecessors in the business community said about him a hundred years ago, perhaps would rethink their holding him out as an icon. And if any of you were to listen to the few remnant speeches that he gave that are on tape . . . [you'd hear the] remarkable things that he was saying about the failure of ethics in the business leadership and the perverse effect on our economy of the cartels that he was pursuing.

Now, today, a hundred years later, nobody disputes that what he did a hundred years ago was not only beneficial for the economy but was absolutely necessary, and that if he had failed to attack the cartels, attack the illegal behavior, failed to open up the economy to permit true competition, then we would not have had the enormous growth that came after Teddy Roosevelt.

I would suggest to you that today we're in the midst of the same debate that occurred a hundred years ago; that what we have on one side is a business leadership that cloaks itself in the language of this free market, but really wants to preserve an ossified system, and they want to act against those who really support competition, transparency, and integrity.

On my side of the aisle, I would suggest to you [that] we have folks who really understand the market, who understand what it takes to permit the market to generate the wealth that has created this marvelous economy that we have, and understand that government must step in every now and again to define the boundary lines and ensure that there is indeed integrity, transparency, and fair play.

What I want to do is run through a few of the cases that we have made in my office and use them . . . in the following way. I want to briefly lay out the facts and then ask what was the response of the other side. How did those who pretend to be the voice of the free market, who pretend to be voices for letting our economy generate the jobs, how did they react when there was evidence—overwhelming evidence—of illegality and impropriety?

ANALYST SCANDALS

The first case was the analyst case. . . . It became eminently clear that the analysts on Wall Street were distorting and misrepresenting their true opinion of stocks in order to encourage folks to buy stocks. Why? Because there is an inherent conflict of interest in the business structure of the major investment houses; and by hawking the stocks and giving them strong buys, they could persuade the issuing companies to bring their underwriting business to the investment banks, and that was ultimately a much more lucrative stream of income.

In other words, they subverted their desire and their obligation—their fiduciary obligation to give honest advice to the investing public—to their desire to get the underwriting business. And as a result, we had an overwhelmingly affirmative, positive report on all sorts of of companies that never should have been taken out into the marketplace in the first instance, and we had a bubble.

Now, we began to reveal the evidence of this underlying problem. And it was rather vivid evidence in the form of e-mails and [more] e-mails. And why anybody still writes those things down is beyond me, but please keep doing it. We need it. It's good evidence. And so we encourage you to keep going in that direction. But when we began to uncover this, Mr. Grubman—and I don't often quote Jack Grubman, who is one of the analysts who were caught in the vortex of this—had made one observation that really captured the problem. He said of his profession, "What used to be viewed as a conflict of interest is now viewed as a synergy." Think about it. They had so rationalized their worldview that, even understanding the inherent conflict of interest, they now said, "Well, but it's a synergy, because we can make money on both sides of the transaction," and they didn't want to own up to the inherent nature, perfidy, of what they were doing.

Soon, before we filed the case, we were negotiating with one of the major companies, trying to resolve it in a way that would get the injunctive relief, the reforms that we wanted, and the lawyer for the other side said something to me that was very revealing and true. He said, "Eliot, be careful. We have powerful friends."

Now, I don't know if he meant this as a threat. If he did, it didn't work. But he was correct. I didn't realize it at the time, but they do have powerful friends. And the "we" that he was referring to probably was just the investment banks, but writ large what he was saying was that the existing system has many powerful friends because the status quo always has powerful friends. Those who benefit from the status quo never want change. And as we have found out as we have moved forward, the impediments to change have been enormous. And only facts in due course will overcome it. But that was only the first interesting interchange.

We charged the company, because having been told "we have powerful friends," I had no choice but to file the lawsuit. I mean, what am I going to do, back down then, and say, "Oh, now you tell me? If you had only told me that last week, we wouldn't be here."

So we filed the case, and then the lawyers for the company come into my office. And what did they say? Now, you all in this room know high-priced lawyers. You know what they're supposed to say: "You don't understand the sector." "You're taking the evidence out of context." "You don't really mean that." "We're nice guys." They didn't say any of that. They said, "You're right, but we're not as bad as our competitors." Now, how is that for a defense? Think about it. Isn't that wonderful? You know, I have three daughters. Even my daughters don't try that defense. And even in an era of moral relativism, it doesn't work.

But once again, they were right. They were right at several levels. Not only were they not as bad as their competitors, which is what we found out, and that's what led to the global deal every major investment bank signed on. But they were right in a more subtle way that every one of the investment banks knew what the other investment bank was doing, or banks, plural, were doing. And rather than collectively get together and say, "You know what, guys. There's a problem here. This is behavior that we really aren't proud of," and elevating their standards through self-regulation or a discussion about what proper standards should be in the industry, every one of them sank to the lowest common denominator. That was important to me, because we found out not only that they knew what the behavior was, knew that it was a conflict, but met the conflict by saying, "We've got to be as devious in how we take advantage of it as our competitors," it reinforced in my mind the notion that we had to step in and do something.

So what happened when we stepped in? Well, what happened was fascinating. I called some of the other regulators in, and I said to them, here's some ideas [about] how we can remedy this problem pretty quickly. And the other regulators said to me, "No, we can't do that," even though they were simple ideas, things that ultimately were made part of the global deal. And I said, "Why not?" And they said the industry won't like it. And I looked at them quizzically, and I said, "Well, so what. It needs to be done." That was the mindset of the regulator community.

Indeed, you know somebody with whom I've locked horns occasionally, Mr. Pitt, [who] was chairman of the SEC for a period of time. Harvey was a fine lawyer. I don't think he understood his job, unfortunately. Harvey Pitt was aware of this problem. He convened a meeting of the CEOs of the major investment houses on Wall Street with the chairman of the New York Stock Exchange. He called them together for the express purpose of remedying the problem of flawed, structurally flawed, analytical work that was being distributed to tens of millions of Americans. But what did he say in his invitation to them to join him for this meeting? "This isn't my problem," he said. "I will leave it to you."

Something that went to the fundamental core of the integrity of the marketplace, and the fact that tens of millions of investors were investing based on knowingly wrong analytical work, he said, "It's not my problem." And that was terrible.

And then worse than that, when the self-regulatory bodies that were supposed to do something about it did absolutely nothing, the SEC under Mr. Pitt went up to Capitol Hill to support a preemption bill that would have precluded my office, that was trying to address this problem, from looking into the problem. So he wouldn't do anything about the problem, but he would support a bill to put handcuffs on the ability of those offices that wanted to pursue it.

Now, the obvious harm that we all understand that resulted from this scandal was that tens of millions of Americans were investing based on bad advice. The other problem that is less often thought about is the misallocation of capital that resulted. If you were to go to AT&T and say to them, "Do you remember that era when WorldCom was getting all those wonderful analytical reports from Jack Grubman and everybody else, and everybody was saying, 'Oh, WorldCom is the future of investing, and Enron,' and you at AT&T or other companies couldn't compete with their numbers?" Now we know why. They were frauds.

And so it's not just that investors were hurt. Companies that were trying to compete for capital, that were reporting honest numbers, that weren't playing the game in the same devious way, were at a competitive disadvantage and consequently had trouble getting access to the capital that they needed.

And yet what did the government—those who pretend to speak for the free market—do? Nothing—and tried to put handcuffs on us.

MUTUAL FUND SCANDALS

The mutual fund scandal is the second sort of case or set of cases that people have paid attention to. Same story. We revealed that there was a significant problem, a trio of problems: timing, late trading, and fees that were driven higher by a failure of fiduciary duty by boards simply to pay attention and do what they were supposed to do.

What has the response been? The response was [that] once again the SEC ran to the Hill and supported a preemption bill. Worse than that, the SEC, when we tried to say to the mutual fund companies, "The failure of your board to live up to its fiduciary duty has generated a delta, a gap, between the fees that should be charged and the fees that are being charged, and it's measurable," and we went to the mutual fund companies and asked them to calculate it, hundreds of millions of dollars a year from one company alone, the SEC disagreed with us and said you can't get into that issue, that's price-fixing. It had nothing to do with price-fixing. It had simply to do with our effort to say to boards of directors: Live up to your fiduciary duty; understand whom you represent and what you have to do to provide integrity in the marketplace.

And where had the SEC been as this enormous scandal in the mutual fund industry unraveled? Nowhere. Nowhere. It was readily apparent, and yet they were nowhere. And that is one of the scandals that is simply out there. And, of course, the *Wall Street Journal*, that paragon of free market double-talk in its editorial page, attacked us, attacked us for actually daring to get into the sector to try to unravel the massive conflicts of interest that existed.

And mind you, keep in mind, $70 billion a year is what the mutual fund companies derive in fees—fees—for managing the mutual funds that are out there. Seventy billion a year in fees. If fees are 10 to 20 percent higher than they should be—which is a conservative estimate—think how much it is costing investors every year. These are enormous, enormous numbers.

INSURANCE SCANDAL

Insurance. Some of you may know the insurance issues that we revealed publicly last October. We settled with Marsh [MMC] this morning, a settlement that I think is wonderful in many respects, not only $850 million, but there's new leadership of the company; there is an entirely new business model that is predicated upon disclosure and transparency so that those who buy insurance in this nation will no longer be victimized by contingent payments that drove premiums up by a significant margin. This is a significant step forward.

But again, what was the response of the Chamber of Commerce? These were just "honest mistakes." Well, "honest mistakes" that already have six guilty pleas; more to come very shortly, many more to come down the road. "Honest mistakes" that constituted bid-rigging and outright deceit and fraud to the point where Marsh [MMC], to its credit—there's now a new Marsh [MMC], and I think this is really a turn for the better—they issued a statement today, as part of the settlement, apologizing, acknowledging that the actions of the individuals, their employees, and others at other companies was unlawful and was shameful.

These were not honest mistakes.

You know, there was a wonderful column in the *Wall Street Journal* written by some apologist or other—I forget whom—in which he said the mistake of these CEOs is not to realize that in the post-Enron era, bid-rigging is unacceptable. Well now, you know, you don't have to be an antitrust scholar to know that bid-rigging was unacceptable even before Enron.

Again, these are the voices of the free market. But they're not. They're the voices for ossification and stagnation.

Now, one footnote to the insurance issues. The president of the United States, whom we all respect, is out there right now attacking the many problems that drive premiums higher. And there are problems, many of them, there are a multitude of problems. I have not heard a single world from the White House saying maybe premiums are higher because the insurance companies formed an illegal cartel. They've pled guilty to it. The record is overwhelming. It is out there. Not a word. Not a single word. Everybody else is the causative factor. The insurance industry has corruption that is rife throughout it, rife. It touches every line of insurance that is purchased, every line. And we will keep going until we find it.

ANTIDEPRESSANTS

Another case that we made, the Paxil case, pharmaceuticals. Not to bore you with details, but Paxil was a drug that was being prescribed for off-label use to adolescents, and GlaxoSmithKline, the company that makes it, was saying to the world it is "safe and efficacious." Those are their words. Well, the problem is, they had done five studies. One of them found it was marginally better than a placebo. The other four found in combination either that it was no better and/or that it generated suicidal tendencies among adolescents. Did they tell people that? No, they didn't. If I were a parent of an adolescent who had been prescribed this drug or if I were a doctor considering whether or not to prescribe it, I would want that information.

So we sued them. We sued them not to say take the drug off the market; that's not my prerogative, it shouldn't be my decision. We sued them on the theory that the information, the clinical testing data, should be revealed to the public. And we said simply create a website, post this data so that people will have a full array of information so they can make informed judgments. And they agreed, of course. They agreed. They said fine, and that website now exists. And Forest Labs has agreed to do the same thing, and other pharmaceutical companies are getting pressured to do the same thing because it makes sense, getting pressured from the medical journals and the doctors who do the testing because it makes sense.

Two observations.

Where has the FDA been on this issue? Nowhere. Silence. It's simply a matter of decency, disclosure, and integrity, and yet this FDA has not said a word about revealing this critically important data so that doctors can make informed judgments.

And not to come back to my favorite editorial page, but the *Wall Street Journal* editorial page, in an editorial where they called me "Paxil man," which I thought was, you know—I don't know how to take it, but there I am—they said, and this is a quote, they said, "The system is working exactly as it should." A system which is denying doctors and patients the critically important information about the known side effects of these drugs? And look at the array of testing data that has since come into the marketplace that has led to changed decisions about what pharmaceuticals should and should not be out there in the marketplace. And yet they, the paradigm of honest and integrity in the free market, said, "The system is working exactly as it should." Ridiculous. Flat-out ridiculous.

PREDATORY LENDING

The last case I want to refer to…is an issue of predatory lending. See, it isn't just financial services. It's pharmaceuticals, it's all over the lot. Predatory lending, where—which—we all know access to capital is hugely important.

Poor fellow who lives in Rensselaer County—which, for those of you not from New York, is a wonderful county just east and southeast of Albany, up the Hudson Valley—poor fellow thirty years ago—remember the number thirty—thirty years ago took out a twenty-five-year mortgage. Took out a twenty-five-year mortgage, there were automatic deductions from his checking account and he made them. They were made automatically.

A year or two ago he woke up and he hadn't really paid attention—he'd been divorced and the mortgage had been bought and sold by a couple companies, securitized as we all know these things are—he woke up and he said, wait a minute, why are they still deducting money from my checking account? A fair question to ask. So he called the bank and the bank gave him a brush-off. He got a lawyer and the lawyer called the bank and the bank gave the lawyer a brush-off. So the lawyer called my office and said, "Maybe you can help us. Maybe they'll pay attention. You know, supposedly people return your phone calls at least"—which, you know, most of the time they do.

And so we called the bank's office and we said, "We think there's a problem." What did we hear back from the bank? They left us a voicemail. It's a wonderful thing, you know, as good as an e-mail. They left us a voicemail, in which they said, "We don't need to answer your questions anymore. The Office of the Comptroller of the Currency (OCC) has told us we can ignore state attorneys general." Why? Because the OCC, in an effort to get banks to move their charter from the state to a federally chartered situation, has offered them preemption—preemption from basic laws, such as complying with mandates against predatory lending. That's what the OCC is doing.

Is the OCC pursuing aggressively cases of predation, predatory lending? No. They'll pretend they are, but they're not. They're extending preemption to banks, handcuffing those of us who are trying to address a critically important issue.

RESPONSE TO CRITICS

Now of all the attacks that have been made on my office for overreaching, for not understanding, whatever the multitude of attacks have been, a couple things that are critically important:

First, not once has the other side said, "You are wrong on the facts." Not once. And the fact of the matter is, you know—and I hope I don't live to regret this comment—we haven't been wrong about the facts we've alleged in these cases. The other side has settled—sides have settled because of it. They've acknowledged the improprieties, as Marsh did today, and Merrill Lynch did, as Goldman Sachs did, Credit Suisse First Boston (CSFB), every one of them. They've acknowledged it, because they understand what's going on.

But those who supposedly speak for the private sector, for the free market, are receding into a shell of ossification, pretending that these issues should not be addressed.

So here's question two. Does anybody out there really believe that the market is better off with those problems, before we revealed them? Does anybody want to go back to an era where this problem of conflicts and analysts—contingent overrides that had bid-rigging in the insurance business; a failure to reveal that Paxil had side effects—does anybody want to go back to that world, just as would anybody want to go back to the world before Teddy Roosevelt, where we broke up the cartels? I think not.

And so even though those who pretend to speak for the free market kick vigorously against us when we reveal these problems, and pretend that somehow we're the ones who are overreaching, the reality is that the market survives only because we reveal these problems, make them eminently clear, and try to confront them in a very real way.

So this has led me to the rule that I have come to live by, which is that only government, at the end of the day, can indeed enforce rules of integrity and transparency in the marketplace. That comment "We're not as bad as our competitors" was too correct. They, unfortunately, will descend to a lowest common denominator. And if we believe that the market depends upon integrity and fair dealing, government must step in to make these cases and make sure that the rules are honored.

Now there are two corollaries to this. The first is that self-regulation has failed. And I say that with real disappointment. We've gone through, in many respects, a legitimate era of deregulation, where an overreaching government bureaucracy has been pulled back. And we were told, "Don't regulate us. We will regulate ourselves. Self-regulation is the answer."

In not one of the instances in which we have uncovered fraud, in not one has a self-regulatory entity stood up to say, "We have a problem here." And I mean not only the NYSE or the other securities self-regulators, but also the industry bodies, the ICI [Investment Company Institute], the AICPA [American Institute of Certified Public Accountants], the SIA [Securities Industry Association]—filled with well-meaning people, but they didn't have the fortitude, even though they understood the problem, to stand up and say, "We have a problem here." And the ICI was professing the purity of the mutual fund industry up until the day that these problems were revealed.

So the first corollary to the rule is self-regulation has failed.

The second corollary. . . . There has been such a failure to adhere to notions of fiduciary duty in every sector we've looked at. That was true with investment banks, mutual funds, insurance agents, and pharmaceutical companies. The failure to adhere to these concepts of integrity is the thread that runs through everything that we have seen. So let me ask a couple questions to those who pretend to be the voices of the free market but are not.

First, how much capital has been misallocated by virtue of what they have done? How much capital would have gone into IRAs and 401(k)s had there not been the bubble that was created by analysts that then generated the enormous losses? How much shareholder equity has been diluted because CEOs have given themselves not only enormous options—which are to a great extent unjustified, in my view—but also change-of-control provisions?

There [was] an article on the front page of the *Wall Street Journal* . . . about change-of-control provisions and the payouts that will be triggered by some of the mergers that are now being discussed in the marketplace. What possible argument is there that a CEO needs a trigger to options or a straight grant of stock merely because they make a decision—that they're suppose to make anyway in the best interest of the shareholder—to merge the company, sell it, or not sell it?

Those trigger this massive dilution of real shareholder equity? What possible justification can there be in an era—in an era between 1980 and the present—when the ratio of CEO comp to the ordinary employee's comp has gone from 43-to-1—43-to-1—twenty-plus years ago, to 530-to-1—530-to-1. Even those who are on the other side have to admit that this is not a viable structure.

Now there are other rules that we have discerned over time that relate to why and when the government should step in, relating to externalities, relating to core values. Because I enjoy the back and forth and the questions with you, I will not go into them other than to make one very quick observation about the third rule. The second rule relates to externalities and why we enforce the environmental statutes, which are a perfect example of it.

The third rule relates to core values. Why does government have to pass laws relating to discrimination and the minimum wage? Because the marketplace alone simply won't get us there. If you ask yourself this question: Before the civil rights statutes of the mid-1960s, had the market alone begun to eliminate discrimination based on race or gender? No. It hadn't. Creating those causes of action and giving government the right to enforce a core value that we believe, which is that there should not be discrimination, is what changed the system.

Do we believe that somebody who works a forty-hour week should be able to live at the poverty line or higher? We do. But if we didn't have a minimum wage, would that be the case? No, it wouldn't be. And that is why there is this consensus that these laws are appropriate and important.

Now I'm not going to go on at length about these. Time is too precious right now. Let me just conclude with one observation.

These issues are more than an abstraction. They affect real people, whether it's the people whose money was lost, the people who were given an improper pharmaceutical, the businesses that couldn't afford to get insurance because the impropriety drove insurance premiums up. Real people are affected.

4

Can Business Help Governments Change the System?

SEB BELOE, JOHN ELKINGTON, and JODIE THORPE

THE NEED FOR GOVERNANCE

Five years ago, UN secretary-general Kofi Annan called on business leaders "to join the United Nations on a journey." He also commented that business was already well down the road with a journey of its own, globalization. At the time, globalization appeared like "a force of nature," seeming to "lead inexorably in one direction: ever-closer integration of markets, ever-larger economies of scale, ever-bigger opportunities for profits and prosperity." However, even ten months before the Seattle protests against the World Trade Organization (WTO), the secretary-general felt it necessary to also warn that globalization would only be as sustainable as its social foundations.

"Global unease about poverty, equity and marginalization," he stressed, "are beginning to reach critical mass." These issues are no less important today, although some focus has shifted to political and security concerns in the wake of 9/11, Iraq, and Madrid—which, some would argue, are intimately connected to unresolved problems of poverty and inequity. Slow progress on the Kyoto Protocol, the limited political traction achieved by 2002's World Summit on Sustainable Development, and the collapse of the Cancún trade talks all underscore the complexity of the challenges we face.

This chapter looks at the emerging agendas for both business and governments. It is based on the report "Gearing Up: From Corporate Responsibility To Good Governance and Scalable Solutions" prepared by SustainAbility for the United Nations Global Compact (see www.sustainability.com/publications/gearing-up). The "Gearing Up" project was guided by a steering group and informed by a mixture of desk research, interviews, surveys, and case studies, which formed the backbone of the research.[1] In this chapter, we quote several of the interviewees, while the appendix outlines our four case studies on climate change, health (including HIV/AIDS and chronic illnesses like Type 2 diabetes), and corruption. The focus on these three areas does not imply that they are the most critical issues we face, although all are important and involve significant scalability[2] issues. Instead, they were chosen as areas where corporate responsibility initiatives seem to be building momentum—initiatives that could help us explore the role of business leadership in preparing the ground for wider policy change.

CORPORATE RESPONSIBILITY, AND A PARADOX

In what follows, we make extensive use of the term "corporate responsibility" (or CR). By this we mean an approach to business that embodies open and transparent business practices, ethical behavior, respect for diverse stakeholder groups, and a commitment to add economic, social, and environmental value.[3] There is a sense, however, that the current approach to CR may be reaching its system limits. While a small but growing number of bold and visionary companies have made considerable strides and are to be commended for their achievements, their numbers will remain small as long as the business case[4] for getting in front of the corporate pack remains weak.

To take a few simple examples:

• Du Pont has achieved its target of reducing greenhouse gas emissions by 65 percent from 1990 levels. Nevertheless, absolute global CO^2 emissions have increased 8.9 percent since 1990, compared with the 60 percent reduction the Intergovernmental Panel on Climate Change has called for by midcentury.

• DaimlerChrysler South Africa provides HIV/AIDS care and treatment to employees and families—with insurance benefits for up to 23,000 people. Yet overall in the world's poorest countries, less than 10 percent of the 6 million people who need antiretroviral medicines currently get them.

• Due to its antibribery policy, BP dismissed 165 people and terminated 29 contracts with third parties in 2003—yet globally, corruption is proving an intractable challenge.

• While some food and beverage companies are beginning to assess their contribution to obesity and chronic disease, Type 2 diabetes—strongly linked to obesity—is rapidly emerging as a global pandemic.

Resolving major sustainable development challenges will likely require a much more systemic approach involving business alongside government and civil society.

The problem, however, revolves around a central paradox with two main dimensions. First, the voluntary CR movement has evolved as a pragmatic response to pressing environmental, community, or human rights issues.

Companies are being asked to address problems and even deliver public goods because governments have been unable or unwilling to do so. But second, because of the weakness—or absence—of appropriate governance systems, CR initiatives are generally disconnected from wider frameworks. As a result, they are at risk of amounting to little more than drops in the ocean when compared to the scale of the challenges. At worst, they may even undermine long-term solutions by deflecting attention from the root problems.

This chapter thus focuses on three questions:

- Does CR have the capacity to deliver real progress on sustainable development?
- Where do governments fit into the CR puzzle?
- Can business play a constructive role in governance by preparing the ground for wider policy change?

Critically, as some of our respondents noted, and a point we strongly endorse, the challenge is not to get companies to take on the responsibilities of governments but to help ensure governments fulfill their own responsibilities. Our case studies (see appendix) all underscore the crucial roles that governments must play, whether in setting the course, developing incentives, or generally helping to create a stronger business case.

We recognize the complexity of the world we are attempting to describe. Clearly none of the key actors we refer to—business, government, or civil society—are homogeneous. And their specific contexts and challenges change at the global, national, regional, and local levels. In addition, involving business in governance is likely to be most straightforward where existing institutions are strongest, especially in the world's well-established democracies. Where governance institutions are weak or absent, there is the greatest potential for relationships between business and government to be perverted due to corruption, "regulatory capture"[5] and other such problems. There is also a risk of local priorities being disregarded in the face of foreign agendas. Yet where governance is weakest is often where the greatest sustainable development challenges and the greatest imperatives for action lie.

RIGHTS, RULES, AND SYSTEMS

Every era has its great challenges. Today, once again, "the world cries out for repair," as Joshua Margolis and James Walsh note in *Misery Loves Companies*.[6] One thing that changes, however, is who we expect to do something about it. In the 1960s and 1970s we turned to governments, while in the 1980s and 1990s the focus was increasingly on markets. Now, in the post-9/11 world, the focus is shifting to issues linked to governance, security, civil liberties, and human rights. In the process, the spotlight is likely to shift from individual company actions and business-led voluntary initiatives to system-level challenges and responses.

"There is a piece missing from the World Summit on Sustainable Development and the MDGs,"[7] notes Oran Young of the Governance for Sustainable Development Program.[8] "There are many aspirations, but the problem is how to achieve them. The missing piece has to do with initiatives to restructure institutional arrangements—the rights, rules, and decision-making systems that establish social practices governing the relations among players. This may not be managed by something conventionally called government—it may be managed by governance systems without formal government agencies at all."

To ensure longer-term success, the CR community will need to make two parallel changes. The first will involve a shift from engagement in a seemingly endless list of special projects, which often fail to address the company's main

ARE THE MILLENNIUM DEVELOPMENT GOALS ACHIEVABLE?

Early in 2004, as part of the "Gearing Up" project, Harris Interactive agreed to include some questions about the millennium development goals (MDGs) in an online poll in the United States. From a balanced sample of nearly 4,000 people, the poll found that just 15% had heard of the goals, with better-educated and better-off people slightly more likely to have done so. Here are some of the other results:[9]

WHICH GOAL IS MOST IMPORTANT?

When respondents were asked to say which of the eight goals they thought most important, the top result (42%) was for eradicating extreme poverty and hunger. This time women, older people, and less well-educated respondents were most likely to vote for this goal. The second highest score (16%) was for ensuring environmental sustainability, followed by developing a global partnership for development (13%), achieving universal primary education (11%), and combating HIV/AIDS, malaria, and other diseases (10%). The other three achieved lower scores: reducing child mortality (4%), promoting gender equality and empowering women (2%), and improving maternal health (1%).

WILL WE SUCCEED?

When we asked how confident respondents were about the ability of the UN and member states to achieve the MDGs by 2015, only 4% were very confident—and less than a third (31%) were either very or somewhat confident. Interestingly, however, the goals that people had said were most important were seen to be least likely to be achieved—relating to poverty and hunger (22%), diseases (30%), and environmental sustainability (30%). The top score (just 38%) was for reducing childhood mortality.

WHO IS DOING LEAST?

Despite the best efforts of billionaires like Bill Gates, wealthy individuals were seen to be doing least (29%), with local, state, and national governments next in line (18%), followed by large, multinational corporations (16%).

WHO SHOULD BE DOING MORE?

This question threw up an interesting set of results (Figure 4.1). National governments topped the list (37%), followed by large, multinational corporations (18%). In the latter's case, respondents argued that more money should be made available, but that essential changes to business practices would also be required to achieve the MDGs. Intergovernmental organizations, such as the UN and World Bank, scored 14%, with NGOs way down at 4%. Interestingly, although respondents felt that wealthy individuals and local governments were doing the least to achieve the goals, they were not high on the list of candidates who should be doing more.

impacts, to a more coherent approach with stronger links between CR and both core business activities and wider governance frameworks. The second change will involve business working harder to overcome the enormous skepticism about its ability to play a constructive role. As David Korten told us, "The idea that publicly traded corporations constituted for the sole purpose of maximizing the short-term profits of shareholders can provide consequential and constructive leadership toward resolving any of the Millennium Development Goals is simply wishful thinking."

Like it or not, surveys of trust in institutions routinely show that Korten's analysis accords with the views of many others—from academics and development practitioners to much of the general public. This need not be the case. What follows is our assessment of how responsible business can help contribute to the necessary restructuring of market economies and the evolution of sustainable governance systems, along with a discussion of some of the steps business must take in order to credibly, legitimately, and effectively play such a role.

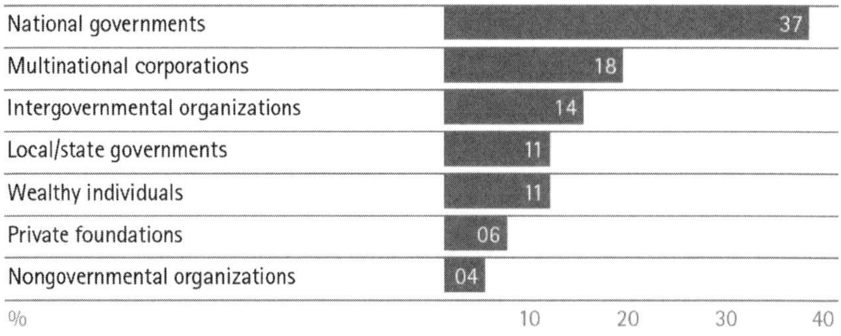

National governments		37
Multinational corporations		18
Intergovernmental organizations		14
Local/state governments		11
Wealthy individuals		11
Private foundations		06
Nongovernmental organizations		04

%   10   20   30   40

FIGURE 4.1.   Who Should Be Doing More to Achieve the MDGs?

Some critics see calls for business to engage directly in governance as dangerously naïve. Business interests are already engaged, for example, through the funding of U.S. presidential campaigns, which—they argue—is a key part of the problem. But there are good examples to range alongside the bad and ugly. Think, for instance, of the vital, constructive role played by some parts of the business community in South Africa in the waning days of the apartheid regime. While many companies benefited from and actively supported apartheid, some far-sighted business leaders helped smooth the transition to democracy.

During the 1980s, representatives of some major companies began meeting clandestinely with the African National Congress (ANC), when it was still a banned (and socialist) movement—worried that the escalating violence and absence of social justice and democracy would lead to irreversible polarization if something was not done. Once the ANC was "unbanned," the business community already had a positive relationship through a group known as the Consultative Business Movement. Ultimately, in collaboration with the South African Council of Churches, it helped broker multiparty peace negotiations.

Clearly, the actions of businesspeople were in their own self-interest, but at the same time they supported the national interest. According to André Fourie of NBI in South Africa, "the initiative was started by a few visionary business leaders—but by the end everyone was behind it. In hindsight it seems so sensible! But at the time, the reaction to the efforts of the early business leaders was that it was 'stupid and dangerous'." In this case, which is easier to "read" because it happened some time back, business leaders took principled steps into the areas of governance and systemic change. And they took these steps because the issues were directly linked to core success factors for their businesses. Our case studies (see appendix) highlight other examples where business is currently forming "progressive alliances" with government and civil society in support of wider systemic change.

GOING TO SCALE

Major sustainable development challenges like health, climate change, and corruption cannot be addressed by a single actor (whether from government, the private sector, or civil society), especially as they are rarely now contained within one geographical boundary. Solutions typically lie in cooperative efforts to change or develop governance frameworks. Yet all too often, traditional CR efforts do not explicitly consider scale issues.

This is a problem. As Mary Robinson of the Ethical Globalization Initiative told us, "Many companies involved in corporate responsibility initiatives are only now beginning to recognize that individual efforts could have a much greater impact if they were scaled up by working more systematically with wider industry groups and with a broader set of stakeholders." And, she continues, "We shouldn't expect that business would be either able or willing to scale up their own efforts in addressing social issues without direct support and involvement from government and civil society. It's a two-way process."

In this context, we offer the following conclusions based on our case studies on the roles of business, governments, and NGOs in creating progressive alliances[10]—and in ensuring that they deliver results. We indicate where the conclusions relate back to our case studies (e.g., Cases 1–4).

• **Market solutions will be crucial in solving global challenges**, but the evidence of current market failures (Cases 1–4) suggests the need for new approaches at the level of governance and market signals, including pricing.[11] Governments have a critically important role to play in these areas.

• **Companies can (and should) take a lead** in initiating new approaches to addressing challenges like the MDG targets, particularly where there are governance failures at the national or global level. Clearly, companies are most likely to take the lead where the business case is compelling (Case 2), although Novo Nordisk's action on Type 2 diabetes suggests that some companies are thinking about long-term strategy as well as shorter-term imperatives.

• Ultimately, however, **scaling requires wider collaboration**, given the limits to what individual companies can achieve (Cases 2, 4). Well-designed and clearly targeted alliances leverage the core competencies of different players, and also help ensure that they become stakeholders in the creation of new rules.

• **Companies can bring innovation, implementation skills, and other forms of know-how to bear** (Cases 1–4), particularly where markets and relevant policies are involved. They also have a good deal of financial muscle. The financial sector, meanwhile, has a key role both in creating real incentives for positive action (Cases 1, 4) and for ensuring longer-term scalability.

• **Governments and multilateral agencies must create the preconditions for scale** by moving CR beyond the leadership companies, retuning market incentives (Case 1), and helping change societal behavior (Cases 2, 3). Multilaterals cannot generally regulate, but they do have influence—including over governments (Case 4). Ultimately, with societies facing competing choices on how to allocate scarce resources, governments' key responsibility will continue to be making judgments about priorities.

• **Civil society organizations potentially bring expertise and credibility.** They can help make the preferences of society known in a more responsive and immediate fashion than most electoral processes allow (although issues of accountability loom large here, too).[12] This role can be strengthened where civil society forms coalitions around issues and positions (Case 4). In addition, civil society is often well placed to bridge gaps between companies, governments, and multilateral organizations and the grass roots, to provide expertise and to act as watchdogs, ensuring that initiatives remain on track.

• **Finally, there is a central role for corporate advocacy.** Our cases show how companies can play a role in developing policy frameworks to address key challenges. Yet generally companies have not made strong, coherent calls for the systemic changes that would be necessary to scale up the initiatives they are involved in (Cases 1–4). Meanwhile, regressive corporate lobbying is a key barrier to scaling up CR responses. Think of the sugar industry and obesity, the pharmaceutical industry and HIV/AIDS, and certain extractive sector companies and corruption.

PROCEED WITH CAUTION

Our case studies include some existing efforts in which business is contributing to—and often taking a lead role in—governance processes. But what are the risks inherent in suggesting that nonelected bodies with profit as a core motive engage directly in governance and public policy processes? Here are some issues raised by our interviewees and respondents:

• **Who should drive?** When it comes to picking priorities, it is clear that only governments have the necessary legitimacy, although business and markets play a critical role in achieving the rapid scaling of solutions. As Elliot Schrage of the U.S. Council on Foreign Relations puts it, "The car shouldn't decide what road to take—rather the driver should decide how to use it. Similarly, it's not that companies and governments are incompatible, but they have different roles." To stretch the metaphor slightly, modern cars and their engines are increasingly efficient in helping drivers reach their destinations more quickly and easily—and, hopefully, the same will increasingly be true of business.

• **What if our failures outnumber successes?** Given the scale of the challenges, experimentation is key, which guarantees failures along the way, some of them spectacular. We need to make the space for experimentation and innovation, with rapid prototyping, shared learning from failures, and a determination to deploy scalable solutions as fast as possible. We must mimic natural evolution, but lacking evolutionary timescales, we will need to fiercely select from the field of innovations those that are most likely to succeed, and invest in them. As noted above, NGO expertise is emerging as key to many innovation processes.

• **What happens where governance is weak?** In some developing countries—and at the global level—there is a risk of unequal relationships dominated by more powerful entities, including large companies. More concerted efforts are needed to strengthen the capacities of governments and civil society. "Southern governments need to consciously invest in the capacity to manage negotiations and relationships not only with global corporations but also with domestic commercial entities," notes Kumi Naidoo of Civicus.

• **What if CR is seen as someone else's agenda?** Several interviewees warned that CR could suffer if it were to be seen as an Anglo-Saxon concept. But most also stressed that, while the language is contested and many of the models currently clustered under the CR label have been most fully developed in the Anglo-Saxon world, there are underlying principles that are universal. Still, there is an urgent need both for a more balanced debate on CR globally, and for global ideas and practices to be translated in a locally meaningful way. "You can't organize these processes of change simply at the global level," explains Sir Mark Moody-Stuart, chairman of Anglo American. "You've got to get the right actors together in the right way at local level to exert influence on government and persuade them to do the things that need to be done."

TRUST AND LEGITIMACY

A final concern voiced by many interviewees and respondents about involving business in new forms of governance links back to negative perceptions of corporate lobbying. David Korten puts it starkly: "The most important responsibility of the corporate sector in addressing the Millennium Development Goals is to stop funding disinformation and lobbying campaigns that seek to undermine any serious effort to achieve them."

Lobbying by business is an inevitable, critically important part of democratic politics, but—almost by definition—is usually reactive. So, is it time to rethink how lobbying is done? True, industry insiders counter that this is a "no go" area: "You can't be transparent about lobbying," said one business interviewee. "Why would a company show its hand?" And many outside industry were equally skeptical.

Not surprisingly, many concerns about involving business more deeply link back to the problematic, controversial history of corporate lobbying against progressive policy on sustainable development challenges. But we conclude that there is an increasingly urgent need to reengineer corporate lobbying and to promote a wider understanding of the favorable business conditions that lobbying[13] seeks to secure. We would advocate three key minimum standards and invite companies to answer three related questions:

1. Single-interest lobbies fighting small points of policy can undermine the achievement of widely held environmental and social objectives. Companies

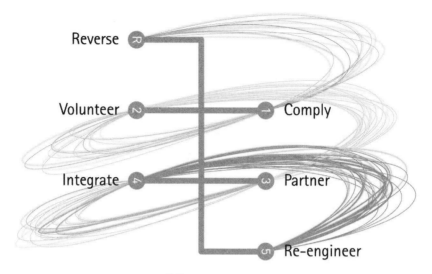

FIGURE 4.2.   Corporate Responsibility Gearbox

that support CR should, at a minimum, not be advocating lower environmental and social standards where these conflict with such objectives.

Q: **Are we advocating the lowering of standards anywhere?**

2. While "mandated trade associations"[14] often represent the lowest common denominator, company membership of such associations is believed to be essential. Leading companies, however, need to ensure that their message to their association is consistent with their CR goals.[15] As Stephen Tindale from Greenpeace UK has put it, "One of the largest reputational risks a company can face is exposure as a hypocrite."[16]

Q: **Are we comfortable that our association positions align with our own?**

3. Companies (and governments) should be as transparent as they can in terms of where they stand on issues about which they are engaging in the public debate or making representations. Transparency will always be limited by the constraints of the law and commercial confidentiality requirements, but even the best companies could do more to make their policy positions clear on key issues.

Q: **Are we doing enough to communicate our public policy positions?**

Furthermore, there is a clear and growing need for companies to speak out in favor of policies that deal proactively with sustainable development issues— and an increasingly robust business case for doing so.[17] This business case rests on a growing recognition that social and environmental pressures are not going to go away, and it behooves companies to lobby governments to address these issues directly as a way of taking the heat off the private sector, which is ill equipped to address these issues.[18] Companies that resist regulation on

RECOMMENDATIONS FOR BUSINESS: "GEAR UP"

While CR has clearly delivered some significant successes, it is also clear that as currently practiced, it is insufficient to solve increasingly pressing social and environmental challenges. Most company CR initiatives are simply too peripheral from core businesses, too isolated from one another, and too disconnected from wider systems to make much of a collective impact.

The challenge for business can be conceptualized in terms of a Corporate Responsibility Gearbox (Figure 4.2). As described below,as companies or sectors shift through these gears, the levels of engagement and integration change. The ultimate outcome of timely gear-shifting should be higher levels of trust in society, enabling greater system change to address sustainable development goals, with significantly less social, political, and economic friction.

1st GEAR: COMPLY

The "business of business" is considered to be business, with some limited acknowledgment of wider society through traditional channels like charitable giving.[19]

- PR and legal departments play a major, defensive role.
- Stakeholder engagement is mainly interpreted as philanthropy.
- Relations with government are seen in terms of compliance with legislation and paying taxes.[20]
- No business case is perceived for going beyond compliance.
- The key drivers are activism, the media, and government.

2nd GEAR: VOLUNTEER

Some companies begin to move "beyond compliance," but the CR emphasis is largely on measuring and managing direct operational impacts.

- The scope of CR widens, though it is still seen primarily as public relations.
- Stakeholder "engagement" is more active, but still often one-way.
- Relations with government still largely focus on taxes, compliance, and lobbying.
- Voluntary industry standards evolve, often independently of governments.
- The business case mainly focuses on risk management and eco-efficiency.
- Corporate peer pressure now emerges as a key driver.

3RD GEAR: PARTNER

Now the company—or sector—is really beginning to motor. But the sheer number of initiatives and partnerships, and their often ambitious nature can mean that corporate executives feel overwhelmed.

- CR experts take center stage, with CEOs and board members "wheeled out" for major events.
- Stakeholder engagement evolves into a two-way dialogue with wider society, including a range of nontraditional stakeholders.
- There are closer working relationships with government, for example through trisector or public-private partnerships.
- The business case now focuses on proactive risk management, reputation-building, and the coevolution of solutions.
- The key drivers are civil society, some parts of government, and leading businesses, with much of the media (because there is less drama) beginning to lose interest.

4TH GEAR: INTEGRATE

By now the issues are being experienced as increasingly strategic, requiring integrated responses across companies and value chains—although tough dilemmas emerge and trade-offs often have to be made between competing priorities.

- Top management and boards are now actively involved.
- The company engages with civil society and governments in progressive alliances working toward common objectives.
- The focus is on embedding CR goals in all business processes, starting with product or service development.
- The business case becomes more strategic as businesses begin to connect the dots between long-term corporate objectives and wider societal challenges.
- The drivers are many and various, including growing interest from the financial sector.
- But companies pushing the envelope still often find that the drivers are inadequate in key areas.

5TH GEAR: RE-ENGINEER

For many people, most of the time, four gears is enough. But there are times when it is necessary to shift into fifth gear, or overdrive. Here the focus shifts to systemic change, addressing future markets, market frameworks, and business models.

- New players come to the table, including "change agents" like inventors, entrepreneurs, venture capitalists, and investment bankers.
- Progressive alliances target system change, focusing both on governance and markets.
- CR moves beyond products or services to reexamine business models.
- The business case is often negative, in the sense that there may be a "first mover disadvantage," at least in the short term.
- There are many drivers of change, including growing financial sector and civil society activity, but governments and governance systems once again must play a central role.

principle may find that a more positive approach can bring opportunities to work with government and other stakeholders in ensuring that rules are efficient, provide a solid basis for long-term planning, and are consistent both within government and across different states and regions.[21]

In addition to rethinking lobbying, greater trust will need to be built through increased transparency and the open, interactive, and reasonably equal involvement of major stakeholders, especially civil society. Many traditional relationships between business and governments that have been most distrusted have been strictly two-party affairs. As Fanny Calder, an associate fellow at the UK's Royal Institute of International Affairs, explains, "Big business has often had very close relationships with governments—this is not new. To be legitimate, however, business should be attempting to influence governments through processes that involve other actors." Good ideas will struggle to get off the ground if the process is seen as illegitimate.

CONCLUSION

Returning to the three questions that began this chapter, our research has suggested several ways to increase the potential for positive change—leading us to conclude that:

• **CR as currently practiced lacks the capacity to deliver real progress** on sustainable development because there are insufficient links to wider governance systems—despite having achieved change within a narrowly defined area.

• **Government has a key role to play in strengthening CR**—by changing or developing incentives and creating a stronger business case. Government can also help achieve critical mass by acting as a convener in "progressive alliances." Most important, government needs to set the course.

• **Business can bring fresh perspectives and innovative, more efficient models**, while mobilizing further weight behind global processes, transferring necessary skills and technologies, and helping create new policy frameworks. Business can also play a positive advocacy role. But in order to be trusted and

---

RECOMMENDATIONS FOR GOVERNMENT

Governments will continue to play a critical role in legislating, regulating, and enforcing, although with a more strategic focus on public policies that are known enablers of efficient markets. In parallel, they will increasingly rely on private initiatives as the first line of enforcement. Companies will be asked to demonstrate "due care" and encouraged to adopt relevant codes of conduct, business principles, and management systems.

Specific recommendations for governments:[22]

- Clearly communicate looming problems and their likely effects.
- Encourage participation from civil society, business, and other stakeholders in progressive alliances.
- Consider how public policy can stimulate key business drivers,[23] taking into account the impact of policies on small business as well as multinationals.
- Given that business is driven by deliverables, specify desired outcomes.
- Encourage the use of metrics that encompass multiple sectors.
- Emphasize innovation, ingenuity, and pragmatic, scalable solutions.
- Support the evolution of markets to price public benefits, such as the elimination of greenhouse gases.
- Develop a portfolio of policy instruments that reward good corporate performance, for example, fiscal incentives, procurement policies, endorsements, labeling, training, and information while also penalizing laggards by using minimum standards, fines, and other disincentives.[24]

Governments in developing countries often face additional challenges in managing and promoting the CR agenda. There is a need to enhance their capacity to implement and enforce existing regulations and to take limitations into account in developing new policies. Another key challenge is to invest in the capacity to handle negotiations and relationships with business, especially multinational companies.

---

taken seriously, business will first need to increase transparency and external engagement, especially as part of progressive alliances, and show more progress on integrating CR into its core business operations.

Shifting into "top gear," companies need to foster progressive alliances with other business actors, civil society organizations, and—above all—governments. The aim: to help scale up CR by linking into system-level change, particularly in governance frameworks. At the macro level, this will involve championing more responsible and sustainable forms of globalization through processes led by agencies like the World Trade Organization (WTO) or, regionally, through market frameworks like the European Union (EU) or the North American Free Trade Agreement (NAFTA). At the micro level, leading companies are building out from purely corporate and supply chain initiatives to coevolve responses like the California Climate Action Registry, the Extractive Industries Transparency Initiative, or Oxford Vision 2020.

Our recommendations will likely prove uncomfortable for those who fear greater government control over business and for those uneasy with greater business influence over governments. To the first group, we would say that stronger government policies in these areas are necessary and probably inevitable. The real issue is how we can make them more effective, consistent, and predictable. Some companies, indeed, already view CR-related public policy as a driver of long-term competitive advantage. To the second group, we would say that while concerns over undue corporate influence on policy cannot be dismissed, there is a growing need for companies to speak out in favor of CR and wider sustainable development issues. However, to be seen as legitimate participants, companies will need to demonstrate significantly greater consistency and transparency across their public policy activities while simultaneously working more closely with civil society organizations on shared policy goals.

WINDOW OF OPPORTUNITY

It is not clear that a role for companies in changing governance structures either at the micro or macro level would have been possible or even desirable until relatively recently. Currently, though, a window of opportunity may be opening up, suggesting a maturation in the types of relationships that are feasible. Although trust in both business and government often remains low, the potential for collaboration clearly exists. Internationally, we are seeing a growing focus on "ethical" or "responsible" globalization. Thought-leaders including Kofi Annan, Bill Clinton, Jagdish Dhagwati, Mary Robinson, John Ruggie, and Joseph Stiglitz are among those making the case that globalization has much to offer the world if undertaken in a responsible way, that is, with adequate governance and safety nets. NGOs such as Oxfam, CARE, and WWF are actively increasing their capacity to work with business in forging solutions to key sustainable development challenges.[25]

This does not suggest that dissent has ceased to exist—which is neither likely nor desirable. However, collaborative relationships such as trisector partnerships[26] are increasingly becoming an alternative and complementary model. True—the focus so far has generally been on delivering specific projects on the ground rather than wider governance impacts, and these collaborations are unlikely to deliver all they have promised. Still, they demonstrate shifting relationships between government, business, and civil society, and an opportunity for more constructive joint working. The question now, however, is whether leading businesses will rise to the governance challenge, or whether they will allow this window of opportunity to close.

RECOMMENDATIONS FOR CIVIL SOCIETY

Specific recommendations for civil society organizations:

- Help establish clear priorities for action.[27]
- Work to strengthen incentives for positive corporate action, by holding all high-impact companies to account, not just branded companies, and by recognizing (and partnering with) leadership companies.
- Invest in progressive alliances and investigate scalability.
- Establish clear "rules of engagement" to protect their integrity and independence.
- Enhance transparency and accountability, ensuring legitimacy in holding business, government, and other actors to account.
- Increasingly promote system-level reforms in addition to changes at the levels of companies and value chains.

While these recommendations are mostly targeted at larger national and international NGOs, grassroots organizations also have a vital role to play. They can act as intermediaries between local communities and private or public sector entities, which often have neither the time nor the skills to engage at the community level. Grassroots organizations can also build bridges to local government and help monitor and report on-the-ground results.

The costs of failure will be enormous. And for business, this potentially means a further weakening of societal trust—the lack of which already undermines the private sector's ability to engage in governance debates and to define where the justifiable and necessary boundaries of CR lie. Moreover, these unresolved problems can seriously undermine the environment in which business operates, with quantifiable financial impacts for companies.

As Harvard's John Ruggie has pointed out, the present state of affairs is unsustainable. "The gap between market and community will be closed; the only issue is how and in what direction. I believe the world needs open markets: business to maximize its opportunities, the industrialized world to sustain prosperity, and the developing countries because an open world provides the best hope of pulling billions of poor people out of abject poverty. But...rollback, a shift away from globalization, is the more likely outcome unless we manage to strengthen the fabric of the global community. Ironically, nobody is better positioned or has greater capacity to play the lead role today than business itself."[28]

While we would agree that business should be taking a lead, and indeed encourage companies to do so, our case studies suggest a wider conclusion. Rather than placing all the responsibility in corporate laps, these examples suggest that multisectoral initiatives should be developed, helping to mobilize world resources and, potentially, achieve new levels of scale. As argued above, the early and ongoing involvement of a diverse range of civil society organizations will be critical. And governments and the wider political system will remain central in deciding priorities and, in the process, making increasingly complex trade-offs.

APPENDIX: THE CASE STUDIES

When we first began to think about the role that business could play in scaling up efforts to tackle major sustainable development challenges, there appeared to be a number of promising examples where the private sector was both showing leadership and preparing the ground for positive public policy responses. These include efforts to deal with HIV/AIDS in the workplace, the development of carbon trading schemes as a response to climate change, and the growing momentum around issues like corruption and chronic illness.

This appendix describes four case studies that explore how business might engage in appropriate efforts toward improved governance for sustainable development. These formed the basis of many of the conclusions that appear in this chapter. The examples in these case studies are not being spotlighted as successful public-private partnerships, although some may be. Instead, the focus was on drawing lessons on how business might contribute to systemic change. We wanted to understand the potential roles, drivers, and dilemmas that businesses—as well as governments and civil society—face in collaborating and in scaling up initiatives. Why, for example, have certain companies become involved policy issues, and what ensures that their role is seen to be legitimate and appropriate? And we also wanted to explore how critical mass had been (or could be) achieved and what barriers still impede progress.

Table 4.1 outlines the four cases, which are described in greater details in the pages that follow.

CASE 1. CALIFORNIA CLIMATE ACTION REGISTRY

Linking to Markets

The United States—the largest emitter of greenhouse gases (GHGs)[29] and, perhaps not coincidentally, a notable "skeptic" on climate change—represents the most important market where business has not yet provided a convincing response to the issue of climate change. One example, though, of how business is helping prepare the ground for an effective response is the California Climate Action Registry.[30]

The Registry was established by the state of California in 2000 to encourage companies and other organizations operating there to increase energy

TABLE 4.1.

	Case 1 CALIFORNIA CLIMATE ACTION REGISTRY Linking to markets	Case 2 WORKPLACE ANTI-RETROVIRALS Showing leadership	Case 3 OXFORD VISION 2020 Providing foresight	Case 4 EXTRACTIVE INDUSTRIES TRANSPARENCY INITIATIVE Offering incentives
Who?	—California state government, city governments —NGOs (e.g., Environmental Defense, CERES, WRI) —46 charter members, mostly companies	—Individual companies in South Africa (e.g., Anglo American) —NGO partners (e.g., Lovelife)	—WHO —Oxford University —Novo Nordisk	—UK government with ten developed and developing country governments —NGOs, including "Publish What You Pay" Coalition —Companies in the extractive sector —46 institutional investors
Aim?	Voluntary registry to encourage companies to increase energy efficiently and decrease GHG emissions	Comprehensive HIV/AIDS management systems, including providing ARV treatment to better control HIV/AIDS in the workforce	Develop for WHO a comprehensive strategy on chronic disease, including obesity	Publication of revenue flows from the extractive sector to host governments, along with government revenue flows from natural resources, so that governments can be held accountable for revenues
Business Role Initiative	—Lead by example	—Lead by providing ARVs and demonstrating potential benefits	—Leadership bringing other companies on board	—Some companies were already publishing

62

Incentive		—Peer pressure		—Encourage host governments to take part —Promise of investment for host governments
Innovation	—Technical expertise	—Share best practice	—Problem definition, strategy formulation, how to maximize leverage from public health care resources	—Reporting protocol
Government Role Initiative	—Registry founded by state of California —City governments as "charter members"	—Help make cheaper drugs available —Multilaterals coinvest in local projects		—UK government creates space for dialogue and brings key actors together
Incentive	—Threat of regulation		—WHO is focusing attention on an "orphan" problem denied by many in business and society	—WSSD provided incentive for UK to act —Participating governments create peer pressure on other governments
Innovation				
Civil Society Role Initiative			—University of Oxford adds convening power	—Initials calls for transparency of revenue flows and for companies to publish what they pay
Incentive	—Raise public awareness and create pressure for action	—Pressure on pharmaceutical companies for cheaper generic drugs —Pressure on government to change its stance on HIV/AIDS		—Create pressure for companies and governments to act

TABLE 4.1. (continued)

	Case 1 CALIFORNIA CLIMATE ACTION REGISTRY Linking to markets	Case 2 WORKPLACE ANTI RETROVIRALS Showing leadership	Case 3 OXFORD VISION 2020 Providing foresight	Case 4 EXTRACTIVE INDUSTRIES TRANSPARENCY INITIATIVE Offering incentives
Innovation	—Develop GHG Protocol which serves as a basis for Registry Protocol —NGOs are represented on the Technical Advisory Committee		—Academic experts and researchers bring considerable intellectual horsepower —NGOs know how to "market" causes that are important to citizens/consumers	
Business Case	Long-term —Influence development of future policy —Protect early action —Encourage consistency in regulation	Immediate —Slow or reverse loss of personnel and productivity —Decrease risk and costs	Long-term —Widen networks —Test business model —Shape market strategy	Medium-term —Reduce corruption and provide more stable operating environment —Create level playing field
System Change?	—Investors drive greater understanding and awareness —Limited progress because business case not compelling —Wider progress requires embedding in government and market systems	—Significant individual efforts but collaborative approach within South Africa is missing —Progress achieved primarily within the business community —Wider progress requires linking into government frameworks and leadership on reform of health systems	—Founding organizations are providing initial vision and leadership —Need for more public and corporate consciousness and involvement, especially in food industry	—Progress achieved by focusing on systemic issue specific for extractive sector. —As yet, critical mass of countries not achieved —Need to create appropriate incentives to bring more governments on board

efficiency and cut GHG emissions. Protocols and tools developed by the Registry enable companies to register GHG-emission baselines for their operations, and then measure changes against this baseline.

The Registry serves as:

- A key component in developing the "market infrastructure" and accounting frameworks for trading carbon;
- A means of engaging the technical expertise of business in crafting solutions;
- An open-source model, allowing stakeholders to review protocols in detail.

The number of Registry members doubled from 23 at its launch in 2002 to 45 in early 2004, including companies such as BP and PG&E Corporation.

Key success factors:

• The involvement of the state of California provides confidence to business that registered GHG reductions will be honored in future regulatory regimes.

• The use of the GHG Protocol developed by the World Resources Institute (WRI) and the World Business Council for Sustainable Development (WBCSD) as a key foundation document encourages NGO support.

• There is a growing sense in the U.S. business community that GHG regulation is coming, coupled with a desire among switched-on business leaders to prepare for (and help shape) regulation.

• There is a growing interest among investors (for example, pension funds) in carbon exposure.

Key Challenges

Although the number of companies participating is significant, it is still minute when compared with the overall business community. But the Registry is working hard to build critical mass.

Potential pitfalls:

• Lack of political traction for action on climate change would leave the Registry vestigial, unconnected to other aspects of market infrastructure.

• The emergence of alternative regulatory approaches or shifting priorities could result in a loss of support from business.

• The loss of support from the NGO community would undermine legitimacy.

• A public perception that the industry is trying to configure the system in its own favor, a concern expressed around emission trading regimes in the United States, would weaken credibility.

Conclusion

The Climate Action Registry demonstrates the value of involving business in the provision of technical expertise in developing and testing of complex economic instruments to reshape market frameworks. The initiative has also provided a framework (known as the Climate Action Registry Reporting On-line Tool, or CARROT) for companies to report their performance over time.

The Registry also illustrates the importance of involving government and NGOs to provide predictability and credibility respectively. Ultimately, how-ever, the example illustrates that with issues of long-term overuse of the public commons, the business case only becomes compelling for companies when regulatory action is expected. This is the critical driver in stimulating business interest in addressing climate change. Companies committed to this regulatory agenda could be taking bolder action. For example, a small group of companies have joined WWF in calling for mandatory caps on carbon dioxide emissions[31] in the United States. Leadership companies could also help the financial com-munity understand the value of effective carbon risk management by disclosing information on how they quantify their risk and what they are doing to protect and boost the company's value.

CASE 2. WORKPLACE ANTIRETROVIRALS (ARVS)

Showing Leadership

An increasing number of initiatives and coalitions seek to involve business in efforts to tackle HIV/AIDS, focusing on both prevention and treatment. So far, the most proactive examples coming from the private sector relate to workplace HIV programs, including the provision of ARV treatment. A handful of companies currently operate such programs—particularly in South Africa, where the government has not been proactive until recently.

But the threat is immense. For example, Anglo American, South Africa's largest private sector employer, estimates that an average of 24 percent of its employees are currently HIV positive, although this varies significantly by business unit. The company has had a workplace program to combat HIV/AIDS for fifteen years, including education and awareness-raising, prevention and treatment, anonymous prevalence testing, wellness programs, combating stigma and discrimination, and support for vaccine research.

The company has also supported community projects, for example through investing in the NGO "loveLife." This project aims to reduce the infection rate among young South Africans by bolstering public sector health infrastruc-ture to make it more attractive and accessible—and helping to prepare for the rollout of the government ARV program.

In 2002, Anglo went well beyond current corporate best practice to provide ARV treatment at company expense to HIV-positive employees who have progressed to a stage of infection where treatment is clinically indicated. ARVs are provided to employees, but not to dependents, contractors, or the com-munity. When Anglo first acted, there was a push back from South Africa's Ministry of Health, ostensibly because of the lack of consultation. Anglo's program to provide ARVs is generating direct benefits to the company as well as to employees, and indirect benefits to families and the wider community. At present, there are 1,300 employees who have been on ARVs over the past twelve months, of whom 92 percent are at work and able to continue playing an active role in society. A further 3,000 employees in earlier stages of infection are on wellness programs.

Key success factors:

• Anglo has its own direct-delivery health care infrastructure and the scale to make an ambitious program work.

• Leadership by local management has been key to participation in voluntary counseling and testing in those operations where uptake is highest.

• There has been collaboration, wherever possible, with trade unions.

• Workers have seen desperately ill colleagues seemingly be restored to "health"—which provides the power of personal experience.

Key Challenges

Anglo and similar companies have demonstrated that progress can be made in the short term by treating employees in the absence of or even counter to public policy. While denial and stigma remain major barriers, awareness-raising, education, and a demonstration that treatment can work are beginning to show results. Yet with 5.3 million HIV-infected South Africans at the end of 2002, it is clear that corporate programs cannot address the problem at the required scale.

There have been important reasons why a more effective and collaborative governance approach toward HIV/AIDS in South Africa has not developed. While some companies have led, other parts of the business community have acted as barriers. The most notable example is the pharmaceutical sector, backed by the WTO, which was initially unwilling to allow cheaper generic drugs to be produced or imported into South Africa.

Until recently, too, the South African government opposed nationwide treatment. While the government had some understandable concerns about the true lifetime costs of the full treatment regime and the impact on long-term public policy and budget choices, communication and execution of its response was poor. The questioning of the causes of AIDS and the emphasis on the toxicity of the drugs hindered progress in combating the disease.

While drug prices have fallen and government policy has changed, the continuing stigma around the disease and the generally high level of distrust between civil society, business, and government in South Africa have been additional barriers, helping to explain the fragmentation of responses.

Conclusion

This case shows the potential for companies to play leadership roles and innovate in tackling major challenges where government is unwilling or unable to take action, at least when the company is convinced that there is a compelling (moral or business) case. However, without this missing government link, individual companies cannot solve systemic issues like HIV/AIDS on their own. Unilateral approaches raise the real risk of creating "islands of influence." Substantial progress in destigmatising the issue, combating discrimination, raising awareness, and providing treatment will ultimately be achieved only with government as the driving force.

CASE 3. OXFORD VISION 2020

Providing Foresight

Preventing type 2 diabetes and other chronic illnesses is much easier than curing them, but prevention takes multisector, long-term initiatives. Three organizations, Novo Nordisk, Oxford University, and the World Health Organization (WHO), have joined forces under the banner of "Oxford Vision 2020"[32] to develop a coherent approach to addressing—and hopefully reversing—the growth in type 2 diabetes and related chronic illnesses.

Oxford Vision 2020 is a significant endeavor, not least because it has successfully engaged organizations from a broad variety of sectors that affect or are affected by chronic diseases. In addition, as one participant put it, "there is no vested interest apparent—this is a vision for public health," creating the potential for partners to foster genuinely innovative approaches.

Among the organizations represented at the first meeting in September 2003 were a range of companies (for example, Novo Nordisk, Johnson & Johnson, JP Morgan, Nestlé, and PepsiCo), civil society organizations (for example, trade unions, NGOs, and academic institutions), and a range of governments and multilaterals (for example, the UK, South Africa, WHO, the World Bank, and the Organisation for Economic Co-Operation and Development, or OECD).

The overall initiative is targeted primarily at policy-makers and politicians as well as consumers and patients. Though still relatively new, a number of important successes have been achieved, including establishing five critical priorities for the initiative:

• Quantify the economic burden of chronic diseases, both in terms of health care costs and of economic productivity—and to define causes, effects, and solutions.

• Mount a successful advocacy program to push chronic diseases higher up the political agenda in health departments as well as across finance, education, employment, and transport.

• Develop a new business model for private industry, to encourage the development of healthier foods and expand the focus of the pharmaceutical industry to include health promotion.

• Use the success of tobacco control strategies to develop a multilevel framework to better manage chronic diseases.

• Explore new partnerships between public and private organizations to communicate to consumers, employers, and health professionals.

Working groups have been set up to address each of these priorities. The next step will then be to test the best ideas at the community level. As Daniel Miller of the World Bank, a participant in the initiative, put it, "We have identified gaps in our knowledge related to the impact of chronic disease on the economies of developing countries and the financial impact of chronic disease on poor households. [We have also] identified critical next steps to radically meet information needs, so a compelling case for chronic disease prevention and control can be made to policy-makers and decision-makers in government."

Key Challenges

The initiative is still at a relatively early stage, and there are a range of challenges and potential pitfalls:

• There is a high level of public ignorance regarding the significance of these issues in terms of public health and the economy.

• The U.S. government has adopted a defensive approach to obesity.

• The enormous complexity of the agenda and the need for multisectoral responses may complicate and slow progress.

• Mistrust between project participants, including between business on the one hand and NGOs and multilaterals on the other, could become an enduring problem.

Conclusion

Oxford Vision 2020 shows how business can take the lead in helping convene far-sighted initiatives to tackle new societal challenges. While there are barriers, there are also some important drivers that ensure active engagement by participants. Companies taking a lead can potentially gain a first-mover advantage in understanding and responding to emerging pressures on their businesses. The academics involved have an opportunity to apply their knowledge in a real-world setting, and for WHO and other multilaterals and governments this initiative represents a potentially powerful opportunity to address an increasingly pressing public health issue.

However, in order to be successful, the initiative will require participants to move well beyond their "comfort zone" in exploring new solutions to type 2 diabetes and other chronic illnesses.

Companies in particular will need to:

• Start "thinking out of the box" in terms of their own direct business interests (with a focus on business models, not public relations).
• Link with leading partners in different sectors, maximizing "core competencies."

CASE 4. EXTRACTIVE INDUSTRIES TRANSPARENCY
INITIATIVE (EITI)

Offering Incentives

The EITI[33] encourages companies in the mining, oil, and gas industries, together with host governments in resource-rich countries, to publish revenue flows from the extractive industries to host governments—and to complement these with the publication of government receipts. The aim is to make it easier for civil society in these countries to hold governments accountable for how such revenues are managed and distributed.

Launched by the UK government at the World Summit on Sustainable Development in 2002, the EITI is supported by a growing number of countries (for example, Azerbaijan, France, and Ghana) and companies (for example, Rio Tinto and Shell). Civil society groups, including the Publish What You Pay coalition, are also active. The EITI has been particularly timely given the increased oil development in West Africa and the Caspian Sea region in the last few years, areas with notably poor records on corruption.

In June 2003 the EITI's principles and actions were agreed upon, and Azerbaijan, Ghana, Indonesia, Nigeria, Sierra Leone, and Trinidad and Tobago volunteered as potential pilots for the scheme. Work has been ongoing since then to create an adequate framework for revenue disclosure within each country. Given the complex nature of corruption and the range of actors and interests involved, priorities and positions are bound to vary enormously. Yet trust is being developed through the process as the EITI focuses on finding common ground and identifying incentives—using the combined persuasive power of the different actors involved to bring companies and countries on board. The narrow scope (one sector and one aspect of corruption) has also made it easier to gain consensus.

In 2004, Nigeria became the first country to host a stakeholder workshop on the initiative. A steering committee has been formed with a view to ensuring full publication of 2004 revenues in early 2005. Also in 2004, the number of signatories to an "investors statement" in support of the EITI doubled to 57, which collectively represent U.S.$6.9 trillion. The longer-term significance of investors in driving this agenda is huge.

Key Challenges

While the initial momentum is promising, some important actors from both business and government have still not signed on. The initiative may risk stalling unless a few key (and successful) pilots are achieved in each world region, creating momentum and pressure for peers to follow suit. Failure to achieve critical mass in a meaningful way would likely result in withdrawal of support by the NGO community and possibly other actors.

A more intrinsic barrier to achieving the aims of the EITI is the lack of well-developed civil society institutions in some implementing countries. Successful implementation will require quite sophisticated advocacy organizations that can engage with policy-makers and companies on fairly equal terms, holding both to account.

Conclusion

Given the negative impact of corruption on the operating environment for business,[34] there is a medium- to long-term business case for companies to engage in anticorruption efforts. There are clear roles that business (including the investment community) can play in influencing governments to curb corruption and in providing mechanisms like reporting frameworks to enhance transparency, accountability, and the quality of governance.

While individual companies can show (and have shown) leadership—including publishing payments unilaterally—this strategy can be perilous in some situations. For example, when BP in Angola promised transparency concerning its payments to the government, the announcement was met with a swift rebuke and a threat to the company's future in the country. BP was forced to back down. The energy giant's experience underlines the importance of collective solutions. In particular, there is a need for collective private sector advocacy to persuade governments and wider society that bribery and corruption are unacceptable and, ultimately, counterproductive.

NOTES

1. SustainAbility is also grateful for the financial support the project received from five corporate sponsors: Novartis, Pfizer, SAP, DaimlerChrysler, and Novo Nordisk.

2. Originally defined to describe the ability of information technology software to handle an increased workload, scalability has now come to mean the ability of any innovation to expand without running into some unknown performance ceiling or bottleneck. (http://support.softwareshelf.com/dictionary/default.asp?l=s)

3. This definition is based on a variety of definitions produced by among others the WBCSD, Business for Social Responsibility (BSR), and International Business Leaders Forum (IBLF).

4. Here and throughout the chapter we use the term "business case" to refer to the extent to which CR improves business value, as conventionally defined. See SustainAbility, (2001), for UNEP, *Buried treasure: Uncovering the business case for corporate sustainability*, and SustainAbility/International Finance Corporation/Ethos Institute, (2002), *Developing value: The business case for sustainability in emerging markets*.

5. The theory that interest groups such as companies seek to promote their interests in the regulatory process, which leads over time to regulatory agencies being dominated by those they regulate (adapted from www.economist.com/research/Economics/alphabetic.cfm?TERM=REGULATION#REGULATORY%20CAPTURE).

6. Joshua D. Margolis and James P. Walsh (2003), Misery loves companies: Rethinking social initiatives by business, *Administrative Science Quarterly, 49*.

7. The millennium development goals or MDGs are part of UN secretary-general Kofi Annan's road map toward the implementation of the United Nations Millennium Declaration, and are a summary of the development goals agreed at international conferences during the 1990s. See www.developmentgoals.org

8. http://fiesta.bren.ucsb.edu/~gsd/about/about.php

9. Our thanks to Joy Sever of Harris Interactive for providing this data.

10. The Copenhagen Centre has developed the following definition of progressive alliances: "People and organizations from some combination of public, business and civil constituencies who engage in voluntary, mutually beneficial, innovative relationships to address common societal aims through combining their resources and competencies." Also called global action networks and social partnerships.

11. A good example of how companies can work with governments to develop effective governance is the UK's Emissions Trading Group, which helped develop a greenhouse gas emissions trading scheme: www.uketg.com

12. See SustainAbility/UN Global Compact/UNEP (2003), *The twenty-first-century NGO: In the market for change*.

13. Lobbying is understood to involve any activity engaged in by individuals or organizations (directly or through hired representatives) and directed to elements of government in an attempt to influence legislation or policies in a way that is favorable to the interests of the lobbying group.

14. Mandated industry associations aim to represent the general position of companies in one industry or region, with their positions based on a "mandate" from their membership. As a result, they often do not represent a progressive or innovative approach.

15. See GPC/SustainAbility (2001), *Politics and persuasion: Corporate influence on sustainable development policy*.

16. Quoted in Simon Caulkin and Joanna Collins (2003), *The private life of public affairs*, Green Alliance.

17. For example participation in the California Climate Action Registry is based primarily on the business need to participate in the creation of new regulatory standards and systems.

18. Adair Turner, former director general of the Confederation of British Industries, quoted in Caulkin and Collins, cited above.

19. See John Elkington, *The chrysalis economy* (2001), Capstone/Wiley. We also acknowledge the influence of *Just values: Beyond the business case for sustainable development*, BT/Forum for the Future (2003), in this mapping.

20. The extent to which companies pay taxes, however, remains a controversial issue.

21. For example, the UK Business Council for Sustainable Energy was set up explicitly to contribute to consistent and efficient UK government policy on sustainable energy.

22. We are grateful to Bernard Sheahan of the International Finance Corporation for his invaluable input in helping inform these recommendations.

23. See also Tom Fox, Halina Ward, and Bruce Howard (2002, October), *Public sector roles in strengthening corporate social responsibility: A baseline study*, World Bank.

24. See, for example, the UK government's Market Transformation Programme: www.mtprog.com

25. See SustainAbility et al., *Twenty-first-century NGO*.

26. See, for example, *Putting partnering to work: 1998–2001. Tri-sector partnership results and recommendations*, Business Partners for Development (2002); and the United Nations: www.un.org/esa/sustdev/partnerships/partnerships.htm

27. One interesting priority-setting initiative is the Copenhagen Consensus project, which focuses on such areas as climate change, communicable disease, governance, and corruption: www.copenhagenconsensus.com

28. John G Ruggie (2004, March 15), Creating public value: Everybody's business, address to the Herrhausen Society, Frankfurt, Germany.

29. Greenhouse gases are heat-trapping gases—both naturally occurring and "synthetic"—that are emitted into the atmosphere. Anthropogenic sources of GHGs have increased markedly in the last century and are a major contributor to climate change.

30. www.climateregistry.org

31. http://worldwildlife.org/news/displaypr.cfm?prid=42

32. www.oxfordvision2020.org

33. www.dfid.gov.uk/news/news/files/eiti_stat_of_principles.htm

34. According to a 2002 survey, 39 percent of companies had lost business because a competitor had paid a bribe. *Facing up to corruption, 2003: Tackling the hard questions*, Control Risks Group (2003).

5

Engaging Governments in Support of Corporate Social Responsibility in Global Supply Chains

ARON CRAMER and PEDER MICHAEL PRUZAN-JØRGENSEN

CONTEXT

We present this chapter in the context of an environment that is simultaneously static and dynamic. On the one hand, there is increasing recognition that the current "system" for achieving good labor and environmental practices in global supply chains, primarily through the mechanism of private codes of conduct and worksite monitoring, is not working. It is not sustainable, nor does it maximize progress. On the other hand, there are still barriers to be overcome for this recognition to be turned into action for change.

The dynamism in the debate is borne of several factors, many of which are unrelated and which together present the opportunity to develop more—and more systematic—change than has been possible in recent years. These change factors include:

• The phaseout of apparel quotas, which threatens to bring fundamental changes in the geography of the apparel industry.

• Fatigue by both buyers and suppliers with current approaches, and a sense that progress available through these approaches has peaked.

• A sense that the atomized models reflected in individual company codes, and competing multistakeholder initiatives, cannot continue indefinitely without losing opportunities for improvement.

• Initial signs that both a political will and an underlying architecture of cooperation are emerging, reflected in a series of collaborations between parties that did not even communicate effectively five years ago.

• A greater willingness on the part of national governments, international institutions, and bilateral donors to engage with these issues, and a willingness on the part of other actors to engage with the public sector in developing countries.

• A growing sophistication in the understanding of the policy, market, and social drivers for the debate.

The static nature of elements of the debate is also very important to acknowledge. Factors that continue to hinder progress include:

• Highly politicized debates in exporting countries, in which labor and management in particular often seek conflict first and conciliation second.

• Lack of resources, especially on the part of exporting country governments, which do not view export sector workplaces as being the highest priority for social and environmental interventions

• Continuing cynicism on the part of suppliers, who do not believe that investments in better social and environmental conditions will bring improved economic performance or greater access to markets.

• Concerns that China's presence in the global market risks making noncompetitive efforts in other countries to secure social and environmental improvements.

• Ongoing holes in the system, owing to very patchy enforcement by governments and uneven enforcement by companies seeking to ensure good practices by their suppliers.

• Lack of internationally accepted principles on environmental matters in a manner equivalent to International Labor Organization [ILO] core labor standards.

We believe that there is a moment in time currently where some of the opportunities can be capitalized on, and some of the barriers overcome by catalyzing greater action by governments, which have a pivotal role to play.

Indeed, this report takes as an underlying premise the notion that codes of conduct to a large extent emerged as a corporate policy solution (though often triggered by public criticism) to a public governance failure. In addition, the current code of conduct trajectory, which emphasizes individual solutions, has exhausted its potential for further progress, in no small part because it does not acknowledge the important role governments play in creating the enabling environment for the achievement of good labor and environmental standards.

Accordingly, although codes of conduct are a force for positive change in terms of labor and environmental performance, current approaches are far likelier to bring sustainable improvements when implemented within a comprehensive, public sector–governed framework.

Governments have good reasons to invest in developing such frameworks. First, such efforts are likely to deliver economic and social spinoffs that contribute positively to national competitiveness. Second, they provide a level playing field for enterprises active in the country. Third, they insert into the debate over supply chains an opportunity for governments to have greater influence over outcomes than they have to date, as "solutions" have often been presented from outside these economies.

Thus, this chapter presents recommendations that identify ways the public sector can mobilize not only its own resources, but also take advantage of the resources, skills, and capacities of different actors in areas such as: capacity-building, training of workers, collaboration with other actors, and the strengthening and diversification of inspection systems.

This report proceeds on the assumption that continued and enhanced efforts on the part of business, both by multinational buyers and local suppliers, is essential and should in no way be seen as letting such actors "off the hook." Further, it proceeds on the assumption that one essential role for government is to create enabling environments that envision strong contributions from civil society (NGOs and trade unions in their respective roles), and also from workers and communities. Such collaborative efforts are at the heart of the approach outlined here.

In fact, the importance of all these actors underlines the need for government efforts since it is only government that can create or ensure an environment in which the main pillars of an enabling environment—drivers, capacity, and tools—point each of these actors in a common direction.

Our recommendations arise from six months of work involving desk research; outreach to numerous government officials; buyers in the apparel and agriculture sectors; NGOs and trade unions in the U.S. and EU; similar organizations in exporting countries; and donor agencies, both bilateral and multilateral.[1] We considered and analyzed the results of these consultations and the information generated by other means.

We would note that the level of experimentation on the part of exporting country governments remains relatively low in quantity and quality, and thus some of the proposals made in this report are based less on extensive, practical experiences and more on analytical perceptions of what may work well in different settings. Moreover, consultations have shown that while there is an increasing sense among various parties to the debate that governments should be engaged more energetically, some actors still find it hard to appreciate the need for a new trajectory that does not center on the performance of the private sector alone. There also remains considerable skepticism about the degree to which exporting country governments are genuinely prepared to compete on the basis of better social and environmental performance.

In short, many seasoned observers continue to see government as the problem rather than the solution. We proceed on the assumption that this is notan immutable situation and that it must be faced directly for progress to be made.

SUMMARY OF RECOMMENDATIONS

The achievement of good, sustainable labor and environmental workplace practices in global supply chains requires a supportive enabling environment. The public sector has a key role as principal overseer of the enabling environment. Developing country governments are likely to be successful in improving social and environmental standards if they develop coherent strategies that address all the critical elements of the enabling framework: transparent and efficient legal and market-based drivers, robust capacities, and useful tools and skills.

In our view, developing-country governments should develop approaches that seek to mobilize the skills, resources, and capacities of multiple stakeholders, including suppliers, buyers, and civil society, and engage them in collaborative efforts focused on particular industries or particular agricultural commodities. Such initiatives should feature collaborative governance, common standards based on local laws and consistent with internationally agreed principles, and financial sustainability.

As noted in the report, we believe that collaborative, industry-focused, and multistakeholder initiatives such as those presently being developed or implemented in the Central American garment industry, the South African wine industry, the Kenyan horticulture industry, and the Cambodian garment industry hold the greatest potential for improving labor and environmental standards in global supply chains.

In developing countries, the public sector can contribute to the development of these collaborative, industry-focused initiatives by endorsing or supporting other stakeholders' efforts; facilitating the creation of these frameworks through its convening power, or by establishing legal frameworks that aid in their development.

Our recommendations for public sector interventions fall into four main categories: (1) standards, including refinement and enforcement; (2) capacity-building; (3) incentives; and (4) worker empowerment. These are further elaborated below.

While the individual proposals falling within these four categories have merit on their own, we suggest that, whenever possible, actions in each of these four categories be implemented through collaborative frameworks that are designed in as comprehensive a manner as possible.

The recommendations we make are included here:

• We recommend that national governments work to ensure that their labor and environmental laws are consistent with internationally agreed principles, as this enables the achievement of good labor and environmental standards. In the field of labor standards, we propose that national governments, as appropriate, benefit from the advisory services of the ILO, which is well suited to carry out such "consistency reviews." In the area of environmental standards, we propose that national governments, as appropriate, seek the advice of, for example, the World Bank Group, the United Nations Environment Programme (UNEP), and UN Development Programme (UNDP).

• We recommend that national governments, as appropriate, seek to ensure that labor and environmental provisions apply equally to all categories of workers, and all workplaces, without exemptions that create or invite lower standards.

• We recommend that the public sector in developing countries seek to engage as appropriate multiple stakeholders representing workers and businesses in distinct industries in efforts to ensure greater clarity of laws as well as guidelines on implementation. Such efforts could take the form of: (1) a users' guide on relevant legal requirements; (2) a management guide on implementation that would help managers identify what actions are necessary to implement the various provisions, and (3) a workers' guide on their rights under the law. The role of government could be to encourage such efforts as well as to play a facilitating and endorsing role to ensure consistency with legal requirements. Such efforts may be carried out in connection with collaborative initiatives, however, they may also yield results when carried out independent of wider efforts.

• In order of priority, governments should focus their capacity-building efforts on suppliers, using a wide array of methods, and, second, explore the new capacities needed within government to undertake the range of actions proposed in this paper. A tertiary priority is the need to build the capacity of workers, trade unions, and civil society organizations.

• Governments should take steps to ensure that a diverse roster of resources is available to support learning by suppliers. Where gaps exist, government should invest in the creation of needed resources.

• Governments should take a range of steps to shift their focus toward greater reliance on capacity-building. This can be accomplished through a number of means, including diversification of the skills present in labor and environmental inspectorates; the creation of new incentives for the staff of such inspectorates; and the creation of new incentives for factories that would access these resources. This may include the establishment of training as a factor in determining which factories will be subjected to formal inspections. Assessments should be conducted to determine the effectiveness of these efforts to allow for decisions about how to invest the time and resources of the inspectorates in the future.

• Government should make an investment in the creation of local networks, pulling together the types of resources discussed in this section.

• Government should facilitate the development of local centers of excellence through funding and incentives.

• We recommend that governments explore the relevance of using the diverse set of positive incentives available. Incentives such as reduced local fees and charges can be used to encourage the adoption of labor and environmental management practices that result in benefits to society that outweigh the costs of granting the incentives. Positive incentives should be used as an integrated element of an overall strategy that promotes better workplace practices. Governments should also explore the relevance of linking access to government "benefits" such as soft lending facilities, participation in trade fairs, and so on to legal compliance. International financing institutions such as the World Bank Group, the European Commission, and bilateral donors should use environmental and social criteria as part of their lending and purchasing criteria, as this will greatly reinforce the message of local governments as well as put additional pressure on local governments.

• We recommend that governments explore negative incentives as a means of promoting legal compliance. The use of industrywide penalties could be considered to encourage a greater degree of self-regulation within industries. Transparency of performance should also be considered; however, attention should be given to ensuring that relevant target groups such as employees, potential employees, competitors, and others have meaningful access to publicized data. Linking these to other efforts, including the targeting of enforcement efforts and the coordination of public and private enforcement activities, will enhance their effectiveness.

• Governments should consider granting Export Processing Zone (EPZ) status to collaborative export-oriented initiatives that aspire to high environmental and labor standards. Additional criteria should be defined, for example, joint inspections by employers and unions, as is the case in some Philippine EPZ. This may act as an incentive to facilitate the development of such initiatives.

• Governments should ensure that all workers in export sectors have reasonable access to clearly understandable information about basic legal protections for workers as well as clear and present environmental risks related to the workplace.

• Governments should take steps to establish, fund, and publicize alternative dispute resolution mechanisms easily accessible to workers.

IMPLEMENTING THE PROPOSALS

In many ways, implementation of these proposals represents more of a political challenge than a technical challenge. There are, in our view, three distinct ways of proceeding to pursue the ideas presented here:

• **National strategies:** The Bank can seek to engage at a national level, to establish an overall commitment to the creation of an enabling environment that is central to the country's export strategy.

• **Industry efforts:** Alternatively, there is the option to engage at a national level in a certain industry, or, in the case of agriculture, a particular commodity.

• **Opportunistic efforts:** There also is the option of pursuing opportunities that arise in particular situations. While this may appear to be less appealing than the other options, because it seems to be less comprehensive and proactive, it is likely that this is the only way to make progress in certain important markets, for example, in China.

While each of these approaches has merits and drawbacks, the reality is likely that no single model is likely to be sufficient. In some cases there may be national economies and situations that will be amenable to a comprehensive approach that will bring the greatest impact. Wherever that is possible, we would welcome such an effort. The Bank's own recent work in Vietnam and El Salvador suggest that such efforts may be possible.

In other cases there may be particular industries or commodities that can be addressed in a relatively comprehensive way. In recent years, the footwear and toy industries, which are relatively concentrated in terms of purchasing and the geography of production, have adopted increasingly harmonized approaches. The cocoa industry, facing serious criticism, also has developed a fairly comprehensive model that could be linked to public policy. The Sustainable Agriculture Initiative, involving several major food companies, also has developed a model that could be integrated with policy solutions on a commodity basis.

Finally, there are undoubtedly opportunistic efforts that could yield solid results. The increased attention that certain export markets (namely China and India) are likely to attract in the aftermath of the phaseout of apparel quotas may create external pressures for governments to address more seriously the issues discussed in this chapter.

A FRAMEWORK FOR PUBLIC SECTOR ENGAGEMENT WITH LABOR AND ENVIRONMENTAL STANDARDS

The achievement of good labor and environmental conditions in global supply chains must be founded in a supportive, enabling environment in which business can work continuously to improve workplace practices in collaboration with stakeholders. The public sector has a key role as the principal overseer of the enabling environment.

Essential Elements for the Creation of Successful Enabling Environments

Based on the work of the World Bank Group with respect to enabling environments (Ward, 2004), consultations with stakeholders, and those practical examples surveyed for the purpose of this study, we believe that any work to promote enabling environments should address either or all of the following three critical elements:

• **Maximum use of drivers:** An enabling environment is considerably easier to create if business and others are pushed to act through the presence of drivers. Drivers can take various forms, including legal, commercial, and social, and they may take both positive and negative forms. A prime example is the impending phase-out of apparel quotas, which is driving many governments to pursue strategies allowing them to compete on the basis of good labor practices. Market-based drivers also have been particularly strong in pushing many of the initiatives referenced in this report, such as the South African wine industry (all producers export to the same market, thus being subject to identical market pressures) and the Philippine garment industry (access to

---

IMPORTANCE OF MARKET DRIVERS

In the nascent Export Success in Central America (ESCA) initiative, there are strong market-based drivers. In this case, access to the large unified North American market and the unique political pressures arising from negotiations over the Central American Free Trade Agreement (CAFTA) have helped engage the attention of all stakeholders. Similarly, the Home workers Code of Practice in the Australian retail and textile-garment manufacturing industry has benefited from strong market drivers, first and foremost intensive NGO campaigns, and, secondly, the need to come in line with Australian law. The Kenyan cut-flower industry, through the Kenyan Flower Council, has developed a social compliance initiative largely in response to the coordinated demand from the Dutch auction houses that source 60 percent of Kenya's exports.

---

quotas has been linked to participation in a WRAP [Worldwide Responsible Apparel Production]-based social compliance initiative).

• **Capacity:** It also is essential that there be relevant human capacities and institutions such as inspectorates, ministerial departments, business federations, and the like to pursue the social, environmental, and economic goals inherent in this agenda. For example, the failure or inability of states to enforce labor standards, despite the presence of legal, social, and, to some degree, commercial drivers of strong labor practices, remains a factor that undermines the enabling environment. Recent progress in Cambodia, for example, presents progress toward an alternate scenario in which trade agreements have provided strong driver, and the ILO has worked to ensure that local capacity exists to make progress toward the social goals.

• **Tools:** A successful enabling environment also relies on the presence of tools to be used in achieving social and environmental goals. Tools that have been identified in our research as well as work performed by others on the Bank's behalf include labels, certificates, guidelines, management systems and so on. One example cited in the text of the report comes from the skilled trades in the Netherlands, where both drivers and institutions were in place to ensure good performance. However, there was a lack of tools available to enable performance that came only when guidelines for the practical application of broad principles were put in place.

Successful strategies should address the critical elements within a coherent framework. While local governments may be effective in building institutions such as robust and credible enforcement agencies, these efforts are more effective when they are coupled with strong and transparent market drivers as well as the practical skills and incentives required to shape business behavior. We also believe, as outlined further below, that such approaches are most effective when they are focused on particular industries engaging multiple stakeholders in collaborative efforts.[2]

In our view, the inherent limits of the present system of codes of conduct to bring about sustainable social and economic change, despite substantial efforts by numerous stakeholders, is based on the absence of a systematic, collaborative framework.

Industry-Focused Collaborative Framework

We believe that strategies based on industry-focused collaboration between multiple stakeholders and within a coherent framework represent a novel departure from governments' traditional approach to promoting labor and environmental standards. Moreover, these arrangements also hold the greatest promise for creating supportive, enabling environments that ultimately will result in improved labor and environmental standards in global supply chains.

While several of the recommendations that we present in this report have merit on their own, we generally believe that the impact of each proposal will be substantially greater if implemented within a coherent, industry-focused strategy that seeks to engage multiple stakeholders in collaborative efforts. Thus, collaborative initiatives can be used to achieve the full range of options presented later in this paper including: (1) efforts to set, extend, and enforce standards; (2) capacity-building; (3) worker education and engagement; and (4) development and implementation of economic incentives for good practices. Before turning to these, below we outline the basic characteristics of such industry-focused collaborative frameworks.

Collaboration

The collaboration we are calling for is not simply the politically driven desire by some to see more transparency on the part of the business sector.[3] Rather, it is practical collaboration within a coherent framework that allows each sector of society to bring its own unique attributes to bear in ensuring that the issues in question can be addressed successfully and result in long-term, sustainable solutions.

There are several reasons for this, including:

• The need to shift away from the ad hoc nature of efforts to date. As we have noted in several places, the present approach is unlikely to yield sustainable results, suggesting a need for developing coherent, collaborative approaches. Collaboration would also seem to be a prerequisite for governments to ensure that efforts are supportive of governments' overall developmental objectives.

• Leveraging and wiser use of resources. Governments will not be able to fully align private, voluntary initiatives to public policy goals unless such efforts are brought within an overall framework. Also, there is widespread agreement among particular businesses (and among many other stakeholders) that the present individualized supplier auditing represents a suboptimization of resources.

This is the rationale behind the growing number of industrywide initiatives such as the German retail sector initiative and the international toy industry initiative. Moreover, the present shift from auditing and policing toward capacity-building and training will require more concerted and cooperative efforts to be successful. However, in the absence of coherent, collaborative frameworks, individualized monitoring risks merely being replaced by individualized capacity-building, resulting in the same suboptimal use of resources.

• Ensuring that complementary competencies are present. While the public sector is the overall "organizer" of the enabling environment, it does not on its own possess the competencies and skills required to bring about change. Thus, collaboration allows each party to apply its expertise and support implementation. For instance, the development of workplace codes in the skilled trades in the Netherlands was a result of collaborative effort in a traditional tripartite setup recognizing that both business and unions had relevant expertise to bring to the table.

• Ensuring broad-based support and credibility. The emergence of codes of conduct should also be seen through the prism of public governance failure to ensure credible and robust enforcement of standards. At the same time, civil society remains highly skeptical of purely private, voluntary efforts to ensure better standards.

In addition to the above, collaboration also appears to be a prerequisite for achieving the critical mass of financial and human resources required to ensure the more widespread realization of labor rights and better environmental protection. Thus, in our view, this is why many of the initiatives to date have failed to contribute to a wider respect of labor rights and environmental protection. They have been too narrow in scope and scale.

The Elements of Collaborative Initiatives

Based on the practical examples cited in this report, we believe that collaborative frameworks could be based on the following organizing principles:

HOMEWORKERS IN AUSTRALIA

In Australia, the issue of homeworking has been addressed through collaborative efforts. The government facilitated an agreement between retailers, trade unions, suppliers, and others to develop a code of conduct that can lead to certification that no homeworkers have been mistreated in the production of goods. Retailers engaged in this process can obtain a "No Sweatshop" label certifying this practice. This example illustrates both a comprehensive, collaborative industry-based approach, the value of developing a clear set of standards that can be understood effectively by workers, suppliers, buyers, and others, and also an example of addressing a gap in standards by enhancing coverage of protections concerning homeworkers.

• **Industry focus:** As noted above, collaborative initiatives are likely to yield the best results when focused on particular industries. Industry is in many respects a highly organizing and defining determinant of the social, political, and economic structures of society. In practice, the critical elements of the enabling environment are likely to be different between industries; for instance, market-based drivers tend to be industry-specific. More important, however, the critical stakeholders are usually organized along industrial lines. This applies to labor unions and employers' federations and also to some NGOs that are focused on particular industries. In addition, the connection between the buyer and the supplier sides follows industrial lines.

• **Shared governance:** The governance of collaborative frameworks should involve participants that reflect the broad concerns and interests of the key constituents affected, including constituencies without institutional representation such as migrant workers, women workers, and the like. Collaboration thus has to extend beyond the mere inclusion of multiple stakeholders to include multistakeholder governance. In some cases, tripartite governance will suffice, and in others additional stakeholders will need to be brought into the picture. Collaborative governance is crucial to the resolution of disputes among the involved parties. For instance, in the executive committee of the South African wine industry initiative, the fact that all constituents participate on an equal footing is seen as essential. In addition, such governance structures may act as a precursor for facilitating institutional dialogue among the tripartite bodies of the labor market. For instance, the project advisory committee in the Cambodian initiative has been instrumental in providing a neutral ground for rapprochement between the Cambodian trade unions and employers' federations. This in turn has created the basis for the development of an institutionalized labor market conflict resolution mechanism that in time should become a permanent institution in the Cambodian labor market.

• **Common standards:** Collaboration should be structured on an agreed-upon set of environmental and labor performance principles, based on national laws and regulations, consistent with international principles, notably core labor standards. This said, we believe that there are reasons to be cautious in promoting labor standards that are markedly "above" the national law, unless there are material differences between national law and international principles. The initiatives in the Cambodian textile industry and the South African wine industry are both considered successful partly because they do not seek to achieve labor standards that are dramatically above what is required by local law. As an observer close to the initiative reported: "Another key issue has been that the code of conduct is based squarely on the law; producers see this as a compliance initiative that in addition may bring skills, capacity, and market access; unions see this as a compliance initiative and not as a process for promoting new union rights/ambitions. If the code aspired to go beyond the law this may have been different."

• **Financial sustainability:** While significant public funding and/or external funding may be necessary to undertake the initial phases of initiatives described here, the long-term financial sustainability of such initiatives would have to be secured by the financial commitment of the involved parties through market mechanisms and/or some limited form of public funding. It is an important premise of the proposals presented that they should not require significant public funding as a prerequisite for successful implementation. In addition, committed collaboration would seem to require an element of financial risk on the part of the private sector.[4]

In addition to the above characteristics of collaborative initiatives, we would like to stress the importance of local ownership.[5] While many of the drivers, capacities, and tools in recent years have come from developed economies, they are not long-term substitutes for the integration of public sector initiatives in developing countries. Moreover, we recommend that the northern industry-wide initiatives seek to interact more profoundly and strategically with local governments as well as work to contribute to local capacity to develop, implement, and govern collaborative initiatives.[6]

The Bank is well positioned to promote collaborative frameworks through its ability to convene governments with other actors and by providing seed capital to develop and adapt collaborative efforts in critical local markets. Indeed, most of the successful multistakeholder initiatives (for example, the ETI, FLA, SAI) in this field have been supported by a multilateral or public sector agency. In addition, it appears that "the stars are aligning" in support of such initiatives, as most parties in this debate—buyers, suppliers, trade unions, and NGOs—are now calling for institutional change. This means that even if

---

NATIONAL VERSUS REGIONAL APPROACHES

The ESCA-initiative in Central America is of interest because it is representative of the collaborative model outlined above, and because it takes a regional approach that mirrors a relatively unified sourcing market. If successful, ESCA could potentially be replicated in other nations or regions, although the region's unique access to the large North American market, and the unique political pressures arising from the negotiations over the Central American Free Trade Agreement (CAFTA) that have helped engage the attention of all stakeholders, may not be equally present in other locations. However, such conditions may not be unique. For instance, in East Africa, Kenya and Uganda are acutely aware of the problem of ensuring similar standards to avoid relocation of industries and/or workers. Some Kenyan consultation partners suggested that regional approaches to some issues might work better in the East Africa region than through national approaches.

such parties are reaching the same conclusion for different reasons, as seems likely, they are indeed far more receptive to the notion that without systematic change, their discrete initiatives are likely to be handicapped.

In summary, the collaborative framework is essential because it seeks to provide precisely what has been missing from the debate to date: This is a coordinated and systematic approach. In addition, the examples cited here and elsewhere in the report demonstrate that it is possible to engineer such approaches with broad participation and good results. Such broad-based initiatives will not be appropriate for all situations, and they may be more time-intensive. However, they hold the promise of greater results, and for that reason we suggest that the more discrete options presented below be considered for inclusion in collaborative frameworks wherever possible.

RECOMMENDATIONS

Governments can engage more fully in promoting compliance with labor and environmental principles by pursuing activities falling into four basic categories: (1) setting and enforcing standards more effectively; (2) building the capacity of private actors to make a maximum contribution toward these goals; (3) empowering workers and trade unions to play a more active role in this debate; and (4) providing targeted incentives, positive and negative, for enterprises to embrace the social and environmental aspects of their businesses more fully.

The four categories are presented in greater detail below and address the following points:

• **Standards:** Setting and enforcing standards are important elements of the drivers, institutions, and tools that create better enabling environments. Recognizing that there are gaps in both the de jure and de facto application of standards, local governments have three primary contributions they can make with respect to standards:

- Clarification of existing standards in a manner consistent with international standards, where available;
- Extension of existing laws and regulations to cover areas such as export processing zones, where they are not currently applied;
- Collaboration with the private and independent sectors in the enforcement of standards.

• **Capacity-building:** Too often suppliers lack the basic management skills to ensure good labor and environmental practices. It is also the case that governments, NGOs, trade unions, and workers have a substantial and distinct ability to participate in the establishment and implementation of codes. Local governments have strong incentives to see the implementation of codes shared by all relevant institutions to reduce the resources they must devote to these issues. Accordingly, governments can achieve improvements by engaging in steps including:

- Wider application of human resources and environmental management practices to achieve the substantive goals embodied in this work;
- The development of local centers of excellence;
- Sharing of technical and management skills.

• **Worker empowerment:** It is clear that workers are not fully able to vindicate their rights in most developing country environments. There are legal, political, and developmental barriers to worker empowerment that can be reduced through a variety of means including:

- Provision of more and better information about workers' rights;
- Removal of barriers to the exercise of freedom of association, allowing workers to protect their own rights through unions;
- Greater attention to the distinct needs of certain categories of workers present in the agriculture and apparel industries (for example, migrants, women, and seasonal and temporary workers) who are less able to avail themselves of existing protections.

• **Economic incentives:** This category of action is the most controversial of the items presented in the report. Some observers do not believe that incentives are appropriate because they are based on a model that provides rewards to private actors for following the law. Others, however, see economic incentives as a temporary way to encourage business to take on responsibilities that they have not been addressing, or believe that capital and/or aid should be conditioned on social and environmental performance. While mindful of the complications presented by incentives, we include consideration of options that have support from some quarters, including:

- Conditionality of export-related financial opportunities such as export credits, loan capital, insurance, and the like, based on achievement of certain social and environmental practices;
- Creation of special export zones available only to companies that commit to achieving social and environmental performance.

Standards

The challenge with respect to standards has two distinct but related dimensions: establishment of standards and enforcement of standards. Both are important on their own and reinforce the other. Both are at the heart of the enabling environment for achieving good labor and environmental practices.

Establishing Clear and Effective Standards

Clear and enforceable standards in content and in application consistent with internationally agreed-upon principles are a critical element of the enabling environment. The public sector in developing countries should attend to the consistency, applicability, and clarity of their national laws to ensure that the legal framework enables achieving good labor and environmental standards.

Consistency with internationally agreed principles. National laws pertaining to labor and environment should be consistent with internationally agreed principles. There are several reasons for this:

• Consistency is an objective in itself. Unless laws are consistent with internationally agreed principles, there is a risk that efforts to achieve good labor and environmental practices in line with the requirements of multinational corporations are undercut by the legal framework.

• Our research indicates that a legal framework consistent with internationally agreed principles enables efforts to achieve good labor and environmental performance. First, the achievement of good workplace practices becomes a legal compliance issue. Second, efforts to achieve good workplace practices are driven by a local rather than a foreign agenda. Third, the two principal drivers of change—incentives and sanctions—becomes mutually reinforcing.

Our research has revealed that some governments in light of new sourcing patterns are conscious about the need to ensure that their national laws are consistent with internationally agreed principles. For instance, in 2003 the ILO prepared a comparative analysis of current labor legislation in each of the countries engaged in CAFTA negotiations, with a particular focus on the core

---

HOW THE LEGAL FRAMEWORK ENABLES ACHIEVEMENT OF GOOD LABOR STANDARDS

Consultations revealed that the commitment of the private sector to the initiatives in the Cambodian textile and the South African wine industries may be partly ascribed to the fact that both initiatives set out to achieve standards that are in line with local law; in both countries local law is materially consistent with ILO standards. One observer noted that this in turn means that both the private sector and the unions see the initiative as a compliance initiative. This dynamic also appears to have played a role in the Kenyan horticulture sector, where the code of conduct defined by the Kenyan Flower Council operates with two compliance levels. The first level aspires to labor standards consistent with the core labor standards of the ILO and environmental standards in line with local law. The second level operates with environmental standards above the legal requirements. In Australia, the Homeworkers Code of Practice is also based on local law and in terms of standards performance, does not require manufacturers or retailers to go beyond the law.

labor standards referred to in the ILO Declaration on Fundamental Principles and Rights at Work.[7]

Ensuring applicability of existing standards. In many developing countries, basic labor law is enforced, if at all, with an emphasis on the formal sector, and in some cases applies only to certain parts of the workforce, leaving a very large part of the workforce with minimal legal protection, including workers who are part of global supply chains. These gaps present problems for three reasons in addition to the obvious point that they leave many workers unprotected.

• First, this lack of legal coverage reinforces the view that codes are somehow an external imposition that is inconsistent with local practice, since codes often require suppliers to ensure compliance throughout their own supply chains.

• Second, these gaps mean that two sets of rules apply: one for companies in a purely local economy, and another for those participating in global supply chains, which creates market distortions and a two-track system for those seeking to enforce applicable provisions.

• Third, these gaps run contrary to clear international consensus.

Some of the collaborative initiatives referenced in this report are seeking to address this issue through nonlegal mechanisms. For example, in the South African wine industry initiative, WIETA, the governing body, also includes representatives of migrant and temporary workers. Similarly, the initiative run by the Kenyan Flower Council in the Kenyan horticultural sector seeks to ensure that labor standards and environmental provisions apply equally to all workers irrespective of their legal status.

Clarity of laws. Standards must be clear and enforceable to allow all stakeholders to work on a common platform toward agreed-upon goals. Empirical research gathered for this report as well as the authors' more general experience makes clear, however, that there is substantial confusion about the meaning of existing standards, as applied.[8] Examples range from the meaning of wage and overtime laws to the application of principles on freedom of association and collective bargaining, to the specific requirements of environment, health, and safety issues. There are several additional reasons why clarification of standards should be pursued:

• Lack of clarity is particularly damaging given that many buyers' suppliers are small and medium enterprises (SMEs), and many workers in agriculture and apparel are unfamiliar with formal industrial work settings.

• There is sometimes (undue) advantage gained by various parties able to claim that the expectations expressed in applicable laws are unclear.

• Clarification of standards would contribute to greater consistency in the requirements expressed by multinational companies to their suppliers. This would limit confusion and inefficiency and contribute to greater transparency in the implementation process.

Research undertaken for this report shows that in several locations stakeholders have sought to address not only what is required, but also how it is done in practice. In these locations, efforts have thus generally sought to

(1) bring greater clarity to the meaning of law, and to (2) guide the supplier to adjust the work practices in meeting these requirements.

The experiences also suggest that clarification is likely to be more successful when addressed at industry level rather than at sector or economy-wide level, as labor and environmental issues tend to be industry specific.[9] These experiences also suggest that multistakeholder approaches rather than government-only attention to these issues should by pursued.[10] Such an approach engages stakeholders in confidence-building processes, where they can address issues such as "What are the problems?" "What are the requirements?" And, "How do we address them?" The industry-specific, multistakeholder approach has also proven to yield results in developed economies as witnessed by the experiences in the skilled trades in the Netherlands. The model used in the Netherlands could easily be replicated as good practice in other countries, including developing countries.

Enforcement of Standards

Enforcement of standards is a key challenge to governments aspiring to create an enabling environment for the achievement of good labor and environmental standards in global supply chains. Poor enforcement is the key aspect of the public governance failure with respect to labor and environmental standards. This is a belief that has been deeply internalized by those consulted for this report, with the result that many are extremely skeptical that the situation will change.

The present enforcement capacity in many developing countries suggests that a system of credible and robust enforcement must rely on other means of enforcement than the traditional policing undertaken by the public inspectorates.[11]

CLARIFICATION OF LEGAL REQUIREMENTS

The initiatives in the Kenyan flower industry, the South African wine industry, and the Cambodian textile industry have all placed great emphasis on developing highly specific implementation guidelines directed at management and middle management. In Cambodia, guides were also developed to workers to allow these to familiarize themselves with their rights and obligations. Similar worker guides are also being considered in the South African wine industry initiative.

In all of these initiatives the role of government has varied, suggesting that the role of government will be different from situation to situation. For instance, in Cambodia the government was an active part of the process, whereas in the Kenyan flower industry initiative it played a very minor role. In South Africa the government played a role by virtue of being represented on the governance board.

INDUSTRY SECTOR LABOR CODES AND GUIDES

The Dutch employers' organization in the skilled trades has developed detailed, easy-to-read and use guidelines for management of workplace issues. The guidelines are structured by an industrial process identifying solutions to potential problems. On each issue it offers advice on how to achieve performance beyond legal compliance. The guidelines have been developed with the relevant trade unions and representatives of government, however the employers' organization is responsible for continuously updating the codes. The codes have been developed at a cost of $15,000. See Case 10 at the end of this chapter.

The absence of robust and credible public enforcement is therefore the principal reason for the rise in private monitoring by multinational corporations in recent years. However, as has been stated several times, while private monitoring and auditing exercised by multinational companies in principle may be seen as a complementary resource to the public labor and environmental inspection systems, in practice the current "system" misallocates and duplicates resources without showing corresponding benefits in social, environmental, or economic terms.

The research undertaken for this paper suggests that public-private collaboration on enforcement presents some opportunities for achieving better and more comprehensive enforcement. The examples identified are very different, each providing different learning experiences. Hence, we have illustrated at some length the most important characteristics of these initiatives.

Public-private collaboration on enforcement of standards. To begin with, the public-private collaboration initiatives studied here shared the following important traits:

• **Tacit cooperation:** In several places it seems as if the public sector tacitly recognizes private monitoring as an effective substitute for public enforcement. This is the case in the South African wine industry (WIETA), where the ongoing monitoring in the exporting part of the industry effectively has allowed the public inspectorates to focus their resources on those producing for the domestic market. The Ministry of Labour is represented at the governing body of WIETA, thereby explicitly endorsing the initiative as well as the standards aspired to and the monitoring methodology employed. Though the Ministry of Labour has not stated that the private, independent monitoring formally substitutes for public inspections, such a move is being considered. Similarly, the industry-led and governed Kenya Flower Council that conducts frequent monitoring of growers according to and beyond legal standards has effectively allowed the public labor and environmental inspectorates to reduce their monitoring. There is no formal agreement to this. Interviews with public inspectorates in other countries revealed that private monitoring in practice often substitutes for public inspections or as a minimum informs the comprehensiveness of the inspections performed.[12]

• **Formal cooperation**: The experiences in Cambodia and the Philippines are different. In the case of Cambodia there is a high degree of formal cooperation in that ILO-driven monitoring has replaced public inspections. In the Philippines, the government endorsed and mandated WRAP-program that relies on private auditors also formally replaces public inspections in the garment industry. The nascent Central American initiative, ESCA, also seems to embark on a highly institutionalized mechanism for private-public cooperation.

• **Self-evaluation**: Whereas all of the above initiatives are highly industry-focused initiatives, the Philippine government has ventured an approach that seeks to rely on self-evaluation as a means of ensuring wider enforcement of labor standards. The recently adopted Labor Standards Enforcement Framework requires companies with two hundred or more employees to carry out self-evaluations. Evaluations are to be carried out once a year by a joint team of workers and management on the basis of guidelines developed by the government. Instances of unreported noncompliance detected during random labor inspections will result in significant sanctions. Similar approaches are being tested in the Indian state Haryana.[13] In the area of environmental standards, the U.S. Toxic Release Inventory and similar pollutant-release and transfer registers (PRTRs) in other northern countries use self-evaluation as a means of enforcement. These registers also use different incentives to ensure "honest" reporting and are noteworthy in that they ensure a high degree of transparency.

• **Accreditation**: During several consultations with public sector representatives, it was suggested that the public sector could accredit a third party to do labor inspections. This was not considered politically impossible. However, with the notable and unique exception of the initiatives in Cambodia and the Philippines (WRAP program), accreditation was not taking place in practice. The multistakeholder initiative HEBI, in the Kenyan horticulture industry, apparently has a goal of training auditors within a third-party framework so they can be accredited; this however is a longer-term ambition, as the public sector presently is only involved as an observer.

These experiences suggest that the public sector can pursue several different approaches to public-private enforcement. Each approach has its merit depending on the industrial setting and the proposed objectives.[14] However, the evidence also suggests that there exists a lack of generic models that may be applied widely across industries and companies of different sizes. Nonetheless, we believe there are models to be tried that build on and/or combine the experiences of existing examples of good practice. We note that these models can be implemented in isolation or combined to achieve wider impact. There are four basic models: self-evaluation, assurance, accreditation, and certification.

Self-Evaluation: We recommend that governments consider self-evaluation as a means of enforcement in larger companies. Self-evaluations should be carried out by a joint team comprised of workers and management to ensure credible and balanced assessments. This in turn means that self-evaluation as a model can be pursued meaningfully only in industries where worker representation is sufficiently strong to balance the power of employers. Where local worker representation is weak, it may be possible to engage representatives of relevant local trade unions. The government should maintain the right to carry out random spot inspections. The government can use various sets of incentives to stimulate sound evaluations, ranging from the threat of significantly greater sanctions when noncompliances are detected during spot inspections to the use of positive incentives, such as offering consulting services to improve labor standards and workplace processes. Companies that voluntarily disclose noncompliance should be given a grace period of six to twelve months to correct the situation. Schemes of self-evaluation can be combined with public registers such as the U.S. Toxic Release Inventory to allow local communities, civil society, and business organizations to engage more effectively on workplace issues, exert greater pressure on poor-performing businesses, and so on.[15]

Using self-evaluation as an enforcement model will allow public sector inspection agencies to focus their scarce resources on industries and/or companies where the scope for improvements is more significant.[16] It may also act as a model for facilitating cooperation between workers and management on these workplace issues. Self-evaluation, in the short term, is unlikely to bring the assurance multinational corporations require to manage their own inspections, but it could allow for these inspections to focus more on training (capacity-building) rather than on policing.

Assurance: We recommend that governments define specific criteria related to such areas as auditing methodology, auditor training, and independence of auditors to allow the public sector to formally recognize private, collaborative, and industrywide monitoring as a substitute for public inspections. This would allow governments to formally approve private monitoring efforts that are based on robust methodologies and sound practices, such as the monitoring efforts in the South African wine industry. This would be one step short of accreditation, as the government should continue to carry out calibration visits and other assurance activities that ensure agreed-upon standards are upheld. Private monitoring results should be made available to the public sector; as agreed in the initiative, such results could also be made available to buyers on request. Instances of noncompliance should be accompanied with grace periods of six to twelve months depending on the issue. Repeated instances of noncompliance should result in penalties. As is the case in the Cambodian textile industry initiative, repeated instances of noncompliance could also result in public disclosure to allow peer pressure to build. This model should apply to industries where industrywide monitoring schemes exist that, in addition to using sound methodologies and trained auditors, ensure balanced representation of all concerned constituencies. Thus, the industry-led monitoring initiative in the Kenyan flower industry would not pass this test, as workers and civil society are not represented either at the governance or implementation levels.

Assurance as an enforcement model would allow the public sector inspection agencies to focus their scarce resources on industries and/or companies where labor standards need the most improvement. It would also allow the government to effectively capitalize on ongoing private monitoring efforts and "legalize" the present tacit consent. In addition, such schemes may encourage other industries to develop identical efforts as well as spur non-participating companies to join these industrywide initiatives. This model can thus be effectively implemented only in locations where industrywide, collaborative initiatives already exist. This model can be incorporated into a framework that uses self-evaluation as a means of enforcement.

Accreditation: We recommend that governments consider accreditation of third-party organizations to carry out labor and environmental inspections based on agreed-upon standards and methodologies. The present work within the International Social and Environmental Accreditation and Labelling (Alliance) (ISEAL-alliance) and the Social Accountability in Sustainable Agriculture project could serve as a basis for the development of appropriate standards, methodologies, and accreditation guidelines. With respect to labor standards, the ILO could play an advisory role drawing upon its experiences with the WISE and Work Improvements in Neighborhood Development (WIND) methodologies, which seek to combine workplace improvements with productivity improvements. Although accreditation may contribute to a process that raises performance standards, removes inconsistencies, and allows for a greater exchange of experiences and learning between the public and private sectors, it is unlikely to result in more extensive enforcement by itself unless it is combined with a legal framework such as assurance and/or self-evaluation schemes. These legal frameworks could recognize inspections performed by accredited auditors as effectively replacing public inspections, provided that private inspection reports are made available to the public inspection agencies. The use of private accredited auditors could be encouraged by various incentives such as a grace period for reported noncompliance, a financial subsidy to cover some of the expenses, preferential treatment, lower insurance premiums, and the like. Accreditation, if based on standards and methodologies consistent with international good practice, could also contribute to reducing the frequency of individual buyer audits.

Certification: The natural extension of accreditation is certification. We recommend that governments define a list of certificates, such as ISO 14001, OSHA 18001, and SA8000, that would exempt certified companies from inspections or result in less comprehensive inspections. This has become part of the new Danish labor enforcement regime that as a key element introduced "customized inspections," which in practice means that companies with robust labor and/or environmental management systems are subjected to less frequent and less comprehensive inspections.[17] Providing additional incentives such as lowering environmental fees, giving preferential treatment in public procurement, and so on could encourage certification.[18] Although the strength of certification in developing countries frequently is met with skepticism, it appears to help inform the public sector in devising its strategies for enforcement.[19]

We believe that the "assurance model" holds considerable promise for effectively combining public and private enforcement capacities. The present model in the South African wine industry provides a good template even if the private monitoring has not yet been formally recognized as an effective replacement for public inspections. The initiative in Cambodia could also provide this kind of learning, however, the initiative is presently too financially dependent on donor support to become a real model. The multistakeholder initiative in the Kenyan horticulture industry, HEBI, could be interesting once it moves toward securing government approval (accreditation) of trained auditors. The "assurance model" could be combined with "accreditation" to lend additional credibility to private monitoring with a view to reassure the buyer and possibly reduce individual buyer monitoring.

Capacity-Building

Increasingly, buyers and suppliers are urging code of conduct efforts to focus less on monitoring and more on capacity-building, recognizing that suppliers often lack the required skills and know-how to sustain good labor and environmental practices.

Government has a strong incentive to engage in capacity-building: When enterprises are better able to achieve social and environmental goals, the costs both of enforcement and mitigation of harm decline. An additional incentive is found in the strong international support network for governments engaging in these activities, such as that from NGOs, buyers, trade unions, and donor agencies. Thus, no one government needs to assume the costs of such activities by itself. It is also widely believed that poor social and environmental practices and poor general management practices are closely connected, suggesting that by addressing labor and environmental standards, local businesses may harness long-term economic benefits and vice versa.[20]

In this section, we make a range of recommendations about how governments can achieve the common goals of competitiveness and good practice by building the skills of suppliers, and secondarily, the institutions that support greater capacity on the part of suppliers to manage labor and environmental issues well. Government's role, with respect to capacity-building, is multifaceted and includes funding; provision of technical expertise; reworking the legal enforcement process; and creating incentives by reducing the mandatory oversight of firms engaged in capacity-building.

Capacity-Building: For Whom?

There are four primary targets for government-supported capacity-building, listed in order of priority: (1) suppliers; (2) public sector staff supporting supplier capacity-building; (3) other supporting institutions; and (4) workers and their representatives.

In this section, we emphasize building supplier capacity. While it is important that the public sector and other institutions develop, we believe that their primary role in this topic is to support the further development of supplier capacity. Furthermore, we address the question of worker empowerment separately, below.

Suppliers. The purpose for building supplier capacity is straightforward: to enable them to perform at a higher level on labor and environmental issues while also improving the efficiency and competitiveness of their enterprises. It has become commonplace among many buyers to say that a fourth element has been added to their traditional criteria of price, quality, and delivery—this is compliance. One of the primary means of accomplishing this is helping suppliers make the transition to become enterprises that manage successfully against economic, social, and environmental criteria. Many suppliers themselves acknowledge that they have not had the opportunity to develop the competencies in human resources, environmental health and safety, and production planning and engineering that lead to the compliance levels their customers are seeking. Too often, efforts to ensure good environmental and labor performance have focused on the symptoms of poor performance when efforts to build new and stronger skills among suppliers are likelier to attack the causes of these problems.

Direct capacity-building for suppliers is therefore needed, and, in addition, there is a need to build the capacity of other institutions so that they can aid suppliers.

Public sector. One of the underlying premises of this chapter is that government officials can use a wider array of instruments and actions to promote the competitiveness and social/environmental performance of suppliers. It is also the case that some additional skills are needed to accomplish these goals.

One critical element of capacity-building is the reorientation of labor and environmental inspectorates away from pure top-down enforcement toward an educational function like that played increasingly by inspectorates in developed economies. This requires a different set of skills from those traditionally played by inspectorates and will likely require some training in a variety of ways, including training methodologies, understanding of the intersection of social, environmental, and economic factors, and also an appreciation of the causes of potential labor and environmental violations. But, as noted above, this is somewhat circular: We are proposing that public sector capacity be developed so that it can aid in the development of suppliers' capacity to address issues themselves.

Supporting infrastructure. Government also can play a constructive role by supporting the creation of a network of institutions enabling code implementation. Such institutions include academia, technical experts, industry organizations, employers' federations, and others. As efforts to apply codes of conduct move into a second decade, it is becoming clearer that more sophisticated training and educational efforts are needed. Many suppliers have had the benefit of broad awareness-raising initiatives. What is needed now is more technical expertise on production planning, human resources management, EH&S, use of chemicals, labor-management dialogue, and similar issues. As noted below, a major effort to develop fledgling industries is not without precedent. In both the United States and Europe, major educational institutions were created to help farmers adopt more modern techniques, and similar initiatives in developing economies could be engines of both economic growth and better social and environmental performance. Other specialized institutions also are important to this discussion. For example, witness the contributions made by the Hong Kong Productivity Council, a private network of technical experts, in helping Hong Kong–owned factories in China address excessive overtime through production planning assistance; see Case 18 at the end of this chapter.

Workers and their representatives. It is widely acknowledged that workers and trade unions have been marginalized until recently in the code of conduct debate. Indeed, many trade unions do not support the widespread development of codes of conduct. However, with the focus of this paper on the role of the public sector in creating an environment in which labor standards and environmental protection can be a greater part of global supply chains, there is a clear opportunity to enhance the role of workers and trade unions linked to supply chains, in part through strengthening their capacity. As this is central to the topics discussed in the paper, we include a separate section focused on worker empowerment, and capacity-building for workers and their representatives.

Capacity-Building Initiatives

The following section outlines specific recommendations that governments can pursue.

Supplier training on labor and environmental standards. There exists in many cases an information gap that prevents suppliers from pursuing the environmental and labor policies discussed in this paper. This corresponds to a clear and demonstrated need in the marketplace. In addition to the information gap, there is a perception gap in that most suppliers still perceive improvement of labor and environmental practices as being inconsistent with productivity and profitability. This was one of the key findings of the ILO's research in support of its Factory Improvement Program (FIP). The research, and the evaluation of the implemented program, suggested that this perception is one of the key barriers for sustained efforts to improve workplace practices. This only serves to underscore the importance of ensuring that supplier training on labor and environmental issues, and other capacity-building efforts, address the twin objective of compliance and competitiveness. To address this issue, which we believe to be a misconception, the experiences from the ILO's FIP in Sri Lanka, which builds on the WISE methodology employed successfully in other Asian countries, could be much more widely shared with labor inspectorates around the world.

Supplier training on human resources. Many observers of supply chain issues have noted that the vast majority of the efforts to date have focused from the "outside in," seeking to mandate performance on social and environmental issues rather than look at the question from the "inside out," by providing basic human resource management training that is likely to lead to better working conditions. This approach has the evident benefit of also bringing production improvements that enhance commercial performance as well.

Several of the examples we cite in this paper have a supplier training element. This reflects the broad desire to enhance the understanding of labor and environmental issues, and also the link to productivity improvements. Training for suppliers should be delivered by a wide range of parties, including:

• **Government agencies:** There is a valuable opportunity to use the resources represented by labor, environment, and agriculture ministries and inspectorates to build the skills of exporters on labor and environmental issues.

• **Buyers:** Buyers already have begun in many cases to shift the resources they devote to promoting CSR in their supply chains away from monitoring and toward educational efforts. This trend should be encouraged. One way to do this is to create some incentives for those supplier firms participating in such activities, or to use such efforts as part of the public-private enforcement collaboration schemes suggested above. While this trend is positive, buyers—and local governments—should be conscious to avoid that a system of uncoordinated individualized ad hoc monitoring is not simply being replaced with a system of uncoordinated, ad hoc capacity-building.[21]

• **Technical experts:** Many issues, notably on environmental practices and health and safety issues as well as human resources and production planning, require technical expertise. These are sometimes unavailable in local markets, or beyond the financial reach of individual suppliers. Government can seek ways to make such resources more widely available to individual suppliers, or, more likely, groups of suppliers. This concept also fits into the centers of excellence concept presented below.

• **Academic experts:** As noted below, many governments have historically supported the development of academic centers that promote learning within industry. The development of professional development and educational centers was at the core of the creation and modernization of agriculture in the United States and Europe, and this model can and should be applied also to the need to develop and modernize the export industries discussed here.

Reorienting inspectorates toward capacity-building. We believe there is a strong opportunity for developing country labor inspectorates to make a transition similar to that which developed nations and many multinational buyers have made, away from a reliance on the enforcement function toward a teaching function that enables suppliers to assume a greater share of the responsibility for performance.

This approach holds the potential to make better use of the scarce resources made available for enforcement. We believe that this proposal does not represent an "either/or" approach, but rather a model that is mutually reinforcing. It has been, for example, at the heart of the Cambodian initiative in the garment industry, where capacity-building for suppliers (and also workers) was viewed as an essential element of the enhanced monitoring framework developed. This developmental approach to enforcement is at the heart of the new Philippine legal framework for enforcement of labor standards.

Accomplishing this goal will require the development of new skills by staff in labor and environmental inspectorates as well as integration of other government agencies not traditionally engaged in such work, such as ministries of trade and commerce. It also requires a change not only in technical skills, but also in the mind-set of institutions more familiar with mandating than with enabling and teaching.

In adopting any or all of these efforts, it is worth including an assessment of the impact of this capacity-building. The approach used by the ILO's FIP in Sri Lanka is instructive here. That program included key performance indicators (KPIs) that measured both the compliance benefits and also the production improvements that resulted from the program.

Create local expert networks. We do not believe that government can or should assume the entire responsibility of building supplier capacity. One additional way of supporting suppliers in their expertise development is to create a network of experts in key sourcing locations to provide technical and educational assistance to suppliers. This is fully consistent with the government's role as facilitator and contributes toward the creation of a decentralized system of support.

In our consultations for this chapter, we heard repeatedly from buyers and others that there is a paucity of expertise available in the most critical markets, with China being cited several times as being a place where capacity-building is strongly desired but without requisite experts to provide such services. There is, therefore, a clear need for government to seed the development of wider networks of independent expertise to support supplier development. Again, the experiences of the ILO Factory Improvement Program and the use of WISE methodology in the Philippines, Cambodia, and Bangladesh suggest that the required tools exist.

Governments also can help establish low-cost EH&S networks to stimulate and facilitate learning, provide simple services via local experts, and pool company resources for training activities. These networks would be run by experts in EH&S, labor relations, and/or human resources, and would be accessible to a small number of companies (for example, ten to fifteen) of equal size, industrial profile, and experience.

While external funding (donors or the public sector) would be required to set up such networks, the cost of running the networks could be covered by the participating companies. They would contribute an annual fee to cover overhead as well as pay a fee for extra services provided. The experiences of the Employers Confederation of the Philippines suggest, however, that there may be a financial barrier that prevents such services from reaching the markets where they are most needed. This often means neglected small and medium-sized companies; see

Case 13 at the end of this chapter. Multinational companies could also consider establishing such networks themselves, and/or providing additional resources to networks.[22] Industrywide buyers' initiatives, such as the German AVE initiative, would be particularly well placed to set up such networks. Indeed, it has been surprising to see that neither local governments nor donors have actively pursued the idea of developing third-party capacity to assist in the process of code implementation through building suppliers' capacity.[23]

Especially in agriculture, there could be a strong case for mobilizing the local community in efforts to sustain good labor and environmental management practices. The concept for facilitating local and/or community-based networks is adapted from an initiative in Ireland, where the local authorities have run a community-based EH&S scheme to improve health, safety, and welfare in smaller communities. The objective is to raise awareness of health and safety issues by encouraging key organizations involved with the local business community to assume greater responsibility for the health and safety of their working populations. The aim is to facilitate their involvement in obtaining sustainable improvements in workplace health, safety, and welfare.

The first step involves identifying and mobilizing relevant local partners, identifying needs and concerns, and engaging organizations such as businesses, fire brigades, police, civil society, and others. The second step is to create awareness of EH&S-related issues through appropriate communications media in the local environment (for example, an effective mix of radio programs, posters, advertisements, flyers, and information stands). The third step involves targeting inspections by multiskilled teams, providing seminars and workshops on EH&S issues, and similar information days. Such approaches go well along with the current thinking in the Kenyan horticulture multistakeholder initiative, HEBI, that seeks to develop more participatory monitoring techniques that also involve the local community.

Develop centers of excellence. One further approach to fostering capacity-building is to establish "centers of excellence" that combine attention to social and environmental issues with the management and technical skills that allow more productive and competitive industries to develop. As noted previously, many multinational companies claim that it is generally difficult in many countries to identify local service providers that can provide such management services.

Such centers could be set up as complementary capacity-building efforts to industrywide monitoring or wider collaborative frameworks.[24] This would allow services and skills offerings to be built around the needs identified in the monitoring to ensure a match between supply and demand of services. It would be critical to ensure that such centers offer services that meet the demands of the market.[25] Both of the ILO-run programs in the garment industries of Cambodia and Bangladesh have a built-in component that seeks to develop production and quality management adviser services around the labor monitoring.

Building on these models can be accomplished by developing centers of excellence that would create ongoing resources for employers and employees. The century-old model of establishing agricultural educational centers in Europe and the United States is in fact instructive as a means of creating the skills needed to transition an economy from one form of activity to another. In other words, just as agricultural extension colleges were considered essential to the development of a modern U.S. agricultural industry in the late nineteenth century, so too could centers of excellence help SMEs selling into the global marketplace develop the skills needed to make the best use of their commercial relationships.

The industry-led compliance initiative in the Kenya cut-flower industry, the Kenyan Flower Council, incorporates aspects of this in its work programme. There, monitors seek not only to audit performance, but also to facilitate the transfer of new techniques and lessons learned. The limited time available to these monitors, along with a lack of skills, means however that this aspect is underprioritized during audits.

The features of such centers could include:

• Engagement of a variety of industry sectors (for example, light manufacturing, heavy manufacturing, agriculture, etc.), to facilitate learning and skills transfer across industries.

• Operation and governance by a combination of academic or technical institutions, business federations, technically skilled NGOs and/or trade unions, or other service providers.

• Services could include EH&S and human resource management as well as productivity, production, and quality management. Services could be delivered through training workshops; problem-solving resources like "hotlines"; a center for stakeholder dialogue; and the provision of basic educational, health, or other services to workers.

In the short term, donor and public sector funding would be crucial to sustain the financial viability of such centers. Donors can also play an important role in developing the initial necessary service delivery capacity of such centers, the organizational setup, and raise awareness among local businesses of the benefits accruing from use of services. In the medium term, these centers must become financially self-sustainable, operated either by private, market-driven actors or semi-public institutions.

Initially, services could be subsidized in way where customers are charged a discounted rate. In the medium term and/or after repeated use of services, customers could be charged the full market costs of such services. The cost of services could also be adjusted according to the size of the customers effectively benefiting small and medium-sized enterprises.

Also, multinational buyers and other multinational companies have a role to play in knowledge and skill transfer, to help their suppliers and other participants in supply chains develop the kinds of basic management tools, specific human resources, and environmental management systems that have become commonplace in companies based in more developed economies.

Mechanisms for Promoting Capacity-Building

In sum, governments can enable capacity-building in a variety of ways.

The first is by changing policy, or changing implementation strategies. This arises most clearly with the reorientation of inspectorates toward a greater reliance on teaching than pure policing.

The second is through funding, as governments have the opportunity to invest in capacity-building that may in the long run bring greater results than existing models do. Every government around the world invests in educational efforts and trade promotion, and there is no reason why the two cannot be linked.

Third, governments also can facilitate capacity-building through incentives. While this category is addressed separately below, we believe that governments can put in place incentives that will lead suppliers to embrace capacity-building, possibly as a way to offset the risks of enforcement actions. Given the sporadic levels of enforcement, this is an effort that could perhaps be linked to co-ordinated enforcement, as discussed above.

Fourth, it may be that simply making existing resources known to target audiences (for example, encouraging exporters' associations to take advantage of existing educational and technical assistance programs) could have a cat-alytic, though more modest, role than the other delivery devices.

Incentives

Governments have several potential mechanisms at their disposal to pro-mote investment in management and workplace practices that improve com-petitiveness and also labor and environmental performance.

These and other examples show how incentives can shape business beha-vior. Still, in the course of considering options for this paper, both the authors and many of those with whom we consulted raised a number of questions about the use of incentives.[26] We generally found little support for incentives that either would erode government revenues or provide positive incentives simply to encourage companies to abide by applicable laws. In addition, there are lingering questions about whether incentives achieve their intended purpose separately, and achieve desired impact only as an element within a compre-hensive strategy.

Targeted Incentives

Governments possess a wide array of incentive-based mechanisms to sti-mulate investment toward achieving good workplace practices. These fall into two categories: positive incentives and negative incentives.

Positive incentives. Positive incentives such as tax breaks, lower environ-mental charges, lower insurance premiums, and other options can be used to spur firms on to meet or exceed compliance baselines. They will be most accepted when the benefits outweigh costs and when they are focused on a result beyond honoring companies for meeting their legal obligations.

For instance, in the Indian state of Karnataka, firms implementing ISO 14001 or similar environmental management systems are eligible for lower environmental charges. The Danish labor inspection framework exempts from comprehensive (and costly) inspections companies that are OSHA 18001 certified or have implemented a workplace management system of an equivalent nature.[27] Similar schemes are in place elsewhere throughout the industrialized world.

In the Philippines, as part of an overall incentive package to stimulate growth among micro-enterprises and small companies, such firms are exempted from enforcement of the minimum wage law as long as employees covered by the act receive the same benefits given to employees in other enterprises, including social security and health care benefits.[28]

Incentives such as awards and other forms of public endorsement can also be used to stimulate good performance. While we question the impact such initiatives may have on the wider enjoyment of labor rights and environmental protection, some consultation partners felt that awards could contribute to the adoption of progressive workplace practices.

For instance, in the Philippines a presidential award has been used to encourage companies to improve workplace practices. This award was instituted in connection with the ILO-driven WISE-program that received nationwide attention (see Case 12), suggesting that such incentives may be brought to greater effect when part of a combined strategy. Similarly, the COYA award (Company of the Year award) in Kenya instituted by the Kenyan Institute of Management has presumably had a significant impact on workplace practices in manufacturing industries.[29] The prize carries a small financial award and covers issues beyond workplace practices and other CSR aspects.

Additional positive incentives based on the conditionality of benefits, capital, or participation in public trade promotion efforts also have great support, and provide an additional mechanism to consider. These work by making compliance with labor and environmental standards an "entry point" for certain

---

CONDITIONALITY

In the Netherlands, access to export credits is linked to "soft" compliance with the OECD's Guidelines on Multinational Corporations. In Denmark, the Danish export credit fund recently signed up to the Equator Principles. Access to Danida's mixed credit facility is conditioned on compliance with a number of labor and environmental criteria. There are numerous similar examples.

government benefits. These can include linking access to public procurement or participation in trade fairs.

For instance, a number of northern governments, including bilateral donors, link access to export credits and similar financial schemes to compliance with labor and environmental standards; see text box. One recent example comes from the International Finance Corporation's (IFC) conditioning loans for the creation of a free trade zone along the border between the Dominican Republic and Haiti on observance of core labor standards. This was highlighted by representatives of the trade union movement as a prime example of an important step forward.

Governments also could require firms and/or managers to undertake mandatory training on labor and environmental management at accredited institutions in order for them to maintain their license to operate. Such a requirement is common practice in many fields, for example, the practice of law in the United States.[30] A variant would be to require companies to undertake a number of training hours at accredited institutions corresponding to the number of employees and/or turnover they have. The number of hours can be reduced or the types of training changed if the company has implemented a labor and/or environmental management system such as OSHA 18001, ISO 14001, or equivalent systems.

Government procurement policies also can play a role in encouraging positive behavior and in fact is one of the most direct steps the public sector can take. The recent announcement that the United Nations system would apply the principles of the UN Global Compact to its own procurement efforts is one example of ways that—if applied by national governments—the public sector can create positive incentives. Given the vast volume of purchasing by public sector agencies, this step has the potential to make a substantial impact.

Negative incentives. Negative incentives such as levying penalties, fees, and other surcharges can also be used. There is a fine line between characterizing an effort as basic enforcement versus "negative incentives," but the main point is to promote certain forms of behavior through means different than checking performance and fining companies for subpar actions.

U.S. TOXIC RELEASE INVENTORY

Companies may become eligible for a number of incentives if they meet nine disclosure criteria. Incentives include (1) no gravity-based penalties, (2) reduction of gravity-based penalties by 75 percent, (3) no recommendation for criminal prosecution, and (4) no routine requests for audit reports. Examples of the nine disclosing criteria include, for example, systematic, voluntary, prompt, and independent discovery and disclosure, speedy correction, and preventive measures. Repeat violations are ineligible, and certain types of violations are ineligible.

For instance, the Philippine labor enforcement framework levies very high fines on companies that, having declared themselves to be in compliance, are not. This approach uses incentives through the availability of self-review and seeks enforcement through fines for misstatements. Negative incentives are also used in systems where certain positive or preventive steps are used to ameliorate penalties for poor performance. An example of this approach comes from the U.S. Toxic Release Inventory, through which companies can be eligible for reduced fines and other incentives if they disclose instances of noncompliance; see text box.

An interesting concept in place in Japan and South Korea, and also under consideration in the Philippines, is the use of industrywide sanctions when industries substantially fail to meet relevant targets set in the area of workplace practices.

Governments in Japan and Korea have set up health and safety funds partly financed by both government and industry to address those industries that need to reduce levels of workplace accidents. The accumulated funds are used to finance investments in industry aimed at improving workplace practices. Since complying and noncomplying companies are equally taxed by this system, business federations are greatly incentivized to encourage noncomplying companies to improve performance.

Increased transparency has become an essential element of the debate over CSR and supply chains in recent years, as exemplified by the disclosure of multinational companies' perceived complicity in human rights abuses in the conflicts in West and Central Africa.[31] While governments do not play the same role as NGOs and trade unions that have raised many public concerns, there is a legitimate role for government in using appropriate measures to enhance transparency with the goal of improving performance.

Public disclosure of performance based on certain well-defined criteria could be considered by governments to stimulate companies to honor their legal obligations by mobilizing peer pressure, public scrutiny, and using other measures. For instance, in the garment sector initiative in Cambodia, poorly performing companies are given two chances to correct instances of noncompliance after

---

SMILING WORKPLACE PRACTICES

The new Danish labor inspection framework classifies companies' performance into three categories, each represented by a colored "smiley." A red smiley suggests that the company has poor performance and has been requested to solicit workplace improvement services. A yellow smiley suggests that the company has been asked to make certain corrections to the working environment. A green smiley suggests that a company is upholding good standards. The result is made public on the Labor Agency's home page once a company has been screened.

which their monitoring reports are publicly disclosed, and these same monitoring reports are then shared between the government, manufacturers, NGOs, and trade unions. Given that the overall performance of the industry impacts the future export opportunities for individual companies, public disclosure can leverage and engage substantial peer pressure.

Similarly, the Danish labor inspection agency publicizes the workplace performance of all companies on the Internet, placing each company in one of three categories.

The principle of public disclosure is at the heart of the U.S. Toxic Release Inventory and similar schemes. In general, transparency can be an effective tool to stimulate changes, however, illiteracy and the lack of access to mass media such as the Internet in many developing countries effectively limit the potential of such initiatives unless other means of publication are used.

It is also worth noting that the use of databases to achieve greater transparency can also serve the purpose of rationalizing the costs of enforcement. There has been substantial movement in the past one or two years toward the development of shared databases, through the SEDEX project in the UK, the Fair Labor Association, the Fair Factory Clearinghouse in the United States, and the AVE and FCD industry-led initiatives in Germany and France respectively. These databases can be used not only to share information about factory performance, but also as a useful tool for focusing enforcement resources where the greatest potential for impact exists. This helps reduce the redundant monitoring and verification that currently marks the apparel industry in particular.

"Green Production" and "Fair Labor" Zones

An additional option, also linked to incentives, is the establishment of manufacturing and/or processing zones based explicitly on strong environmental performance and fair labor practices.

As buyers and consumers of the products made in free trade and export processing zones are increasingly seeking assurances of good social and environmental practices, there may be an opportunity to create zones that can serve as best practice centers.[32] This model would, in theory, also appeal to exporters and governments seeking new ways to achieve and demonstrate that their products are the result of processes reflecting good environmental and labor conditions. Incentives to be used could include gradually phased-out tax breaks that are combined with a payback scheme if companies fail to uphold good labor and environmental standards; the availability of workplace improvement services at a reduced cost as well as relevant worker education programs; and credible and robust multistakeholder monitoring based on high standards backed up by third-party verification.

The advantages of such a model also include the ability to achieve economies of scale in terms of compliance. Companies in the zones could pool resources, buyers of products in the zones could achieve desired assurance with less expense, suppliers in the zones could pool resources to achieve both compliance and better productivity while likely lowering the enforcement costs for governments. This could also serve national governments by providing a basis for attracting inward investment on the basis of sustainable and supportable business practices.

Such zones could represent a next and more sustainable phase in the development of the concept of free trade zones, delivering improvements in productivity, knowledge, and technology transfer, increased inward investment, and improved labor and environmental conditions. This would present a model that could usefully synthesize commercial and social concerns, and could also provide an environment in which the public-private partnerships described in this paper could be tested and refined for application more broadly. The phase-out of apparel quotas may represent an opportunity to consolidate production organized around principles of responsible business.[33]

We are also aware that several multinationals have begun to express interest in developing models that consolidate various aspects of the production process, such as the "Supply Chain City" concept being modeled in south China.[34] This consolidation is a "double-edged sword," presenting both the opportunity to promote good practices more effectively while at the same time risking the possibility that SMEs grow ever less able to compete as greater sophistication and investments are needed to become part of global supply chains. In considering this approach, they have also considered demonstrating support for fair labor/green production zones that cross industry sector lines.

Should fair labor or green production zones be developed, caution would be required to avoid having these zones become isolated enclaves, or having the standards in other workplaces decline as attention shifts to these locations. It

---

SUPPLY CHAIN CITY

A recent article in the *Wall Street Journal* noted the creation of a "Supply Chain City" in Dongguan, China, in which numerous processes from product design to manufacturing are brought together in one location. Here lies a potential model workplace for the embrace of leading-edge labor and environmental practices. This site is being designed for four thousand workers and was seen as a model that could "radically alter apparel production in the future."

One interesting element of this model, for present purposes, is that this factory setting brings jobs that rely not only on inexpensive labor, but also greater value-added components like design and technologically advanced manufacturing. As such, this production model presents a clear opportunity for government to create incentives for social and environmental elements of production, especially if more buyers can be enticed to consolidate production as a result.

should be considered how positive linkages could be established to communities and local economies outside the zone.[35]

Worker Empowerment

Workers in global supply chains have too often been shut out of efforts to ensure good labor and environmental practices that affect them directly. In many cases governments have been reluctant to ensure protection of core labor standards and failed to protect the right to organize, and businesses have often acted in a similar manner.

It is now evident that engaging workers more directly in the process of ensuring good labor and environmental practices is essential to sustainable progress. Better labor and environmental performance is enhanced through more educated workers better able to vindicate their rights, more effective trade unions with free access to workers, and better labor-management dialogue.

In the long run, many now express the view that worker engagement and engagement with unions could be as effective or more effective in raising standards than codes themselves. In the nearer term, there also are opportunities for improvements to be attained through sustained efforts to empower workers. There is a strong need therefore to find ways to ensure that workers understand labor and environmental laws designed to protect them, and are able to play a more vibrant role in pursuing these goals.

This is a role for governments to play, through the clarification and enforcement of existing laws; bringing of existing laws into conformance with core labor standards; ensuring that labor-management relations can operate smoothly and within the bounds of core labor standards; and in finding ways to serve in the role that only it can play: that of a neutral party tied neither to management nor labor.[36]

Worker education and empowerment is a good in itself, and at the same time worker empowerment can and should be an aspect of each of the other three categories addressed in this chapter. We note ideas and examples in this section that are specific to progress on worker empowerment. However, we also propose that worker empowerment be integrated into the other concepts promoted and illustrated in this paper.

For example, both the WIETA program in South Africa and the comprehensive approach being implemented in Cambodia encompass worker involvement, and serve to promote worker empowerment. The Philippine legal enforcement framework that mandates joint employer-employee self-assessment in companies with more than two hundred employees is a model system, which, if implemented widely and effectively, could be quite useful. Each of the collaborative structures discussed in this chapter has the potential to be strengthened by engagement of workers and trade unions.

The initiatives discussed here need to consider the makeup of the workforces in question. The agriculture and apparel industries generally are comprised of a highly diverse workforce that includes a large cohort of workers from sectors of the labor market that often receive less complete protection than others, namely migrant workers, women, and seasonal/temporary workers. Many of these groups face distinct challenges in understanding and exercising their rights. In addition to the benefit of having governments ensure that laws apply to all classes of workers, including migrants, temporary workers, and others, there is a need to develop educational and other programs that target these workers. In addition to addressing the specific classifications of workers in the apparel and agricultural industries, it is essential that the educational levels of workers in these industries be addressed so that efforts and materials are appropriate and effective.

Please note that in this section of the chapter there are few examples of good practice from which to draw. This is reflective of the secondary importance many governments and businesses have placed on this topic, and in some cases the direct opposition to progress in this area. It also reflects the sheer challenge of reaching out to any significant number of workers in cost-effective ways, further underlining the crucial role to be played by trade unions in promoting such efforts.

Educating Workers about Their Rights

There is a substantial need for workers to become more familiar with their rights at work as well as the environmental, health, and safety issues that can arise in apparel and agricultural manufacturing.

Government can support such efforts in a variety of ways, including the following:

• **Mandating provision of basic legal information to workers:** In some economies, notably in the OECD countries, it is required that workers be made aware of information concerning basic legal protections, and this is something that could be extended to countries that are main exporters of apparel and agriculture. The advantage of having this work done by the government is that the information would be made available at a lower cost, and the message would be consistent, clear, and accurate. When early efforts to develop codes of conduct emerged, buyers rushed to translate their codes into local languages for the purpose of placing posters on their suppliers' factories walls. There is substantial evidence that this activity did not serve the ultimate purpose of educating workers, in part because of the sometimes inconsistent, sometimes confusing messages sent by having numerous standards posted in a single workplace. Given that these codes rely to a very substantial degree on applicable legal standards, a more rational and effective approach is likely to result from having governments post applicable legal standards in language understandable by the average worker.

• **Supporting educational efforts by local organizations:** While government can and should take new steps to educate workers on their rights, government also could help to ensure that community groups, and NGOs have the opportunity to engage in efforts to educate workers.

• **Promoting general educational programs for workers:** Programs such as the (soon to be defunct) Global Alliance for Workers and Communities have successfully provided educational resources for workers in global supply chains. These programs, which focus more on general educational efforts than the provision of information specifically about workplace conditions, also hold the promise for improving conditions in workplaces. The ILO WIND-methodology may also be used to increase awareness among agricultural workers of issues in the workplace.

As stated above, incentives also can be created for businesses to engage in educational efforts aimed at building workers' understanding of their rights, and, as noted below, trade unions have a central role to play.

Note also that there is a direct link here to the clarification advocated in the section above discussing standards. Without clarification of existing legal requirements, it is difficult to envision effective educational efforts that are needed to empower workers further. There also is a link to collaborative enforcement methods, which can and should involve workers, as illustrated by the Cambodian and Philippines examples. Finally, there also is a link to the changing role of labor and environmental inspections, which could include these government workers in any shift toward more of an educational role as opposed to a pure policing mind-set.

Removing Barriers to Worker Representation

In many countries that are major exporters of apparel and agricultural products, there are de jure and de facto limitations on unions' abilities to operate. Governments can achieve the objectives described in this paper by providing more space for workers to choose freely whether to participate in independent trade unions, and this holds the potential for decentralizing the monitoring of workplace conditions by engaging workers more directly. As noted earlier in this chapter, this would also seem to be a prerequisite for the further development of effective, credible, and balanced self-assessment models that involve joint employer-employee inspections/assessments.

The inability of trade unions to operate in a manner that allows workers to exercise their right to freedom of association and collective bargaining distorts and limits the effectiveness both of local laws and of codes of conduct. These organizations are also likely to play a key role in delivering required training and information to workers, including the development of simple and popular tools that will help workers address EH&S issues in the workplace.

In many locations, notably including EPZs, unions often have difficulty gaining access to workers. Government could take steps to ensure that security provisions established for the legitimate purpose of managing trade restrictions are not applied for inappropriate purposes.

Many observers—including workers—have also noted that trade unions have not always acted as independent organizations seeking to represent workers. Some in the international trade union movement have indeed acknowledged this privately. Government, possibly acting in concert with international institutions,

List of Organizations Consulted

	Public Sector	Buyer	Donor	Civil Society
China				
Ann Taylor*		1		
Asia Monitor Resource Centre*				2
City University of Hong Kong*				1
Disney*		1		
Gap*		2		
Guangzhou Occupational Health and Occupational Rehabilitation Resource Center*				1
HK Christian Industrial Committee*				2
IPS (subsidiary of Limited Brands)*		1		
Li & Fung*		1		
May Company*		1		
Narrowgate*		2		
Nike*		1		
Participatory Development Appraisal Network*				1
India				
Karnataka State Pollution Control Board	1			
Karnataka Factories and Boilers Department	1			
Kenya				
Kenya Human Rights Commission	1			
Kenya Investment Promotion Agency	1			
Kenya Tea Development Agency	1			
Philippines				
Occupational Safety and Health Center	1			
Employers Confederation of the Philippines	1			
Bureau of Working Conditions, Department of Labor and Employment	1			
South Africa				
Department of Economic Development and Tourism	1			
WIETA				1
Sri Lanka				
Export Development Board	1			
Department of Labour	1			
Ministry of Labour	1			
Board of Investment	1			
Central Environmental Authority	1			

United States			
Fair Labor Association			1
Maquila Solidarity Center			1
Clean Clothes Campaign			1
Solidarity Center, AFL-CIO			1
USLEAP			1
Workers Rights Consortium			1
Europe			
ICFTU			1
ILO		6	
DFID		3	
DANIDA		3	
SIDA		2	
GTZ-Programme Office for Social and Ecological Standards		2	
BMZ-Public Sector Cooperation		1	
European Commission DG Development		1	
European Commission: Occupational Health and Safety Agency	1		
LO/FTF Council (Danish Trade Union's international development arm)			2
Environmental Protection Agency	1		
Oxfam International			1
Natural Resources Institute			2
Hennes & Mauritz*		1	
Karstadt Quelle*		1	
IKEA*		1	
Marks & Spencer*		1	
Adidas*		1	
Chiquita*		1	

*Consulted in a group that was larger than two persons

can help professionalize the actions of trade unions and help remove inappropriate political and other barriers to the effective functioning of unions as the representatives of workers.

Enhancing Dispute Resolution Mechanisms

Governments also can help empower workers by creating more easily accessible means through which workers can express concerns about workplace practices.

In the past ten years an entire new global industry has been created to produce a monitoring "police force" that roams the world to identify and help remedy labor and environmental issues. Too often overlooked has been a set of dispute resolution mechanisms that can serve a useful role in deterring and mediating issues. As noted by one international trade union leader interviewed for the project, labor-intensive industries are often rife with disputes, especially where, as in the apparel industry, incentive based compensation is the norm.

This person suggested, and we agree, that exploration of mediation services be considered. Nations in North America and Europe have longed used such services as a relatively nonbureaucratic way to prevent and address disputes, and it is possible that such concepts could be developed outside these regions as well. This union leader suggested that by shifting some labor disputes to this type of forum, it also would make freedom of association easier to implement, as his view is that employers become less wary of unions once alternative dispute resolution mechanisms become available.

The experiences from the Cambodian garment industry provide useful and instructive learning lessons, even if the quota-based system may not continue after phaseout at the end of 2004. The ILO representative responsible for the program noted in consultations for the purpose of this report that the development of a dispute resolution mechanism in the industry in the long run may end up being the most important contribution of the ILO project to labor standards in the industry. In addition to having solved certain conflicts, the mechanism has effectively turned out to be a confidence-building measure that eventually may allow for less antagonistic and more constructive relations between the labor market parties.

Governments also can streamline the bureaucracy devoted to addressing workplace conditions by creating special adjudicating bodies for particular types of workplace issues, such as workplace injuries or wage disputes. Such efforts, when coupled with raising awareness of workers about their availability, and relative ease of access, can serve a useful purpose as well.

LIST OF CASES OF GOOD PRACTICE

Case 1:   Australia—Homeworkers Code of Practice
Case 2:   Bangladesh—Collaborative ILO-initiative in the garment sector
Case 3:   Cambodia—Collaborative ILO-initiative in the garment sector
Case 4:   Central America—Export Success in Central America Partnership
Case 5:   Asia—ILO Factory Improvement Project
Case 6:   India—Fair Wear Foundation's Tirupur Committee
Case 7:   Ireland—A community-based approach to health and safety
Case 8:   Kenya—Horticulture Ethical Business Initiative (HEBI)
Case 9:   Kenya—Kenya Flower Council
Case 10:   The Netherlands—Industry Sector Codes and Guides
Case 11:   Philippines—Private Sector Self-Assessment of Labour Standards
           Compliance
Case 12:   Philippines—Work Place and Productivity Improvement in Small
           Enterprises

NOTES

Aron Cramer, Business for Social Responsibility, and Peder Michael Pruzan-Jørgensen,
PricewaterhouseCoopers, with the support of the World Bank Group's Foreign Investment Advisory Service. This chapter is an adaptation of a report prepared by the
authors for the World Bank Group and financed by the Royal Danish Ministry of
Foreign Affairs, and is published with permisson of PricewaterhouseCoopers Denmark
and the World Bank Group. For complete text of the report, including methodology
and case examples, go to: http://www.ifc.org/ifcext/economics.nsf/AttachmentsByTitle/
Implementation+of+CSR+in+Global+Supply+Chains/$FILE/Implementation+of
+CSR+in+Global+Supply+Chains.pdf

1. A full report of the parties with whom we consulted is contained at the end of
the report.

2. As indicated above, many of the practical examples that follow should illustrate
the relevance of these key assumptions. We also would note that we do not consider
these assumptions to be necessary in 100 percent of the efforts we propose, and there
will continue to be relevant interventions that fall outside the scope of these assumptions. For instance, the extension of labor laws to all sectors of society to ensure
widespread realization of labor rights is not industry-specific. Similarly, as has been the
case in the both South African wine industry and the Kenyan horticulture sector,
external (northern) actors can undertake crucial roles in bringing forward a locally
governed process. There are also examples where nonstate actors have been the key
driver behind initiatives to achieve higher social and environmental standards but with
the public sector in an engaging role, for example, the social compliance initiatives of
the Philippine Employers Confederation.

3. By this we refer principally to many civil society organizations' push to ensure
that supplier auditing to a greater extent relies on participatory techniques involving
local communities, NGOs, and trade unions. While this has significant merit in its own
right, as present auditing techniques are not yielding the desired results, we do not see
greater transparency in auditing as being sufficient to deliver sustainable, effective, and
credible solutions to the real challenges. Rather, as noted elsewhere, to deliver sustainable solutions, a departure from the present trajectory of auditing is required.

4. Financial risk does not necessarily come as the donation of financial capital, but
also in the form of in-kind contributions such as participation in training activities, test
implementation of new techniques, and so on.

5. The WIETA-initiative in the South African wine industry is an interesting example of how a northern actor has served to incubate an initiative where it is arguably

more meaningful—in the exporting countries where collaboration is needed most acutely.

6. It is noteworthy that even now, northern institutions are largely driving many of the most prominent industry initiatives pertaining to codes of conduct. For instance, the social compliance initiative in the German retail sector supported by the German government's development cooperation arm, BMZ (and GTZ), has only a superficial cooperation with southern governments. Similarly, many of the U.S.-based multi-stakeholder initiatives such as the WRC, FLA, and SAI have limited formal cooperation with southern governments. WRAP is the exception to the rule in that the organization has sought to develop cooperative relations with a number of developing country governments.

7. ILO (2003), Fundamental principles and rights at work: A labour law study—Costa Rica, El Salvador, Guatemala, Honduras, and Nicaragua. Geneva.

8. In our first report to the World Bank Group, lack of clarity was also identified as one barrier to more efficient implementation of codes of conduct at the level of suppliers. Buyers in consultations undertaken for the purposes of this report restated this message.

9. There may be issues that are more suitably addressed at the national level.

10. This was also confirmed in interviews with representatives of labor inspection agencies in the Philippines, India, and Sri Lanka.

11. In countries such as Cambodia, the Philippines, and Vietnam, the number of labor inspectors is less than three hundred, suggesting that even major increases are unlikely to have any significant impact on the enforcement capacity. In addition, labor inspectors often are poorly remunerated, making them easy targets to corruptive practices.

12. For instance, in India companies chosen for inspections are identified randomly by a computer system, however, once inspectors visit companies that have been subjected to private monitoring they adjust the scope of their inspection accordingly. Also, in situations where insurance companies undertake monitoring activities as part of assessing their risks, the public inspectorates adjust their own inspections accordingly (instead of testing equipment, they only check documentation that equipment has been tested by an independent third party).

13. We were unable to identify additional information on this initiative that was mentioned during an interview with a representative of Factories and Boilers in Karnataka, India.

14. For instance, it is important to distinguish between efforts aimed at improving the competitiveness of local industries and those aimed at serving a social objective, such as improving general enforcement of standards.

15. Another challenge would be to ensure the public's access to data since PRTRs publish data on the Internet. The Danish Environmental Protection Agency showed great interest when presented with this idea.

16. This is the basic setup in the Philippine enforcement framework, where "policing" inspections are focused at medium-sized companies, and "training" inspections are focused on small enterprises.

17. Companies are grouped into different categories reflecting their level of performance. This in turn impacts the penalties that can be levied: Good-performing companies will rarely receive a direct penalty, but will be given a grace period to correct the

situation, while poorly performing companies will receive immediate penalties. The new Danish law also requires companies to finance inspections themselves.

18. In the state of Karnataka, India, ISO 14001–certified companies are exempted from certain environmental emission charges. The region of Umbria, Italy, adopted a law in 2003 which states that SA8000-certified companies will receive preferential treatment in public procurement; this decision, however, is presently being reviewed by the European Commission in anticipation that it is in violation of European Union procurement rules.

19. The buyers consulted for the purposes of the report expressed profound skepticism of the quality of certification in many developing countries.

20. For example, overly long work hours result in part from poor production planning; worker mistreatment occurs in an environment where human resources training is completely absent; occupational hazards can often be addressed through readily available safety information that is otherwise ignored; and managers often are unaware of the efficiencies that can be made available by basic resource management, so that material inputs, and therefore costs, can be reduced.

21. Buyers consulted for the purposes of this study stressed that while the bottom-up approach was required to deliver sustainable performance, it was also an extremely resource-consuming process that individual buyers were ill equipped to undertake.

22. Again we would refer to the initiative by the Employers Confederation of the Philippines that has tested such business networks in which a larger company assists its small suppliers to embrace a rights-based approach to workplace improvements; see Case 13.

23. The involvement of the German bilateral donor agency, BMZ, in the German retailers' initiative (AVE Social Compliance Initiative), has been limited to sponsoring awareness-raising activities.

24. Most public sector consultation partners found the concept of centers of excellence attractive, although several were unsure about the capacity of government or the private sector to initiate and finance such centers.

25. Bilateral donors consulted stressed the importance of ensuring that such centers were built around clearly identified market demands, and not just supplier needs. As evidenced by the experience of the Employers Confederation of the Philippines (see Case 13), needs do not necessarily translate into demands, as the latter require a financial capacity not always present with small and medium-sized companies.

26. Some public sector representatives expressed great enthusiasm for the use of incentives of all kinds, including tax exemptions and/or deductions.

27. As the Danish labor inspection framework requires companies to pay for the costs associated with labor inspections, the incentive to adopt good labor management practices is further strengthened.

28. The overall incentive package also includes exemption from income taxes as well as lower local taxes, charges, and fees.

29. Thus, the Kenyan Human Rights Commission spoke very favorably of the award, which was believed to have contributed significantly to the adoption of better workplace practices in manufacturing industries.

30. Firms should fund their own participation. The penalty for not participating could be the equivalent of the training fee plus a fixed amount that in principle would outweigh the possible advantage of attending to work.

31. See the various reports by a UN panel of experts issued as part of the UN's involvement in the conflicts in Liberia, Sierra Leone, Angola, and Democratic Republic of Congo.

32. In the past fifteen years in particular, there has been an increase in free trade zones and export processing zones as a favored mechanism for promotion exports, especially in the apparel, textiles, and consumer electronics sectors. Many critics have claimed that these zones have been locations where general labor and environmental laws do not apply, and also that the culture of such zones interferes with respect for workers' rights and reflect poor environmental practices.

33. This has been the case in Cambodia and also is part of the backdrop for the ESCA initiative in Central America. The authors acknowledge that substantial social and economic dislocation may occur in sourcing countries that lose jobs. This is an issue to address with seriousness. At the same time, it also appears that consolidation of production may create some opportunities to further labor and environmental practices, and that is the main focus of this paper.

34. This thinking seems inspired by the national competitiveness thinking of the 1990s propelled by Michael E. Porter's theorizing on clusters of competitiveness.

35. This point was strongly stressed by several consultation partners. In Kenya, there are some efforts being made in this direction, however so-called green zones with free access to efficient sewage systems have been unable to attract the critical mass of investments hoped for.

36. The question of worker empowerment is perhaps one of the most politicized topics addressed in this paper. Governments have, therefore, an important role to play in demonstrating their ability to act as "honest brokers," enabling workers, trade unions, and business to interact within the bounds of fairly administered national legal frameworks consistent with core labor standards.

REFERENCES

Berman, J. et al. (2003). Race to the top: Attracting and enabling global sustainable business. Washington, DC: World Bank Group.

DANIDA. (2004). *Guidelines for integration of working environment concerns into Danish development assistance.* Copenhagen.

Department for International Development (DFID). (2004). *Labour standards and poverty reduction.* London.

Fox, T., Ward, H., and Howard, B. (2002). *Public sector roles in strengthening corporate social responsibility: A baseline study,* Washington, DC: World Bank Group.

Jørgensen, H. B. et al. (2003). *Strengthening implementation of corporate social responsibility in global supply chains.* World Bank and International Finance Corporation. Washington DC: World Bank Group.

Ministry of Foreign Affairs et al. (2004, March 22–23). "How donor agencies are supporting and enabling corporate social responsibility": A summary document prepared for the conference on development cooperation and corporate social responsibility, exploring the role of development cooperation agencies. Stockholm.

Oxfam International. (2004). *Trading away our rights: Women working in global supply chains.* Oxford.

Polaski, S. (2004, October). "Cambodia blazes a new path to economic growth and job creation. Washington, DC: Carnegie Papers No. 51.

Ward, H. (2004). *Public sector roles in strengthening corporate social responsibility: Taking stock.* Washington DC: World Bank Group and International Finance Corporation.

III
CORPORATE GOVERNMENT AFFAIRS STRATEGIES

6

Corporate Public Affairs: Structure, Resources, and Competitive Advantage

JENNIFER J. GRIFFIN, STEVEN N. BRENNER,
and JEAN J. BODDEWYN

R ebuilding trust with investors, the public, employees, and customers has been burdened by the breech of faith evidenced in major business scandals such as Enron, Parmalat, Adelphi, and WorldCom. Few companies survive (for example, Arthur Andersen, AirTran; the verdict is still out on Tyco) let alone thrive (for example, Johnson & Johnson's Tylenol scare, Ford's tire recalls). Strategically managing these public relationships as well as strategically managing the corporate public affairs (PA) function has been a key difference in the survivors. As a boundary-spanning function, effectively managing relationships, images, reputations, and issues stemming from both external and internal sources can be a competitive advantage when survival is called into question.

This article briefly traces the history of the modern public affairs function throughout the past three decades. Initiating with multinational companies in a hostile and turbulent 1970s, the PA function was born. By examining the expansion of corporate public affairs in scale, scope, resources, and issues throughout the 1980s and 1990s, the future prognosis of public affairs is created. By returning to its roots of managing five primary stakeholder sets, public affairs can strategically transform the relationship between business and its relevant constituencies.

INTRODUCTION

Incorporated firms have always had to account for their performance—from skimpy financial statements to elaborate reports to the Securities and Exchange

Commission and other public agencies on their objectives, prospects, and performance in various economic, political, legal, and social arenas. Their relations with, influence among, and impacts on various constituencies now called stakeholders have become very important.

Such multifaceted communications with stakeholders are now the function of knowledge-management public affairs (PA), whose purpose is to gather *information* about the firm's interactions with stakeholders and to translate it into *actionable knowledge* for its executives and employees as well as *responsible accounting* to its constituencies, including shareholders. This function has grown from being an appendix of advertising to becoming a corporate unit reporting to top executives and boards of directors in the context of new governance structures. It has collected resources—people, skills, and budgets—to match these new responsibilities and to translate superior knowledge into real competitive advantages complementary to those deployed in economic markets.

This chapter analyzes the domestic and international challenges and responses that account for the state of the PA function during the 1990s and in the early twenty-first century, particularly the varied structures and resources that companies have created to be known and preferably renowned in private and public arenas where transparency, responsibility, and reputation provide lasting advantages.

DOMESTIC AND INTERNATIONAL FORCES: 1970 TO 2000

The 1970s witnessed much inflation and recession because of the oil crisis of 1973, the winding down of the Vietnam War, the devaluation of the U.S. dollar after 1971–1973, and the incipient decline of U.S. competitiveness. While prosperity also generates discontent, a declining or sluggish economy highlights certain problems such as consumer protection (a hot topic in the 1970s under the leadership of Ralph Nader) and employment discrimination (related to civil and women's rights). Deregulation, privatization (Mitnick, 1993; Russo, 1992; Mahon and Murray, 1981) and e-commerce policies change the economic playing field for entire industries.

The 1973 oil crisis turned petroleum companies into scapegoats; ITT's political behavior in Chile raised questions about multinational enterprises (MNEs) interfering with national sovereignty; "foreign corrupt practices" were discovered and outlawed by the United States in 1977; Barnet and Muellers's *Global Reach* (1974) attacked MNEs for their behaviors in less developed countries (LDCs); the UN's Group of Eminent Persons provided a critical report that led to the creation of the Commission on Transnational Corporations and the continuous drafting of various codes of conduct; governments in France, Japan, the UK, and West Germany as well as the European Common Market's Commission were engineering various industrial policies designed to curb IBM and other U.S. MNEs, while Congress kept alive from 1971 to 1974 the threat of the Hartke-Burke bill that would have negatively impacted U.S. foreign trade and investment.

Changes in National, State, and Local Governments

The Vietnam War and President Nixon's "Watergate" generated dissatisfaction with the U.S. political process as well as divided America. Revealed instances of hidden political contributions at home and abroad resulted in the authorization of political action committees (PACs) in 1974 as well as in demands for greater transparency in political matters and broader access to legislators, executive departments, and agencies. These developments gave much greater "voice" to groups hostile to business or to those that had a "social" agenda. Repercussions stemming from the civil rights and social/environmental movements in the 1960s and 1970s reverberated in the form of social regulations. In addition to economic regulations (Epstein, 1990), social regulations continue to fill many legislative and regulatory agendas. Social regulations change the operations and activities for multiple firms across industries (Post, Lawrence and Weber, 2000). Enforcing health and safety regulations affects manufacturing firms in the chemical, telecommunications, aerospace, food and beverage, electronics, forest products, and pharmaceutical industries, for example.

"Environmentalism" entered the consciousness of people on account of Rachel Carson's *Silent Spring* and progressively assumed international dimensions. The 1970s brought significant expansion of business regulation in response to societal awareness of significant problems and excesses. The increase in regulation created threats and economic burdens for America's corporations (Sonnenfeld, 1981; Ryan, Swanson and Buchholz, 1987). In response to the imposition of controls and regulations (for example, environmental, affirmative action, health and safety), firms needed additional information, expanded skills to either shape or avoid regulation, and/or strategies to deal with the public policy process (Keim, 1985).

During the 1980s, congressional procedures were modified, taking power from entrenched, longtime committee chairpersons and making the process far more open. Corporations saw that such reforms would allow greater access and result in potentially more benefits if more careful and coordinated efforts were deployed (Keim, 1985). At this same time, a stronger economy allowed an expansion in the allocation of resources for such activities (Marcus and Kaufman, 1988).

Heightened awareness of governmental impacts on firms (potentially both positive and negative) was one result of the ideologically charged Reagan/Carter presidential election in 1980. The increased political conservatism of the electorate provided encouragement for firms that sought to either eliminate or modify what they saw as onerous limitations on managerial prerogatives. During that same election, corporate political action committees (PACs) grew and played a significant role in electing both Ronald Reagan and a more balanced Congress (Ryan, Swanson and Buchholz, 1987).

As the turn of the century approached, the demand for more transparency and accountability within the public sector created initiatives to eliminate the Departments of Commerce, Education, and Energy as well as the Environmental

Protection Agency. Eliminating unfunded mandates and increasing demands for a more "neighborly government" raised expectations for decision-making on health care, welfare, and education at the state and local level. New Federalism and the devolution of power to the states caused firms such as AT&T to create focused strategies for their state governmental relations functions (Griffin, Shaffer and Mahon, 1997).

Globalization

Perlmutter (1969) made popular the "attitudes" of *ethnocentrism, polycentrism, and geocentrism,* which later informed the policy/strategy issue of "global integration versus national responsiveness," which is particularly evident in international public affairs. Policy diffusion across borders required keeping a closer eye on international developments that became salient domestic and business issues: international trade negotiations through GATT; foreign direct investments into the United States; relations with OPEC countries and the recycling of huge amounts of petrodollars; flexible exchange rates, and other dynamics. Consequently, U.S. governments had to simultaneously regulate large U.S. firms for various economic and social reasons, and harness them to national interests in the face of greater international hostility or—at least—challenge.

Global policy issues and industries spanning global borders became interesting topics for public affairs research. Examining global policy issues such as the Montreal Protocol (Getz, 1995), the WTO (Young and Brewer, 1999) and international bribery (Windsor and Getz, 1999) with complex stakeholder negotiations were of interest. The arenas of resolution as well as the arenas initiating policy were changing. For example, genetically modified organism (GMO) debates have been very spirited in the EU yet below the radar screen of the general public in the United States. The worldwide web of policy networks creates opportunities and challenges for senior public affairs executives. Industries spanning the globe such as the steel industry (Schuler, 1996) and the U.S. construction equipment industry (Johnson, Lenn, and O'Neill, 1997) were examined by drawing on political science, international business, strategic management, and public affairs literatures. More broadly, Meznar (1996; Meznar and Nigh, 1995; Kennelly and Gladwin, 1995; Meznar and Johnson, 1996) focused on U.S.-based MNC responses to globalization via buffering and bridging activities.

THE CORPORATION RESPONDS: ANTICIPATING AND SHAPING POLICY ISSUES

Conceptually, Talcott Parsons (Parsons and Smelser, 1956; Parsons, 1960) and James Thompson (1967) argued that there is a qualitative break among the technical, managerial, and institutional *roles* in organizations. This breakthrough allowed us to associate the PA *function* with the institutional *role* of the organization. As part of the institutional role, PA is a *window in* the organization so the public, the media, prospective employees, and community leaders can transparently view the goals, ideals, and shared values of the organization. PA is also a *window out* of the organization for the CEO and executives to help shape opinions, policy, and perceptions of the firm and its activities (Post, Murray, Dickie, and Mahon, 1982, 1983; Adams, 1976). Compared to public relations, which is exclusively external in orientation ("This is our company: Think well of us!"), public affairs can transform the organization, both in its internal and external aspects. This perspective anticipated what, in organization theory, were later called "bridging and buffering" structures, processes, actors, and strategies.

At the same time, corporations were also very attuned to attacks about the "social *responsibilities* of business." Public affairs research focused on specific action steps taken to manage relations with the firm's public constituents and the "corporate-responsiveness" approach to public affairs (Ackerman, 1975). Hirschman's (1970) *Exit Voice and Loyalty* has implicitly or explicitly shaped typologies of PA activities and organizational "responses" to environmental developments. Recognition of the changing domestic and international ways of doing business was acknowledged by early writers such as Ed Epstein's *The Corporation in American Politics* (1969) and Raymond Vernon's *Sovereignty at Bay* (1971).

But it wasn't until Jean Boddewyn began addressing the internal firm responses to these changing business environments that an academic interest in PA was expanded. Jean and colleagues John Fayerweather and Ashok Kapoor began exploring the question: "What are MNEs doing—or should be doing—about largely hostile developments at home and abroad?" Boddewyn focused on U.S. MNEs operating in Western Europe in the 1970s (Fayerweather, 1969; Boddewyn and Kapoor, 1972; Boddewyn, 1973, 1974, 1975, 1977; Dunn, Cahill and Boddewyn, 1979; Kapoor and Boddewyn, 1973). He examined the structure, staff, and resources of the PA function at the local (community), national, regional (European), and global levels in some forty firms through more than two hundred field interviews. He identified and analyzed its development at the foreign entry, ongoing, and exit stages in the light of: (1) industry characteristics; (2) firm size, growth, and structure (product, geographical, functional), and (3) personal attitudes of top and middle executives.

Developing corporate PA as a viable organizational function meant *greater internalization*—essentially: (1) distinct, larger, and fairly integrated PA staffs and budgets; (2) greater recognition of the institutional role of the chief executive (and of local foreign managers) to represent, commit, and account for the organization, and (3) growing awareness that "external/public affairs begin at home"—meaning that it cannot be the exclusive responsibility of the PA staff but must ultimately involve and implicate all managers and (preferably) all employees—an early version of "grassroots mobilization."

More, and larger, PA functions within *Fortune* 500 firms grew throughout the 1970s and 1980s (Brenner, 1980; Dickie, 1981; Post, Murray, Dickie, and

Mahon, 1982, 1983). One study showed over 50 percent of *Fortune* 500 firms having a formal PA function by 1980 (Keim, 1981, p. 45). At the same time, resources allocated in both people and dollars grew (Post et al., 1982, 1983; Marcus and Kaufman, 1988). One explanation for this initial growth was that the number and complexity of public issues facing corporations had themselves grown explosively, creating a need for firms to have a more organized and strategic response (Sonnenfeld, 1981).

Corporate public affairs functions were becoming more formalized. Mission statements became more common, along with some "codes of conduct" and "social audits." In addition, there were various attempts to fit the PA function into shifting organizational structures based on function, product, geography, and even a matrix of them. Usually the PA function was adapted to these changing structures, but, occasionally, the PA institutional-role imperative dictated that structures be adapted to "the political imperative" of "national responsiveness" and coloring. For example, there was no "ITT France" because each ITT subsidiary had to be French-looking rather than part of a foreign MNE in order to get French-government contracts.

By 1996, 64 percent of respondents from a national U.S. corporate public affairs survey said they had a formalized mission statement, 70 percent regularly prepared a public affairs plan, and 36 percent had a formalized "vision statement" for the PA department. Three years later, a similar survey of a similar population indicated a jump to 89 percent having a formalized code of ethics and 69 percent having a formalized crisis management plan (Post and Griffin, 1997; Foundation for Public Affairs, 1999a). Formalization of public affairs is due in large part to professional associations throughout the world educating, sharing best practices, and surveying current corporate public affairs practices (Centre for Corporate Public Affairs, 1996; Canadian Council for Public Affairs Advancement, 1999; Foundation for Public Affairs, 1999a).

Senior corporate public affairs executives remained involved in top management decision-making. By the late 1990s, more than half of all senior PA executives were reporting to the CEO, chairman, or president; more than half are currently members of the firms' senior management committees (or equivalent); and one-fifth have a board-level committee that focuses primarily on their companies' interactions with the external environment such as public policy, social policy, or public affairs (Post and Griffin, 1997; Foundation for Public Affairs, 1999a).

Doing More with Less

During the1980s, the growing size of firms' Washington presence is at least partly the result of an increasingly broad set of federal government relations activities managed by corporate public affairs units (Dickie, 1981; Marcus and Kaufman, 1988). Concomitantly, in the 1990s a myriad of activities beyond the traditional U.S. business-government relations focus were under the responsibility of the senior PA executive (Post and Griffin, 1997; Griffin, 1997). By the turn of the century, fifteen activities, on average, supplemented governmental relations (Foundation for Public Affairs, 1999a) including: PACs, community affairs, media relations, investor relations, coalition development, grassroots advocacy, Internet policy, and issues management, among other activities.

Human resources allocated to PA functions have decreased from the early 1980s to mid-1990s. Due to re-engineering, downsizing, "rightsizing," and being "McKinseyed," public affairs functions have, on average, fewer people (Griffin, 1997). And, PA budgets have remained unchanged over the same period after correcting for inflation (Griffin, 1997). PA executives are being asked to do more with fewer resources.

To effectively manage increased responsibilities with diminishing resources, some PA functions became a hodgepodge of disparate activities reporting to a single executive—much like a diversified conglomerate. Alternatively, some PA functions purposively integrated disparate activities to better focus their resources (Fleisher, 1999), customize their PA responses with consistent messages across various audiences, and selectively engage in relevant political/social activities (Getz, 1993). In some organizations, issues management, for example, was integrated into strategic planning (Greening, 1992; Greening and Gray, 1994) to facilitate a proactive and interactive engagement of relevant stakeholders. By actively shaping issues as they gain momentum in the court of public opinion, firms are gaining a competitive advantage (Mahon, 1982, 1983, 1989).

To do more with less, some organizations through their PA office *mobilized and tapped external resources*. The traditional use of trade associations of the "umbrella" type (for example, industry associations, the capstone Chamber of Commerce of the United States, and the National Association of Manufacturers) was complemented by ad hoc coalitions (for example, to protect freedom of foreign trade and investment) and by the use of well-placed lobbyists, "political" law firms, communications experts, "free-enterprise think tanks," and the like.

Other PA offices use technology as a tool to help manage the volume of queries, calls, and interactions with government stakeholders, community leaders, and employee groups (Foundation for Public Affairs, 1999a, 1999b; Canadian Council for Public Affairs Advancement, 1997). Tracking voting records of politicians, corporate contributions, yield rates of get-out-the-vote initiatives, grassroots fax blasts, and momentum of corporate mentions in the media has transformed the depth and breadth of corporate PA offices.

Articulate and Demonstrate Value-Added

Downsizing, rightsizing, re-engineering, and doing more with less have forced a performance-based accounting on corporate PA offices. "Public affairs is an earning function" rather than mere overhead began to be heard and advocated. However, to this day, ways of measuring such "earnings" or "effectiveness" remains elusive in most cases. Like the Swiss army, the PA function has to keep explaining why its deterrent effect is needed even in the absence of wars.

Resources being allocated to public affairs activities were nontrivial in magnitude and directly observable by top management. The expectations for a return on those expenditures were very likely growing. The need to justify the existence and importance of PA became critical. The Asian financial crisis in the late 1990s continued to emphasize the need for appropriate business-government relations that rationalized resources effectively. In general, the legitimacy, efficacy, and future viability of business political behaviors remained under scrutiny and required justification (Meznar and Nigh, 1993; Boddewyn and Salorio, 1999; Shaffer and Hillman, 2000).

In some organizations, justification for corporate PA is based upon being a narrowly honed asset directed at selected targets, tightly coordinated with corporate strategy (Fleming, 1980; Marx, 1986; Miles, 1987; and, Sonnenfeld, 1981). The focusing of resources and people on a narrow set of issues (esp. on congressional legislation) and the coordination of PAC contributions to PA actions are examples of selective and strategic use of PA resources and capabilities.

Another result of the increased scrutiny was the importance on measuring and assessing the perceptually "soft" outputs of corporate PA. Performance measurement became a major research agenda in the early 1990s (Fleisher, 1992, 1993a, 1993b). Management by objectives (Post and Griffin, 1997; Foundation for Public Affairs, 1999a; Centre for Corporate Public Affairs, 1996), a balanced scorecard approach (Fleisher and Mahaffy, 1997) and benchmarking (Fleisher, 1998) were partially successful as practical tools for management assessment.

By responding to internal corporate demands for change, the PA function was changing from the inside out. At the same time, the PA function was responding to external triggers for change and growing from the outside in. These dual acting pressures have continued to fashion vastly different PA functions, reflecting each individual firm's personality and culture as well as common industry issues and political realities. Consequently, a "typical" PA function does not exist. Opportunities for differentiation, distinctive competencies, and competitive advantage abound. Different combinations of prioritizing five primary stakeholder groups create capabilities not easily imitated as well as different roles for PA within organizations. While creating identity, legitimacy, and institutionalization issues for the PA function, the wide range of PA functions also creates opportunities for competitive advantage and unique PA strategies. Various corporate public affairs strategies are examined in the next section.

CORPORATE PUBLIC AFFAIRS STRATEGIES

Cogently responding to external and internal pressures for change has forced a strategic orientation on corporate public affairs functions. That is, PA executives must incorporate political and competitive strategies (Dickie, 1984;

Marx, 1992; Baron, 1995; Schuler, 1999), and local/international strategies (Young and Brewer, 1999; Mitchell, Hansen and Jepsen, 1997), to satisfy internal and external stakeholders (Meznar and Nigh, 1995; Griffin, 1997; Schuler, 1999). Integrated strategies (Baron, 1995) are critical.

Corporate PA functions add value to corporate strategies in a variety of ways. Value can be added via: enhancing the firm's image, building corporate reputation (Healy and Griffin, 2005), eliminating barriers to entry for new product/market offerings (Schuler and Rehbein, 1999), building capacity for future growth strategies via political engagement in foreign countries (Schuler, 1996, 1999), or tax breaks. These externally oriented programs to gain corporate advantages can be supplemented by improving activities along the firm's value chain. Public affairs can aid in gaining access to raw materials such as technical skills (for example, H1B visa) and global information systems, positioning products for governmental contracts, and by using effective political involvement systems (Keim, 1985; Griffin and Dunn, 2004). *How* PA adds value by creating viable political strategies is the focus of the remainder of this section.

Generic political strategies (Hillman and Hitt, 1999) for diversified firms (Shaffer and Hillman, 2000) suggest a lockstep approach incorporating relational/transactional and collective/individual action dimensions. Widespread use of generic strategies for a firm's political environments has been, however, difficult. By definition, a generic strategy is easily imitated—it is "generic." Yet, an easily imitated capability does not create and sustain a firm's competitive advantage *over time*. Nor does a "generic" political strategy recognize nuances that have created individualized PA functions. Previous research suggests that PA activities and strategies are affected by industry, senior management commitment/leadership, structure, and issue life cycles, among other factors. We examine how industry differences, issue life cycles, and leadership challenges affect public affairs strategies below.

Issues vary significantly by *industry* (for example, pharmaceuticals versus soft drinks) and *geography* (for example, "nationalism" is a hot issue in one country but not in another), thereby emphasizing the role of specific trade (for example, for pharmaceutical firms) and foreign associations (for example, American chambers of commerce abroad). Miles (1987), and Bhambri and Sonnenfeld (1988), described the profound differences among members of a single industry when it came to planning and implementing PA activities. Their work, done in the insurance industry and forest products industry, respectively, shows that choices of both position and actions were linked to the philosophy of the firm's management about how to deal with public issues. In both industries a set of firms had a "cooperative" stance while other firms had an "adversarial" one. In both studies firms that took the more cooperative approach were seen as having a more effective social performance. Mahon (1982, 1983) found that larger firms had multiple levels of governmental interaction (for example, local, state, and federal as well as legislative and regulatory branches) and used a wider selection of the nine activity areas he identified.

Issue life cycles (Wartick and Rude, 1986; Heath and Nelson, 1986) suggest that issues move from birth to growth (or early death), maturity, and decline; and firms must position themselves differently at each stage through variations on Hirschman's (1970) themes of "[entry], exit, voice and loyalty." Post, Murray, Dickie, and Mahon (1983) suggest managing an issue life cycle by using different strategies: ignore, try to anticipate, become better at reading the environment, expand public affairs efforts, and having the public affairs effort pervade the company. A four-step scale was developed: reaction, defend, anticipate, and proaction (RDAP). *Reaction* to external developments needs to be complemented by *proaction*—unless *inaction* is appropriate ("That too shall pass, and there is little or nothing significant that we can do in the meanwhile"). The proactive view led to what scholars (for example, Wood, 1986) would later call "the strategic use of public policy."

Post and Mahon (1980) suggest that the "fit" between the environment, the firm, and the public affairs unit's approach can have a profound effect on the success of issue life cycle strategies. Mahon (1989) proposes that the relationships among industry type, level of regulation, and sophistication of corporate interaction as well as the escalation of the issue help determine the senior management commitment as well as the depth and breadth of PA strategies.

For all the logic of adopting and integrating appropriate PA strategies on account of industries, *leadership* and senior management commitment must be factored in (Griffin and Dunn, 2004). For better or worse, CEOs and PA leadership matter. CEOs or senior PA executives may have individual preferences for a "high versus low profile" (Boddewyn and Marton, 1978; Marton and Boddewyn, 1978). PA executives' professional backgrounds affect PA decisions (for example, are financial and legal types more attuned to public policies than managers with engineering, production, and even marketing experience?). In addition, organizational brands, CEO reputation, philosophy, and attitudes affect PA decisions (Perlmutter, 1969; Miles, 1987).

Various business associations and consulting bodies have taken leadership positions by publishing reports on the rationale and practices of domestic and international public affairs: the Conference Board; the Public Affairs Council; Business International, Inc.; International Business-Government Counsellors, and the Committee for Economic Development, among others. In the early 1970s, business leaders took action as thought leaders to inspire and motivate firms as well as reassure (up to a point) various external constituencies: Sol Linowitz (Xerox), David Rockefeller (Chase), Pépé de Cubas (Westinghouse), Jacques Maisonrouge (IBM), to name a few. Yet, the charismatic leader at the turn of the century was accused of focusing more on branding of the CEO or the corporation while providing increased returns to shareholders (for example, Jack Welch of GE; Ken Lay of Enron; Bernie Ebbers of WorldCom) rather than external constituencies.

Responding to the industry differences, issue life cycle challenges, and leadership opportunities, corporate PA functions have grown from being a part of the strategic planning function (Marx, 1990) to being a transformational change agent for continued competitiveness (Mitnik, 1993; Fleisher, 1999; Foundation for Public Affairs, 1999a). As a strategic function aligned with the corporate strategy (Fleisher and Hoewing, 1992; Fleisher, 1999; Fleisher and Stephan, 1996), PA has become integral to some modern corporations as a knowledge management function. PA executives gather, assess, and translate information into knowledge-rich, actionable activities focused on critical corporate opportunities.

PA executives have created webs of like-minded organizations. Drawing from their competitors, suppliers, and shareholders as well as special interest groups and trade associations, PA functions are amassing a wealth of internal and external assets to manage with changing societal expectations. RJR Nabisco (now Altria) with its controversial products has aptly managed changing expectations by minimizing legislation or actively shaping regulation when the tipping point had been reached. The DOJ antitrust suit against Microsoft, for example, has resulted in the need for Microsoft to develop a DC presence, and forge relationships in the legislative, administrative, and judicial branches of government. Not only is there increased opportunity for public policy participation, organizations are learning how to effectively participate interactively. Building coalitions of like-minded interests are important (Foundation for Public Affairs, 1999a, 1999b) in today's interactive regulatory and legislative environment.

The Internet has facilitated the accelerated growth of dot-com companies and special interest groups with targeted missions and committed memberships. Firms are strategically rebuilding trust by engaging relevant stakeholders. Organizations actively pursue their interests via individual action, coalitions (Lord, 2000), grassroots advocacy (Lord, 1996), and in international (for example, WTO) or transatlantic forums (for example, NAFTA). Recognizing governmental agencies as definitive stakeholders (Mitchell, Agle and Wood, 1997), organizations have actively created and maintained relationships to gain a competitive advantage (Dyer and Singh, 1998). Corporations are developing strategies integrating multiple political involvement tactics including PACs (Mullery, Brenner and Perrin, 1995; Lord, 1996; Gray and Lowery, 1997; Dean, Vryza, and Fryxell, 1998) alongside grassroots advocacy (Lord, 1995) and lobbying. Lord (2000) has recently shown that coalition-building is the most important political involvement tactic from both congressional and corporate perspectives.

Research at the intersection of political science, management, and organizational theory suggests that organizations are actively engaging in the public policy process from issue creation via special interest groups, the media, and crises to legislation and enforcement (Greening and Gray, 1994; Getz, 1997). Bridging the gap between political science and organizational theory, Schuler and Rehbein (1997) propose and test (1999) a combined model using internal, firm-specific variables with external, environmental variables to better determine political involvement effectiveness. Governmental audiences are recognized as a viable, legitimate arena to set, or change, the rules of the competitive marketplace (Mahon and McGowan, 1996; Boddewyn and Salorio, 1999). Insights from these literatures, however, generally remain separate and distinct (Epstein, 1998). Opportunities for competitive advantage via public affairs and understanding the strategic importance of PA remain as challenges in the future. Additional opportunities and challenges for public affairs executives and scholars are highlighted below.

THE FUTURE OF CORPORATE PUBLIC AFFAIRS IN THE TWENTY-FIRST CENTURY

With the implosions from Enron, WorldCom, and Parmalat reverberating through the investor and corporate communities, corporate public affairs executives have a unique opportunity to solidify their strategic positioning within their company and transform relevant relationships. By returning to the initial ideas of public affairs executives as thought leaders; in creating alternative arenas for thoughtful interactions benefiting organizations, citizens, and consumers; by using policy to enable new business initiatives; and by using the public policy process as an opportunity for innovative thinking and new ways of operating, senior public affairs executives can provide leadership. As top managers intimately involved in public debates on relevant business issues, PA executives are uniquely positioned to effectively broker the multifaceted business-government-citizen relationships. Three different opportunities for public affairs executives are highlighted below: developing value-based enterprises; seeking alternative arenas of resolution; and exerting thought leadership.

Developing Value-Based Enterprises

In an ever more crowded public issues arena with complex business policy issues such as taxes, health care, welfare, offshoring, employment, and wage rates, many constituencies are questioning the interests of corporations. Firms, quite appropriately, are unapologetic in creating wealth, employing millions, and providing an enhanced quality of life for millions more around the globe. But existing employee, consumer, investor, and community activities are not meeting the moving targets demanded by firm's constituencies. Rather, civil society is demanding to understand, support, and "buy into" the firm's position on a host of issues not necessarily considered by business as "core" business issues. Rather, more constituencies are questioning the philosophy, governance, and decision-making of management. Issues such as living wages, product liability, corporate boards, social investments, expensing options, and retirement benefits are creeping into the domain of salient business issues.

In response, some firms are branding themselves to position their core values as a significant differentiating factor. Given choices, consumers are increasingly interested in purchasing branded products representing core values with specific messages on lifestyle choices connoting prestige or position. Building an articulated value-based enterprise is becoming critical (Healy and Griffin, forthcoming). The core competencies and distinctive acts of a firm are not enough in an increasingly competitive market. Consumer product companies such as Nike, Luna, Whirlpool, ING, and The Gap are leading the way in clearly articulating core values upon which the company is based.

Building a perception (as well as the reality) of being a value-based enterprise creates choices for firms, their employees, their consumers, their communities, and their constituencies. Benefits of a value-based enterprise include increased choices in hiring the best prospective employees, choices in partnering with legitimate special interest groups, choices in being asked to testify on Capitol Hill, and opportunities to give a public rejoinder when a crisis of confidence occurs. The "stickiness" or "halo effect" of a value-based enterprise changes the question from: "Is this a bad company dealing with yet another business problem?" to "Is this a good company dealing with an occasional hiccup?" (Harsanyi, 2004). Trust, integrity, and legitimacy are at the heart of being a value-based enterprise. Being given the benefit of the doubt when issues arise is just an added benefit of a value-based enterprise.

Trust and integrity are enhanced by enhancing transparency (Tapscott and Ticoll, 2003; Harsanyi, 2004) and anticipating the sharks that are just below the water surface (Catania, 2004). Anticipating the sharks—anticipating controversial issues and problematic stakeholders—is not just a matter of serendipity. Anticipation requires being positioned at the right time, with the right resources, and a clear understanding of how the sharks (e.g., issues and stakeholders) can impact your firm over time (Dentchev et al., 2004; Griffin and McGowan, 2004).

Public affairs functions actively anticipating controversial issues monitor blogs and Internet chat sites to understand what stakeholders (competitors, legitimate advocacy groups, consumers) are discussing. Is an issue newsworthy? Is momentum building on an issue? Are more, legitimate, and catalytic stakeholders (that is, Congress, the media, and others) becoming involved? Who is shaping the issue(s)? Collating and prioritizing issues is the first step. Implementing responses based on the values of the enterprise is also important although an oft overlooked step.

Value-based enterprises seek out various stakeholders to cooperatively work on public issues. Signing cooperation contracts with groups that might detract, distract, or undermine your initiatives is critical. These cooperation contracts can be made very noisy—with lots of media fanfare. Else, these contracts can be quietly pursued. Regardless, media exposure is a critical element of a cooperation contract. Some special interest groups need media exposure to satisfy their memberships. For example, Whirlpool has signed contracts with the National Resource Defense Council, the Friends of the Earth, and the Sierra Club as partners to solve problems in energy efficiency cooperatively.

Value-based enterprises actively promote loyalty and quality as part of the firm's organizational DNA. Loyalty to core values helps define, explain, and expand the organization's strategy. Rather than embracing a separation between the economic aspects of a business and "everything else," a value-based enterprise creates situations to embrace the economic, political, legal, and social realities facing a business. Some firms reinforce the importance of being a value-based enterprise by actively recruiting executives into prestigious positions within the company publicly demonstrating those values, noisily firing individuals not demonstrating the values, developing educational programs, creating on-the-job training, and very actively mentoring future leaders in the behaviors expected of them (Harsanyi, 2004).

Proactively engaging relevant stakeholders means understanding policy issues from all sides. A new activity for values-based enterprises is identifying the disadvantage of an issue before the competition does. Effectively managing the disadvantage may include mitigation, building collaborations, stalling, or communicating the benefits and downside risks to politicians, consumers, analysts, and other constituents. Managing unintended consequences of a policy issue is becoming as important as effectively managing the public policy process. Drawing from multiple disciplines such as the law, the sciences, engineering, and policy requires a broader conceptualization of the boundary-spanning role of public affairs. Professional association workshops, networking, business schools, certificate programs, and listservs are important tactical activities for developing professionals within a value-based enterprise. Doing more with less requires leveraging assets not normally assigned to PA to understand the role and implications of products and polices on the enterprise.

Seeking Alternative Arenas of Resolution

"Glocalization" suggests broadening arenas of resolution to include the global level while simultaneously paying strict attention to local matters. Strong federal government relations in the U.S. are often supplemented and complemented by a strong state government relations function as well as an active grassroots capability (Public Affairs Council, 2004; Lord, 2003). Simultaneously coordinating efforts on critical issues cutting across multiple arenas of resolution is mandatory for twenty-first-century public affairs executives. Critical business issues are initiated in political arenas as well as public arenas like local news that escalates to national attention.

Issues are often migrating across geographical barriers and political jurisdictions. For example, the genetically modified organism (GMO) debates are very contentious in the EU while GMOs are largely ignored in the United States. Pan-national agencies such as the WTO and the United Nations Cartagena Protocol call for substantially different positions on GMOs. Much debate continues in a wide variety of arenas of resolution. Standing back and waiting for others to lead the issue can be disastrous for firms playing catch-up.

Tracking issues as they migrate and morph across international borders is an zopportunity for preemptive public affairs functions. Tracking issues can be enhanced by effectively using trade associations. Trade associations can collate disparate information from international sources, but taking a specific stance on an issue may be problematic for large trade associations with conflicted stakeholders (Griffin and McGowan, 2004).

Creating flexible public affairs capabilities is critical in fast-moving issues. When the arena of resolution is a technical forum based on information, reports, scientific data, and academic studies, trade associations can add value by distilling the volumes of data. Legal opinions and expert witnesses affect technical areas of resolution. Yet, when issues escalate and the arena of resolution changes to political forums or to the court of public opinion, advocacy, special interests, and political sophistication must be leveraged with civil society–based activities.

Exerting Thought Leadership

Corporate public affairs executives are uniquely positioned to be effective thought leaders within their corporation and with relevant stakeholders. Intuitively, a CEO might be thought of as the company's only opinion leader with the power, credence, and authority to drive the change incumbent within a CEO's position. Yet, ideas can stem from multiple sources within the corporation. Thought leaders can initiate and execute ideas at any position within the firm. Having the ear of the top management team and reporting directly to the CEO, 'he senior PA executive can exert leadership on social, political, and legal initiatives affecting future business initiatives, its products, and employees.

Thought leaders are far more than the public relations spokesperson who focuses on delivering the company's message to the organization's constituents. Rather, thought leaders engage in conversations with academics, in global forums, in the media, and build big moments that can be leveraged across audiences (Healy and Griffin, forthcoming). Thought leaders inspire, motivate, cajole, and at times assert peer pressure. In the past, numerous CEOs were effective thought leaders. Now, where are their equivalents in the new millennium? Well-known CEOs such as Bill Gates focus their business on business. Johnson and Johnson may have a superb reputation, but can you name its chairman?

Complicating the role of thought leaders within global businesses is the question of who is the salient thought leader when several product divisions operate within a country. Consistency of messages, coordination among constituencies, and integration of activities remain critical challenges to the legitimacy of effective thought leaders. Further complicating the role of senior PA as thought leaders may be the educational training of many PA executives. Senior PA executives are predominantly lawyers. A legal education provides excellent skill sets for examining complex issues as well as working with politicians who are former lawyers. Yet, if an organization's response to public issues is lawsuits and legal showdowns, then a capability in law can become a barrier to creating win-win business and public policies (Catania, 2004).

CONCLUSION

Altogether, the PA function is here to stay and will grow in the twenty-first century. Its managers are well positioned in firms that have the objective and potential to emerge as thought leaders and action exemplars. Their expertise lies in translating information into the knowledge needed to build reputation, trust, and legitimacy around core values reflecting the philosophy of top management. PA professionals are both the "message" and the "messenger" when firms face conflicts, but also when they seize opportunities to position themselves competitively through their creed and its delivery to multiple stakeholder groups.

The future is bright for public affairs executives. Strategically positioned within companies having unlimited potential to emerge as thought leaders on substantial public policy issues, public affairs executives can leverage many core assets. PA executives are at the heart of developing viable value-based enterprises. Building reputation, trust, and legitimacy around core values reflecting philosophy of top management, PA executives are critical to being healers of conflict. In time, the problems stemming from Enron, WorldCom, and Parmalat can be identified as outliers in an effective business market.

NOTE

Continued thanks to John Mahon (University of Maine), Jim Post (Boston University) and Dan Kane (George Washington University) for their comments on earlier versions of this chapter.

REFERENCES

Ackerman, R. W. (1975). *The social challenge to business*. Cambridge: Harvard University Press.

Adams, J. S. (1976). The structure and dynamics of behavior in organizational boundary roles. In Dunnette, M. D., ed. *Handbook of industrial and organizational psychology*, 1175–1199.

Baron, D. P. (1995). Integrated strategy: Market and nonmarket components. *California Management Review, 37*(2), 47–65.

Bhambri, A., and Sonnenfeld, J. (1988). Organization structure and corporate social performance: A field study in two contrasting industries. *Academy of Management Journal, 31*(3), 642–662.

Boddewyn, J. J. (main reporter). (1975). *Corporate external affairs: A blueprint for survival*. New York and Geneva: Business International, Inc.

Boddewyn, J. J. (main reporter). (1977). *Multinational government relations: An action guide for corporate management*. Washington, DC: International Business-Government Counsellors, Inc.

Boddewyn, J. J. (1973). The external affairs function in American multinational corporations. In Fayerweather, J., ed. *International business-government affairs*. New York: Ballinger, pp. 49–62.

Boddewyn, J. J. (1974). External affairs: A corporate function in search of conceptualization and theory. *Organization and Administrative Sciences*, 5(1), 67–111.

Boddewyn, J. J., and Kapoor, A. (1972, December). The external relations of American multinational enterprises. *International Studies Quarterly*, 433–453.

Boddewyn, J. J., and Marton, K. (1978). Corporate profiles: Low, high, and right. *IPRA Review*, 2(2), 9–12.

Boddewyn, J. J., and Salorio, E. M. (1999). Business political behavior is as universal, strategic, effective, and legitimate as economic and organizational behaviors. Unpublished paper.

Brenner, S. N. (1980). Corporate political activity: An exploratory study in a developing industry. In Preston, L., ed. *Research in corporate social performance and policy: A research annual*. Vol. 2. Greenwich, CT: JAI Press, 197–236.

Canadian Council for Public Affairs Advancement. (1997). *The impacts of information technology on public affairs management*. Waterloo, Ontario: Canadian Council for Public Affairs Advancement.

Canadian Council for Public Affairs Advancement. (1999). *1998 state of corporate public affairs survey*. Waterloo, Ontario: Canadian Council for Public Affairs Advancement.

Catania, T. (2004, August). Whirlpool's corporate social responsibility initiatives: Building actionable knowledge. Presented at the Annual Academy of Management meetings.

Centre for Corporate Public Affairs. (1996). *Report of Australia and New Zealand corporate public affairs survey*. Sydney, Australia: Centre for Corporate Public Affairs.

Dean, T. J., Vryza, M., and Fryxell, G. E. (1998). Do corporate PACs restrict competition? An empirical examination of industry PAC contributions and entry. *Business & Society*, 37(2), 135–156.

Dickie, R. B. (1981). Playing the government relations game: How companies manage. *Journal of Contemporary Business*, 10(3), 105–118.

Dickie, R. B. (1984). Influence of public affairs offices on corporate planning and of corporations on government policy. *Strategic Management Journal*, 5, 16–34.

Dunn, S. W., Cahill, M. F., and Boddewyn, J. J. (1979). *How fifteen transnational corporations manage public affairs*. Chicago: Crain Books.

Dyer, J. H., and Singh, H. (1998). The relational view: Cooperative strategy and sources of interorganizational competitive advantage. *Academy of Management Review*, 23(4), 660–679.

Epstein, E. M. (1969). *The corporation in American politics*. Englewood Cliffs, NJ: Prentice Hall.

Epstein, E. M. (1990). Business political activity: Research approaches and analytical issues. In Preston L. E., ed. *Business and politics: Research issues and empirical studies*. Greenwich, CT: JAI Press, 1–55.

Epstein, E. M. (1998). Business ethics and corporate social policy: Reflections on an intellectual journey, 1964–1996, and beyond. *Business & Society*, 37(1), 7–39.

Fayerweather, J. (1969). *International business management: A conceptual framework*. New York: McGraw-Hill.

Fleisher, C. S. (1992). Modeling the role of evaluation and measurement in the achievement of corporate public affairs management effectiveness. Unpublished doctoral dissertation, University of Pittsburgh.

Fleisher, C. S. (1993a). Assessing the effectiveness of corporate public affairs efforts. In Mitnick, B., ed. *Corporate political agency: The construction of competition in public affairs*. Newbury Park, CA: Sage Publications, 274–316.

Fleisher, C. S. (1993b). Public affairs management performance: An empirical analysis of evaluation and measurement. In Post, J. E., ed. *Research in corporate social performance and policy, 14*, 139–163.

Fleisher, C. S. (1998). A benchmarked assessment of the strategic management of corporate communications. *Journal of Marketing Communications, 4*, 163–176.

Fleisher, C. S. (1999). A systems-based analysis of public affairs as a strategic communication function. *Asia Pacific Public Relations Journal, 1*(1), 1–26.

Fleisher, C. S., and Hoewing, R. L. (1992). Strategically managing corporate external relations: New challenges and opportunities. *Journal of Strategic Change, 1*(5), 287–296.

Fleisher, C. S., and Mahaffy, D. (1997). A balanced scorecard approach to public relations management assessment. *Public Relations Review, 23*(2), 117–142.

Fleisher, C. S., and Stephan, A. R. (1996). To be or not to be assessing the strategic management of corporate public affairs. In Logsdon, J. M., and Rehbein, K., eds. *Proceedings of the seventh annual international Association for Business and Society*. Santa Fe, NM, 206–211.

Fleming, J. E. (1980). Linking public affairs with corporate planning. *California Management Review, 23*(2), 35–43.

Foundation for Public Affairs. (1999a). *1999–2000 state of corporate public affairs*. Washington, DC: Public Affairs Council.

Foundation for Public Affairs. (1999b). *Creating a digital democracy: The impact of the internet on public policy making*. Washington, DC: Public Affairs Council.

Getz, K. A. (1993). Selecting corporate political tactics. In Mitnick, B., ed. *Corporate political agency: The construction of competition in public affairs*. Newbury Park, CA: Sage Publications, 242–273.

Getz, K. A. (1995). Implementing multilateral regulation: A preliminary theory and illustration. *Business & Society, 34*, 280–316.

Getz, K. A. (1997). Research in corporate political action: Integration and assessment. *Business & Society, 36*(1), 32–72.

Gray, V., and Lowery, D. (1997). Reconceptualizing PAC formation: It's not a collective action problem and it may not be an arms race. *American Politics Quarterly, 25*, 319–346.

Greening, D. W. (1992). Integrating issues management activities into strategic planning: An empirical analysis of inter-industry differences. In Wall, J., and Jauch, L., eds. *Academy of management best papers proceedings*, 343–347.

Greening, D. W., and Gray, B. (1994). Testing a model of organizational response to social and political issues. *Academy of Management Journal, 37*(3), 467–498.

Griffin, J. J. (1997). Corporate public affairs in the 1990s: Structure, resources, and processes. Unpublished dissertation, Boston University.

Griffin, J. J., Shaffer, B., and Mahon, J. F. (1997). The "new federalism" and the devolution of power from Washington: Determinants of business political activity at the state government level. Paper presented at the Academy of Management annual meeting.

Harsanyi, F. M. (2004, August 14). Restoring confidence at Tyco: Lessons in value-based leadership. Keynote speech at the Academy of Management, Social Issues in Management Division.

Healy, R., and Griffin, J. J. (2005, forthcoming). Building BP's reputation: Tooting your own horn, 2001–2002. *Public Relations Quarterly*.

Heath, R. L., and Nelson, R. A. (1986). *Issues management: Corporate public policy-making in an information society*. Beverly Hills, CA: Sage Publications.

Hillman, A. J., and Hitt, M. A. (1999). Corporate political strategy formulation: A model of approach, participation, and strategy decisions. *Academy of Management Review*, 24(4), 825–842.

Hirschman, A. O. (1970). *Exit voice and loyalty: Responses to decline in firms, organizations, and states*. Cambridge: Harvard University Press.

Johnson, J. H., Lenn, D. J., and O'Neill, H. (1997). Patterns of competition among American firms in a global industry: Evidence from the U.S. construction equipment industry. *Journal of International Management*, 3(3), 207–239.

Kapoor, A., and Boddewyn, J. J. (1973). *International business-government relations: U.S. corporate experience in Asia and Western Europe*. New York: American Management Association.

Keim, G. D. (1981). Foundations of a political strategy for business. *California Management Review*, 23, 41–48.

Keim, G. D. (1985). Corporate grassroots programs in the 1980s. *California Management Review*, 28(1), 110–123.

Kennelly, J. J., and Gladwin, T. N. (1995). Patterns and trends in the management of global public affairs. In Nigh, D., and Collins, D., eds. *Proceedings of the International Association for Business and Society*, 255–260.

Lord, M. D. (1995). Corporate grassroots political strategies: An empirical assessment of corporate constituency building activities. Working paper, Center for Competitiveness and Employment Growth, University of North Carolina at Chapel Hill.

Lord, M. D. (1996, August). PAC contributions and variation in corporate political strategies: An empirical examination of corporate legislative influence activities. Presented at the Academy of Management annual meeting, Cincinnati.

Lord, M. D. (2000). Corporate political strategy and legislative decision-making: The impact of corporate legislative influence activities. *Business & Society*, 39(1), 76–93.

Mahon, J. F. (1982). Public affairs structures and activities in large American corporations. *Academy of Management Proceedings*, 366–370.

Mahon, J. F. (1983). Corporate political strategies: An empirical study of chemical firm responses to superfund legislation. In Preston, L., ed. *Research in corporate social performance and policy*. Greenwich, CT: JAI Press, 5.

Mahon, J. F. (1989). Corporate political strategy. *Business in the Contemporary World*, 2(1), 50–63.

Mahon, J. F., and McGowan, R. A. (1996). *Industry as a Player in the Political and Social Arena: Defining the Competitive Environment*. Greenwich, CT: Quorum.

Mahon, J. F., and Murray, E. A. (1981). Strategic planning for regulated companies. *Strategic Management Journal*, 2, 251–262.

Marcus A. A., and Kaufman, A. M. (1988, March–April). The continued expansion of the corporate public affairs function. *Business Horizons, 58–62.*

Marton, K., and Boddewyn, J. J. (1978). Should a corporation keep a low profile? *Journal of Advertising Research, 18*(4), 25–31.

Marx, T. G. (1986). Integrating public affairs and strategic planning. *California Management Review, 29*(1), 141–147.

Marx, T. G. (1990). Strategic planning for public affairs. *Long Range Planning, 23*(1), 9–16.

Marx, T. G. (1992). Linking political strategy and competitive strategy: A synthesis. In Post, J. E., ed. *Research in Corporate Social Performance and Policy, 13,* 235–244.

Meznar, M. B. (1996). Public affairs management in multinational corporations: Who makes the decisions? *Journal of International Management, 2*(3), 149–175.

Meznar, M. B., and Johnson, J. H. (1996). Multinational operations and stakeholder management: Internationalization, public affairs strategies, and economic performance. *Journal of International Management, 2*(4), 233–261.

Meznar, M. B., and Nigh, D. (1993). Managing corporate legitimacy: Public affairs activities, strategies, and effectiveness. *Business & Society, 32*(1), 30–43.

Meznar, M. B., and Nigh, D. (1995). Buffer or bridge? Environmental and organizational determinants of public affairs activities in American firms. *Academy of Management Journal, 38*(4), 975–996.

Miles, R. H. (1987). *Managing the corporate social environment: A grounded theory.* Englewood Cliffs, NJ: Prentice Hall.

Mitchell, R. K., Agle, B. R., and Wood, D. J. (1997). Toward a theory of stakeholder identification and salience: Defining the principle of who and what really counts. *Academy of Management Review, 22*(4), 853–886.

Mitchell, N. J., Hansen, W. L., and Jepsen, E. M. (1997). The determinants of domestic and foreign corporate political activity. *Journal of Politics, 59,* 1096–1113.

Mitnick, B. M. (1993). The strategic uses of regulation—and deregulation. In Mitnick, B., ed. *Corporate political agency: The construction of competition in public affairs.* Newbury Park, CA: Sage Publications, 67–89.

Mullery, C. B., Brenner, S. N., and Perrin, N. A. (1995). A structural analysis of corporate political activity. *Business & Society, 34,* 147–170.

Parsons, T. (1960). *Structure and process in modern societies.* New York: Free Press.

Parsons, T., and Smelser, N. J. (1956). *Economy and society.* New York: Free Press.

Perlmutter, H. V. (1969). The tortuous evolution of the multinational corporation. *Columbia Journal of World Business, 4,* 9–18.

Post, J. E., and Griffin, J. J. (1997). *The state of corporate public affairs final report.* Washington, DC: Foundation for Public Affairs.

Post, J. E., and Mahon, J. F. (1980). Articulated turbulence: The effect of regulatory agencies on corporate responses to social change. *Academy of Management Review, 5*(3), 399–407.

Post, J. E., Murray, E. A., Dickie, R. B., and Mahon, J. F. (1982). The public affairs function in American corporations: Development and relations with corporate planning. *Long Range Planning, 15*(2), 12–21.

Post, J. E., Murray, E. A., Dickie, R. B., and Mahon, J. F. (1983). Managing public affairs: The public affairs function. *California Management Review, 26*(1), 135–150.

Russo, M. V. (1992). Managing deregulatory tensions: Changing patterns of public policies and political strategies. In Post, J. E., ed. *Research in Corporate Social Performance and Policy, 13,* 219–234.

Ryan, M. H., Swanson, C. L., and Buchholz, R. A. (1987). *Corporate strategy, public policy, and the* Fortune *500: How America's major corporations influence government.* Oxford, UK: Basil Blackwell.

Schuler, D. A. (1996). Corporate political strategy and foreign competition: The case of the steel industry. *Academy of Management Journal, 39*(3), 720–737.

Schuler, D. A. (1999). Corporate political action: Rethinking the economic and organizational influences. *Business and Politics, 1*(1), 83–97.

Schuler, D. A., and Rehbein, K. (1997). The filtering role of the firm in corporate political involvement. *Business & Society, 36*(2), 116–139.

Shaffer, B., and Hillman, A. J. (2000). The development of business-government strategies by diversified firms. *Strategic Management Journal, 21,* 175–190.

Sonnenfeld, J. A. (1981). *Structure, culture and performance in public affairs: A study of the forest products industry.* Boston: Auburn House Publishing.

Tapscott, D., and Ticoll, D. (2003). *The naked corporation: How the age of transparency will revolutionize business.* New York: Free Press.

Thompson, J. D. (1967). *Organizations in action.* New York: McGraw-Hill.

Vernon, R. (1971). *Sovereignty at bay: The multinational spread of U.S. enterprise.* New York: Basic Books.

Wartick, S. L., and Rude, R. E. (1986). Issues management: Corporate fad or corporate function? *California Management Review, 29*(1), 124–140.

Windsor, O. D., and Getz, K. A. (1999). Regional market integration and the development of global norms for enterprise conduct. *Business & Society, 38*(4), 415–449.

Wood, D. J. (1986). *Strategic Uses of Public Policy.* Marshfield, MA: Pitman.

Young, S., and Brewer, T. L. (1999). Global firms, the government affairs function, and the WTO. Paper presented at the European Academy of International Business.

7

Multinational Enterprises and Governments: An Analysis of New Trends

ALAN RUGMAN, ALAIN VERBEKE, and
NATHAN GREIDANUS

In this chapter we explore the linkages between multinational enterprise (MNE) strategy and government policy. A synthesis of the relevant literature and related economic data suggests three recent shifts in MNE-government relationships. At the macro level, we observe a shift from goal conflict between MNEs and governments toward more goal complementarity. We also find evidence of corresponding shifts at both the institutional and firm strategy levels. Rugman and Verbeke (1998a, 2001a) identified these shifts first, and this chapter extends their analysis.

MNE-government linkages deserve renewed scholarly attention, given the increased importance of MNE activity in many economic sectors and the potential for government policies to influence MNE behavior in a substantive fashion, including their location decisions and subsidiary role assignments. Overall, MNE sales now represent $18 trillion, and the total number of workers employed by these firms exceeds 53 million individuals (UNCTAD, 2003). MNEs contribute significantly to raising living standards around the world, and they have acted as engines of development and growth through the economic activity they generate. Well-documented, positive spillover effects include, inter alia, technology and skills transfers to economic actors outside the firm as well as improved labor, health, safety, and environmental conditions (Liu, Siler, Wang, and Wei, 2000; Caves, 1996; United Nations Department of Economic and Social Development, 1992).

Governments interact with MNEs and affect MNE behavior through many mechanisms. The principal, distinct areas of government intervention include taxation, competition policy, and innovation policy, which is increasingly aimed at the creation and transfer of technological know-how (Caves, 1996). The precise impact of specific government policies on MNEs cannot always be predicted accurately, but government policies that develop national infrastructure, and promote growth and exchange rate stability, generally appear to encourage inward foreign direct investment (FDI) (Peck, 1996; Globerman and Shapiro, 1999).

The debate is ongoing regarding the impacts of MNEs on governments, and on the nation-state. MNEs are sometimes viewed as powerful economic entities that have the ability to avoid or hamper the enforcement of government regulations by withdrawing or threatening to withdraw from economically dependent nations (Strange, 1988). Some of the more sensible observations regarding the relative power of the MNE versus the nation-state can be found in Vernon (1971), Bergsten, Horst and Moran (1978), Behrman and Grosse (1990), and Rugman (2000).

The main point made in this chapter is that MNEs, as efficiency-driven institutions, have recently been faced with changes in incentives, triggering new strategies toward government policy. Specifically, MNEs and governments appear to be shifting toward a more complementary relationship, and from a transaction cost economics (TCE) perspective, this shift can be interpreted as serving economizing purposes.

APPROACHES TO MNE-GOVERNMENT LINKAGES

Rugman and Verbeke (2001a) suggest there are three approaches to analyzing MNE-government interactions. Two of these approaches are described in Caves' (1996) acclaimed textbook *Multinational Enterprise and Economic Analysis*. In the tenth chapter of his book, Caves first utilizes neoclassical welfare economics to review the benefits and costs of government policies. In the second half of the chapter, Caves then turns to "behavioral" approaches to public policy, based on the assumption that there are self-interested actors in the political domain who influence the formation of public policy. Rugman and Verbeke (1998a) introduce a third approach to analyzing MNE-government interactions that utilizes the resource-based view of the firm. In this section we briefly review both the welfare economics and behavioral approaches to analyzing MNEs and public policy. We then turn our attention in the next section to a more detailed analysis of Rugman Verbeke's framework for studying the MNE-government linkages.

Building on the foundation of neoclassical welfare economics, efficiency approaches to analyzing MNE-government linkages focus, as the name suggests, on the efficiency aspects of MNE activity. This focus on efficiency does not necessarily line up with the equity-distributional rationale inherent in many of the government policies toward MNEs. As Rugman and Verbeke (1998a) note, the distinction between efficiency and equity is useful from an economist's viewpoint and has been used by such writers as Safarian (1966, 1993), Rugman (1980), Casson (1987), and Dunning (1993a). As Caves (1996) highlights, however, efficiency approaches assume away distributional issues. In fact, Caves lays out all the assumptions required for efficiency approaches based on neoclassical welfare economics to be valid. For example, each state is assumed to maximize real national income; each enterprise has a single home country; and government policies can discriminate between foreign and home-based MNEs.

The efficiency approach is fully consistent with the use of internalization theory as the key theoretical explanation for the existence of MNEs. This TCE-approach to MNEs was pioneered by Buckley and Casson (1976), Rugman (1981), and Hennart (1982). Internalization theory argues that natural market imperfections may arise because agents are boundedly rational, and thus these agents do not always know all relevant prices (especially of intermediate outputs such as knowledge), nor are they always capable of measuring all relevant outputs. In addition, they cannot always trust others to carry through on open-ended promises (Williamson, 1975, 1985). When these market imperfections are high, the expansion of firms across national boundaries through FDI may be comparatively more efficient than the use of other entry modes such as licensing (Hennart, 2001).

Similarly, from an efficiency perspective, Caves (1996) suggests that the MNE, as a global profit maximizer, will tend to react to host-government policies so as to minimize their negative impact on expected profits. Thus, policies that maximize, respectively, the income of individual MNEs, MNE home countries, host countries, and the world as a whole are not necessarily identical, and conflict can be expected.

Due to discrepancies between observed policies and the prescriptions provided by the efficiency approach, Caves (1996) also presents "behavioral" approaches to the analysis of MNE-government linkages. These "behavioral" approaches recognize that government decisions may result from self-interested agents interacting in a political setting. These approaches can explain governments' focus on distributional issues instead of income maximization. Caves offers two versions of the behavioral approach, with both including discriminatory measures imposed on foreign MNEs. In the first version, utility-maximizing electoral behavior can lead to redistribution at the expense of the MNE. This approach emphasizes that investors from abroad lack voting rights, and elected governments may propose packages of measures to appeal to a majority of domestic voters in an effort to remain in power (Caves, 1996). In principle, such policies could also benefit the MNE. For example, Blomstrom and Kokko (2003) note that governments may make excessive long-term financial commitments, such as offering incentives to attract foreign MNEs, in order to increase employment and obtain short-term political gains. Here,

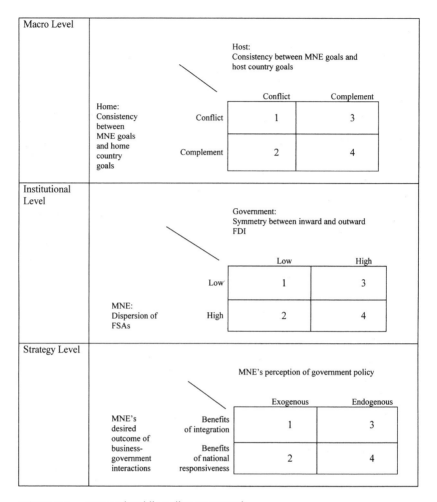

FIGURE 7.1. MNE and Public Policy Framework

some of the perceived benefits (jobs created) are easily observable in the short run, while some of the costs (tax breaks and fiscal incentives) may be distributed over long periods of time. In Caves' (1996) second version of the behavioral approach, government policies are assumed to be the work of a coalition of government officials who resent foreign MNEs because of their ability to avoid various types of regulations. Although these behavioral approaches do offer some insight into the dynamics of MNE-government interactions, they neglect factors such as government support for domestic MNEs engaged in outward FDI. In the next section we will review Rugman and Verbeke's (1998a; 2001a) analytical framework, which better captures the complexities of MNE–public policy dynamics.

RUGMAN VERBEKE'S FRAMEWORK FOR ANALYZING
MNE-GOVERNMENT INTERACTIONS

Rugman and Verbeke (1998a, 2001a) have developed an analytical frame-work to incorporate the work synthesized by Caves (1996) and other more recent literature on MNE-government interactions. The framework consists of three sequential components that offer a macro-level, institutional-level, and strategy-level analysis of the MNE-government relationship. Each of the three components can be represented visually in a two-by-two matrix that reflects key variables critical to MNE-government interactions. We provide a graphical summary of these components and related matrices in Figure 7.1. In this section, we describe each of the components of Rugman and Verbeke's framework and position the MNE-government literature within the frame-work. With this foundation in place, the following section then explores the recent shifts in MNE-government interactions identified through application of this framework.

Macro-Level Component (Goal Consistency)

The macro-level component of the framework reflects the degree of con-sistency between MNE goals and government goals of both the home and host country. As shown in Figure 7.1, at the macro level, MNE and government goals can either conflict or complement each other, thus leading to four pos-sible combinations of MNE and home/host government goal consistency. In Quadrant 1 of this framework, the interactions between MNEs and both home and host governments are supposedly driven by goal conflict. As described in our previous review of efficiency and "behavioral" approaches, the goal conflict found in Quadrant 1 stems largely from the divergence between micro-efficiency-driven behavior of MNEs and the macro-efficiency, or distribu-tional, objectives of governments (Rugman and Verbeke, 1998a). Thus, in this quadrant we would have the Hymer (1976) quasi-Marxist view of conflicts between (home and host) governments and MNEs. We can also place Vernon's (1971) *Sovereignty at Bay* position in this quadrant. Although Vernon (1991) himself states he did not argue that the MNE would dominate the host nation, he did suggest there would be an antagonistic relationship between them. Kojima (1973, 1975, 1978, 1985) also reveals an MNE-host and home gov-ernment conflict in his hypothesis on the effects of trade and FDI as substitutes in the U.S. experience but complements in the Japanese case.

Quadrant 2 of the framework displays a consistency between MNE and home-country goals, but conflict with host-country goals. In this quadrant we place Porter's (1990) view of MNEs relying on a strong home base. This view suggests there can be a synergistic relationship between a home government and its MNEs; appropriate government policies from the home nation will strengthen the domestic firms' home base and increase the likelihood of international success. At the same time, foreign-owned firms are in conflict with the host nation, as the ability to attract inward FDI is not seen as a competitive advantage for host nations but rather as a weakness. This quadrant is also representative of the literature which suggests, perhaps inadvertently, that home governments can subsidize their MNEs to develop first-mover advantages in a zero-sum game with other nations (Krugman, 1986; Brander and Spencer, 1985). We note that in reality such policies have predominantly failed, as few governments have the necessary capabilities to guide a domestic firm toward becoming an internationally competitive MNE (Rugman and Verbeke, 1990). The Aliber (1970) theory of FDI, which argues that a strong currency allows home-based MNEs to capitalize expected earnings at a higher rate than host-country firms, would also fit in this quadrant. Quadrant 2 also encompasses the more conventional literature on political risk management (Kobrin, 1982; Brewer, 1983, 1985; Ghadar, 1982; Nigh, 1985). This literature focuses on the host government's ability to regulate foreign MNEs. From this perspective, MNEs are often seen as instruments of economic colonization, bringing with them unwanted approaches from their home nation. Related to this literature is the obsolescing bargaining hypothesis (Encarnation and Wells, 1985; Kobrin, 1984; Grosse, 1996). This model assumes the MNE and host nation have conflicting goals and that negotiations are seen to initially favor the foreign firm (due to risks and uncertainty) and then are renegotiated in favor of the host country as the risks and uncertainty for the host country dissipate, namely when the MNE has engaged in sunk costs. Bergara, Henisz and Spiller (1998) adapt this model to their study of potential expropriation of investments associated with large sunk costs in the utility industry. Eden, Lenway and Schuler (2004), however, argue that the classic obsolescence model is now viewed by many scholars as an inappropriate description of present-day reality. The authors suggest that entry bargaining is minimal as few governments restrict inward FDI, and that case studies testing the obsolescing model reveal that MNEs are able to retain relative bargaining power and prevent opportunistic behavior by host governments. In a reconceptualization of the obsolescing bargaining model, Eden et al. (2004) develop the political bargaining model, which appears to fit better in Quadrant4 of the Rugman and Verbeke framework, given the assumption of co-operative goals.

Quadrant 3 depicts a conflict between MNEs and their home governments, but complementary relations with the host nation. One illustration of this quadrant is the case of MNEs allegedly engaging in escape investments, fleeing tight home market regulations, and moving operations to lax host nation regimes, as is often observed in maritime shipping, where flags of convenience are used. MNE relocation decisions driven by the attractiveness of cheap labor, offshore assembly platforms, and tax havens would also reflect a positioning in this quadrant. In more general terms, these types of relocation arguments, even if misguided conceptually, as they miss the efficiency-driven rationale for most

MNE behavior, are consistent with the "race to the bottom" hypothesis, where MNEs seek out the nations with the most lax environmental and labor policies (see Scherer and Smid, 2000, for a brief overview). Meyer (2004) suggests that the "race to the bottom" is of concern only in specific industries, such as textiles, footwear, and electronics assembly. In contrast to the race-to-the-bottom hypothesis, other authors argue that MNE activity usually has positive effects. For example, they can provide pollution reduction halo effects by introducing environment-friendly technology, which is subsequently diffused locally (Buysse and Verbeke, 2003; Rugman and Verbeke, 2001b; Eskeland and Harrison, 2002). Further, Dowell, Hart and Yeung (2000) find that MNEs adopting a single, stringent global environmental standard experience higher market values than firms satisfied with less stringent host-country standards.

Quadrant 4 indicates a complementary relationship between MNEs and both home and host states. As noted above, this quadrant is consistent with early views of internalization theory (Buckley and Casson, 1976; Rugman, 1980, 1981; Dunning, 1981; Hennart, 1982), whereby the internalization of technological and managerial know-how within the internal market of the MNE overcomes the Coase (1937) problem of knowledge as a public good and the appropriability issues associated with this (Rugman and Verbeke, 1998a, p. 125). The process of internalization is efficiency-based as from a comparative institutional perspective, the MNE helps both home and host countries develop. Thus, we place much of the literature surrounding trade liberalization in this quadrant, as such liberalization usually reflects the complementarity between the firm-level and government goals of efficiency and economic gain (Dunning, 1993b). These cooperative goals emerge largely from national host governments' understanding the value of access to MNEs' firm-specific advantages (FSAs), and the impossibility of simply unbundling FSAs from MNE control or purchasing these FSAs as intermediate goods. We will elaborate on this quadrant in the fourth section of this chapter, where the apparent shift toward Quadrant 4 within the macro-level component of Rugman and Verbeke's framework is explored.

Institutional Component

Beyond the macro-level analysis, Rugman and Verbeke (1998a) also provide an institutional-level component to their framework. This component recognizes that the institutional characteristics of specific MNEs and specific countries largely determine MNE-government interactions. At the institutional level, the key MNE issue is the dispersion of its firm-specific advantages (FSAs). (As Rugman and Verbeke [1998a] point out, in terms of the resource-based view, an MNE's FSAs reflect its core competencies and dynamic capabilities). The MNE's FSAs can be either highly or lowly dispersed. For example, an ethnocentric MNE will concentrate its FSAs in the home country and simply replicate home-country production and managerial approaches in host nations, thus being characterized by low FSA dispersion. On the other hand, highly dispersed FSAs are characteristic of polycentric and geocentric MNEs. These types of firms have their FSAs dispersed over the various host-nation subsidiaries, or concentrate some FSAs in the home base, while other FSAs are developed autonomously in various host-country subsidiaries.

At the government level, the key institutional factor determining MNE-government relations is expressed by the symmetry between inward and outward FDI, or the lack thereof. Symmetry need not imply that inward and outward FDI stocks and flows are similar in size; it merely implies that a single country is both the origin and recipient of substantial FDI volumes. Rugman and Verbeke (1998a) consider this factor an "institutional element because a high symmetry represents an ex-post reflection of the willingness of governments to allow inward and outward FDI" (p. 121). Thus, policies toward MNEs will depend on whether the nation is primarily an exporter of FDI, a recipient of FDI, or a dual player with substantial outward and inward FDI. As Dunning (1993b) suggests, in terms of regulating MNEs, the incentive structure facing governments varies in each of the above cases.

As shown in Figure 7.1, at the institutional level, the degrees of FSA dispersion and FDI symmetry (low or high in each case) lead to four different types of expected MNE-government interactions. Quadrant 1 is characterized by low symmetry between inward and outward FDI and low dispersion of MNE FSAs. The literature synthesized in Caves (1996) can be largely positioned within this quadrant. Here, MNEs have centralized organizational structures (FSAs concentrated in the home base), and governments adopt either the pure home or pure host perspective. Vernon's (1966, 1971) as well as Porter's (1990) work would also fit in this quadrant, as their work assumes that non–location bound FSAs (that is, internationally transferable competencies, leading to economies of scale and scope as well as benefits of exploiting national differences) are created exclusively in the MNE's home country. MNE strategies in Quadrant 1 consist of replicating home-country practices abroad, and there is no recognition of the need to develop location-bound FSAs (conferring benefits of national responsiveness) in host countries; a point we shall discuss further in the next section.

In Quadrant 2, characterized by low symmetry in FDI but high FSA dispersion, firm-driven national responsiveness becomes more important, and therefore the likelihood of governments responding by providing national treatment at the macro level also increases. The work of Doz (1986) and the later work of Bartlett and Ghoshal (1989) fit well in this quadrant. The latter authors do not limit themselves to demonstrating that national responsiveness may be important, but they suggest that once MNEs feel sufficiently confident about the competence-building potential of a specific subsidiary, then non–location bound FSAs may begin to develop there. This view offers the host nation a characteristic conventionally reserved for the home nation, that is, to become a source country for new innovations.

In Quadrant 3, the high FDI symmetry provides governments with incentives at the macro level for nondiscriminatory regulation of foreign MNEs. Although MNEs in this quadrant have low FSA dispersion, the nondiscriminatory treatment induces them to become more nationally responsive at the micro level. The occurrence of symmetry in inward and outward FDI, as found in Quadrants 3 and 4, constitutes an important departure from the conventional literature covered by Caves (1996). A number of international institutions, such as GATT, have focused in the past on tariff cuts and negotiating trade barrier removal. This focus was on "shallow integration" (Ostry, 1997; Brewer and Young, 1998). Such shallow integration assumed that little could be achieved on trade in services or in the FDI area because governments were viewed as either sole exporters or sole recipients of FDI. In relation to symmetrical FDI, the new agenda of the WTO and the OECD's Multinational Agreement on Investment (MAI) is to negotiate "deep integration." The objective of the MAI is to make domestic markets internationally contestable through the principle of national treatment, where host governments treat all MNEs in the same manner as domestic firms.

In Quadrant 4, the symmetry between inward and outward FDI, and the dispersed FSAs at the firm level "lead to complexities in terms of optimal business-government interactions that cannot be solved at the national level" (Rugman and Verbeke, 1998a, p. 121). Specifically, it can be argued that both MNEs and governments will lean toward supranational approaches to government policy in order to institutionalize norms of reciprocity at the government level and common standards regarding appropriate MNE behavior. With FSAs found commonly in host country subsidiaries, and host governments acting as both sources and recipients of FDI, this quadrant diverges the most sharply from Caves' (1996) approach, and the neoclassical economics approach to MNE-government linkages in general. In spite of this divergence with Caves' (1996) approach, we view the Quadrant 4 positioning as an increasingly representative reflection of the incentives facing MNEs and governments.

MNE Strategy Component

The final component of our (1998a) framework analyzes the various strategies MNEs can adopt vis-à-vis government policy. Two parameters are important here. First is the perceived exogeneity of government policy. The MNE may perceive government policy as being exogenous, whereby the firm will work within the rules set by the government, or as endogenous, whereby the firm will attempt to influence actively the content or process of government policy. Along the desired outcomes axis, firms may either pursue benefits of integration or benefits of national responsiveness. These benefits relate to the vital, resource-based distinction between location-bound FSAs (leading to benefits of national responsiveness), and non–location bound FSAs (leading to the integration benefits of scale, scope, and exploiting national differences) (Rugman and Verbeke, 1991).

As shown in Figure 7.1, the variables described above lead to four possible MNE strategies vis-à-vis public policy. In the first quadrant, MNEs view public policy as exogenous, and their objective is to achieve the benefits of integration (for example, conventional efficiency benefits such as scale economies and economies of exploiting national differences). In this quadrant, government policy is used as a lever for international competitiveness. Porter's (1990) work fits well within this quadrant as he uses a home base/cluster concept, stimulating domestic firms to adopt an integration strategy (largely scale and innovation-driven) and views government policy as exogenous. Domestic government policies should thus attempt to improve the "diamond conditions" for domestic firms only. Within Porter's framework, there is no room for subsidiary managers or foreign governments to contribute to the MNE's FSAs, except in the implementation stage of integration-based strategies. This view has also been applied to trade and environment issues, whereby government policies aim to create a first-mover advantage internationally for domestic firms (Porter and van der Linde, 1995).

In Quadrant 2, government policy is still viewed as exogenous, but MNEs do voice their preferences and develop strategies building upon public policy to capture the benefits of national responsiveness in the various countries where the firm operates. Arguments purporting that public policy should provide a level playing field fit in this quadrant. This perspective is reflected in the academic work on the negotiation of subsidies at the GATT and the WTO, and the OECD's work on the MAI. The research of Guisinger et al. (1985), Hufbauer and Erb (1984), and Gladwin and Walter (1980) is also relevant to this quadrant.

In Quadrant 3, government policy is endogenous, but the MNE aims to achieve the benefits of integration-based, or non–location bound FSAs. In this quadrant, MNEs develop companywide bargaining strategies for dealing with subnational, national, and supranational public agencies. "The danger associated with active MNE strategies in this area is that they often represent a Trojan horse approach. Firms themselves use strategic trade policy arguments to obtain government favors. First-mover advantages at the international level, strategic entry deterrence, technological spillovers, learning curve effects, credible retaliation to foreign support programs, etc. may be among effects lobbied for by the firms" (Rugman and Verbeke, 1998a, p. 130). Such lobbying often disguises shelter-seeking strategies, whereby the firms requesting government favors, allegedly to improve their competitive position internationally, are in fact unable to compete without artificial government support. Boddewyn (1988) and Boddewyn and Brewer (1994) have defined these behaviors as political strategy (or at least a subclass thereof), whereas Rugman and Verbeke (1990) describe them as the "fourth generic" strategy.

In Quadrant 4, MNEs have a decentralized or matrix-type organizational structure, and they compete based on national responsiveness (Doz, 1986;

Prahalad and Doz, 1987; Bartlett and Ghoshal, 1989). The focus on national responsiveness in this quadrant extends to one of nation-bound bargaining, potentially resulting in the MNE developing location-bound FSAs in government relations for each country in which it operates. Strategies positioned in this quadrant have been observed, inter alia, in the realm of environmental regulations (Rugman and Verbeke, 1998b). In this work, government policies are viewed as a parameter that can be actively influenced (endogenized) through negotiations and lobbying. In the following section we describe a shift toward Quadrant 4 and further review literature representative of this quadrant that suggests strategies of proactive national responsiveness.

SHIFT IN MNE-GOVERNMENT RELATIONS

International business has undergone immense changes over the last thirty years. Improvements in transportation, technology, and communication have all played a role in the internationalization of the world economy (Dunning, 1998). In this context, a critical observation is the recent shift in MNE-government relations from Quadrant 1 to Quadrant 4 in all three components of Rugman and Verbeke's (1998a, 2001a) framework. Thus, at the macro level we note a shift from conflicting MNE-home and host-government goals to one of complementary goals. At the institutional level we note a trend from both low dispersion of MNE FSAs and low FDI symmetry at the level of nation-states to one of high FSA dispersion and high FDI symmetry. Finally, at the MNE strategy level, we also see a corresponding shift from an MNE perception of government policy as being exogenous (especially in host countries) and a focus on benefits of integration, toward the view that governments can be influenced and that the focus of business-government relations should be on benefits of national responsiveness. Below, we explore some of the underlying drivers of these recent trends.

Trend toward Complementary Goals

Throughout the 1970s and 1980s, MNEs and governments were characterized in the relevant academic literature as having conflicting goals. This view is apparent in much of the neoclassical welfare economics literature that we placed in Quadrant 1 of the macro-level component of this chapter's framework. The firm-government conflict paradigm extends back in history to such writers as Hobbes (1651); he argued that the state can potentially be weakened by corporations, which were viewed as parasites. Even in the works of Adam Smith we note that the two roles of "trader" and "sovereign" were considered inherently incompatible. As discussed earlier, the underlying assumption for the conflict between MNEs and governments largely stems from the micro-level, efficiency-seeking behavior of the MNE being contrasted with government's focus on national welfare and income distribution. Despite the history and rationale for this conflict-based paradigm, we note that more recently, authors have started characterizing MNE-government relations as potentially cooperative, and shifting away from a focus on conflict (Dunning, 1993b; Stopford, 1994; Luo, 2001). This trend from conflicting to complementary goals is reflected in the framework by a shift at the macro level of analysis from Quadrant 1 to Quadrant 4.

From the government's perspective, the shift to complementary goals is shown by the liberalization of government trade policies. Starting in the early 1980s, both developed and developing nations began substantial efforts to liberalize their economies, cutting trade barriers and opening their doors to FDI (UNCTAD, 1999). Dunning (1993b, 1997) traces the changing nature of the interactions between MNEs and governments over the last thirty years. He observes that governments have switched their attention from a quasi-sole focus on the distribution (that is, appropriation) of (alleged) rents and structural issues of technology transfer toward policies aimed at attracting knowledge-based, mobile FDI. Dunning (1998) further identifies the reduction in trade barriers as one of the key features in the changing world economic scene affecting international business over the last twenty years. The fact that host governments have shifted toward a more favorable view of FDI is supported by recent statistics. For example, nearly 95 percent of the almost twelve hundred changes in FDI legislation during 1991–2000 were favorable to foreign investors (UNCTAD, 2001). The move toward more favorable FDI regulations can also be observed in Table 7.1. Note the increasing trend in number of countries, regulatory changes, and favorable regulatory changes over the 1991–2002 period.

Although the shift toward more favorable FDI regulations is unambiguous, some debate surrounding the benefits of FDI still exists. Goldberg (2004) recently concluded from a review of the relevant research that FDI is typically

TABLE 7.1. Changes in FDI Regulations (UNCTAD, 2003)

	1991	1992	1993	1994	1995	1996	1997	1998	1999	2000	2001	2002
# of countries that introduced changes in investment regimes	35	43	57	49	64	65	76	60	63	69	71	70
Number of regulatory changes	82	79	102	110	112	114	151	145	140	150	208	248
More favorable to FDI	80	79	101	108	106	98	135	136	131	147	194	236
Less favorable to FDI	2		1	2	6	16	16	9	9	3	14	12

associated with improved allocative efficiency, higher technical efficiency, more efficient use of existing resources, higher rates of technology transfer and diffusion, and higher wages. However, she did acknowledge the ongoing debate on whether the above benefits from FDI accruing to host countries justify large incentives. A related debate revolves around the effectiveness and ability of government policy to attract FDI (Oman, 2000).

MNEs have also shifted their goals in a way that has led to more complementarity with government goals. This is reflected in the OECD's (1986) nonbinding code of good behavior for MNEs. This code suggests that MNEs should: take into account host countries' general economic objectives; make available any information needed by the host government; cooperate with local community and business interests; avoid predatory practices toward local competitors; hire national citizens; and heed environmental goals and regulations (Caves, 1996). Real-world expressions of these actions abound. For example, Hart and Christensen (2002) suggest that an increasing number of MNEs build on disruptive innovations to serve the "bottom of the pyramid," that is, the 4 billion poor people across the globe.

In addition to the above intentional attempts to broaden goals, perhaps the most significant factor in the shift toward increased MNE-government goal complementarity over the past decade has been the rise in MNE FSA dispersion and the rapid growth of strategic asset-seeking FDI (Dunning, 1998). In the following section, we elaborate on the trend toward dispersed FSAs and the corresponding increase in "deep integration."

Trend toward Dispersed FSAs and FDI Symmetry

Corresponding to the macro-level shift from Quadrant 1 to 4 described above (and partly responsible for that shift), we note a recent trend from Quadrant 1 to 4 at the institutional level. Thus, there has been a shift from low dispersion of MNE FSAs, as reflected in the home base/centralized decision-making model of the 1970s and 1980s, to more dispersed FSAs, as characterized by matrix and decentralized organizational structures. The dispersion of FSAs is also supported by an UNCTAD (1998) report on the top one hundred MNEs, which found a continuous trend toward greater internationalization in terms of foreign assets, sales, and employment.

At the government level there has been a shift away from low FDI symmetry, as seen in the 1970s and 1980s, with most countries acting as either sole exporters or sole recipients of FDI, to more symmetrical FDI positions. For example, in developing countries the inward FDI stock approached one-third of GDP in 2001, up from a mere 13 percent in 1980. Outward FDI stocks held by developing countries have grown even more dramatically (at least in relative terms, from 3 percent of their GDP in 1980 to 13 percent in 2002) (UNCTAD, 2003).

Rugman and Verbeke (1998a) suggest that the institutional shift to dispersed FSAs and more symmetrical FDI positions in Quadrant 4 will lead to a common preference, by both MNEs and governments, for supranational regulatory frameworks. These supranational frameworks range from WTO processes to regional trade agreements such as NAFTA and the EU.

Trend toward Strategies of National Responsiveness and "Endogenous" Government Policy

It is perhaps the most difficult to identify a trend or shift between quadrants at the strategy level. Part of this difficulty arises from MNEs moving toward a "transnational approach" (in the sense of Bartlett and Ghoshal, 1989) to government policy. Rugman and Verbeke (1998a) suggest that the transnational approach may encompass all four, strategy choices, with a set of contingency variables determining which strategy option will be selected in specific circumstances. A transnational strategy seeks to achieve high levels of both national responsiveness and global integration simultaneously by overcoming the trade-off between the conflicting demands arising from the two pressures on strategy. However, Dunning's (1998) findings surrounding the higher-order activities of subsidiaries, the deepening of the value chain, and the rise of intangible assets that are difficult to move across national boundaries all point toward the increasing importance of national responsiveness. The trend toward benefits of national responsiveness is further demonstrated by research on host-country subsidiaries that perform specific value-creating activities, which are embedded in the knowledge development systems of these host countries (Cantwell, 1989, 1992, 1995; Dunning 1994, 1995; Florida, 1997; Shan and Song, 1997; Kuemmerle, 1999; Rugman and D'Cruz, 2000; Rugman and Verbeke, 2001b). The paradox is that MNEs seek benefits of integration through supranational intervention, but simultaneously see national government policy as being critical to successful strategy implementation. The move toward viewing government as an endogenous strategy variable is illustrated by Ramamurti (2001) and London and Hart (2003), who highlight the importance of negotiations between MNEs and local governments.

The past decade has also seen the proliferation of global policy networks, and MNEs participating in such networks. These networks are loose alliances of government agencies, international organizations, corporations, NGOs, and religious groups joining forces to achieve what no single organization could accomplish on its own (Reinicke, 2000). In 1999 the World Bank identified fifty different networks, noting that most have emerged over the past decade. In some respects, the increasing power of NGOs forces the MNE to participate as a stakeholder in government policy formation (Ostry, 1997).

To summarize, and as shown in Figure 7.2, we note a general move from Quadrant 1 to Quadrant 4 in all three components of Rugman and Verbeke's (1998a) framework on MNE-government linkages. The three components appear strongly interrelated. The shift toward complementary goals of MNEs and governments (macro level) facilitates international FDI flows and

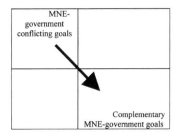

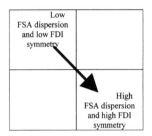

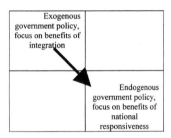

FIGURE 7.2. Trend in MNE–Public Policy Relationship

increases the symmetry in country-level FDI positions (institutional level). Higher symmetry pushes governments to adopt policies of national treatment, which in turn facilitate the processes of knowledge transfer and greater FSA dispersion. Such dispersion, coupled with the need to embed subsidiaries deeper into local economic systems in order to fully access the location advantages present, leads naturally to firm-level strategies with a greater focus on national responsiveness (strategy level). This in turn provides an incentive to influence government policy more proactively, that is, to consider government policy an endogenous variable.

The interrelated moves in Quadrant 4 can also be given a "bottom-up" interpretation. For example, an MNE's shift to national responsiveness (strategy level) will facilitate the embeddedness of host-country subsidiaries and thus the development of new FSAs in those countries. This implies higher FSA dispersion (institutional level), while the related value-added contributions made to

host countries will facilitate goal complementarity with those of host governments (macro level).

TRANSACTION COST ECONOMICS (TCE) ANALYSIS

In TCE-based analysis, the firm is described as a managerial hierarchy and is
contrasted with other forms of organization, most notably markets, where
transactions take place without internal, managerial oversight (Williamson,
1975, 1985). Firms exist when they can reduce the costs of negotiating
and enforcing terms and conditions of exchange relative to market transacting
(Coase, 1937). In essence, TCE describes an institutional setting in which
uncertainty prevails, individuals are boundedly rational, the legal enforcement
of agreements is costly, and attempts to escape from fulfilling open-ended
promises cannot be ruled out (Yarbrough and Yarbrough, 1990).

TCE-based analysis suggests governance mechanisms will be selected that
economize on bounded rationality (scarcity of the mind) and bounded reliability (scarcity of making good on open-ended promises). This type of analysis can be applied to both a firm's internal contracts—with its managers,
employees, and shareholders—and its external contracts with other parties
that sell to, buy from, and, in the context of this chapter, develop public
policy relevant to the firm. Thus, to the extent that government actors pursue economizing goals, TCE is suitable for analysis of the shifts in MNE-
government relations. In this case, TCE addresses decisions about the optimal
organization of discrete economic activities that involve multiple economic
actors, who are dispersed across borders (Rugman and Verbeke, 2003). Further, internalization theory, the mainstream conceptual framework in international business theory, is the MNE version of conventional TCE (Rugman
and Verbeke, 2003).

From a TCE perspective, the shifts in MNE-government interactions described in this chapter occur largely because they economize on bounded
rationality and bounded reliability, and therefore lead to greater efficiency. In
TCE-based analysis, efficiency is defined as an outcome for which no feasible
superior alternate can be described and implemented with net gains (Williamson, 1996). Thus, the shifts from Quadrant 1 to 4 in the three components
of the framework addressing MNE-government linkages can be interpreted as
the result of both governments and MNEs economizing on bounded rationality
and bounded reliability.

From a TCE perspective, the macro-level MNE-government goal conflict
found in Quadrant 1 is fraught with bounded reliability problems, including
opportunism. In this quadrant, MNEs incur ill will and restrictions from
governments. Although FDI occurs as a micro-level response to natural market
imperfections, governments react by imposing "unnatural" market imperfections (Rugman, 1981). This is done in an effort to "unbundle" the efficiency
properties of FDI (desired by nation-states) and MNE strategic control (viewed

as undesirable and conflicting with macro-level efficiency goals as well as distributive equity goals) (Caves, 1996). Thus, from the government's perspective, FDI as an entry mode leads to a perception of additional transaction costs, resulting from the MNE's control over its FSAs and the associated ability to renege ex post on open-ended promises, or at least public policy expectations of specific FDI effects.

As demonstrated by Hennart (1989), this perception of higher transaction costs incurred by governments is wrong, at least from a comparative institutional perspective, as FDI is chosen as an entry mode precisely as a result of inefficiencies associated with alternative entry modes. Governments simply cannot expect access to MNE FSAs without simultaneously accepting MNE control over these FSAs. This last point has been accepted by most governments since the mid-1980s, when they started to realize the negative effects of such restrictive policies on inward FDI. In addition, MNEs incur increased transaction costs stemming from uncertainty surrounding future government actions, and the potential opportunistic behavior of governments reneging on *ex-ante* commitments, especially after the MNE has engaged in substantial sunk costs (the obsolescent bargain challenge).

The trend toward Quadrant 4 at all three levels implies the creation of relational governance, whereby increased familiarity among participants economizes on bounded rationality and bounded reliability costs. Behavioral uncertainty can arise from an actor's lack of information about the other actor's actions; yet in the contractual world, traders are not anonymous, and their names and identities serve to lower the costs of exchange (Yarbrough and Yarbrough, 1990). The depth of relationship and familiarity between parties increases as governments shift toward more MNE-friendly policies (when understanding the comparative efficiency properties of FDI) and MNEs become more embedded over time in host countries (with dispersed FSAs, nationally responsive strategies and perceptions of government policies as endogenous). This familiarity reduces the *ex-ante* uncertainty as well as the information asymmetries inherent in predicting what actions might be undertaken by the other actor (Granovetter, 1985, p. 498).

The shift from Quadrant 1 to 4 not only increases MNE efficiency through reduced transaction costs from enhanced familiarity among actors, but such a shift also offers further reductions in transaction costs. For example, MNEs adopting socially progressive and environment-friendly goals in developing countries that are complementary to both host and home government goals help reduce the potential hazards from host governments that have lax social or environmental policies (Meyer, 2004). Such hazards in, for example, exploiting global brands, are increasing as globalization intensifies competition, facilitates reactions by consumers to unethical production, and increases the transparency of working and living conditions in host countries. Thus, MNEs' adoption of goal complementary to those of governments serves economizing purposes, as it reduces the transaction costs associated with the above hazards.

The shift toward Quadrant 4 also has economizing effects benefiting governments. Transaction costs will be higher for governments that have a track record of poor treatment of MNEs, as such governments will have a reputation for untrustworthiness (Argyres and Liebeskind, 1999). MNEs then incur related transaction costs, as in those cases, not even the accumulation of experience in a country is enough to diminish the negative influence of political hazards on FDI entry rates (Henisz and Delios, 2001). (Political hazards are defined by Henisz [2000] as the feasibility of policy change by the host-country government, which either directly [seizure of assets] or indirectly [adverse changes in taxes, regulations] diminishes multinational enterprise's expected return on assets. Henisz further operationalized political hazards as the feasibility of policy change [the extent to which a change in preferences of one actor may lead to a change in government policy].) Where policy credibility is low, firms minimize commitments to a market or avoid investment. Bergara, Henisz and Spiller (1998) analyze firms' investment decisions in utility infrastructure across a wide sample of nations. The higher the political instability of a country, the higher the potential for governments not to respect open-ended promises, and hence the more inefficient the performance of the sector considered. High sunk-cost investments provide governments with incentives to behave opportunistically. To protect their assets, MNEs will therefore invest in less specific assets, thus less efficient but more flexible technologies may be chosen, limiting the social value of the enterprise. Such examples illustrate that uncertainty associated with government policies toward MNEs increases transaction costs for MNEs and reduces the asset specificity of MNE investments, thereby resulting in an overall reduction in efficiency. These costs can be reduced, however, by the shift to Quadrant 4, as MNEs and governments develop relationships that reduce uncertainty surrounding government policy and correspondingly increase the efficiency (both at the micro and macro levels) of MNE investments.

The point to be drawn from the above discussion is that governments that pose political hazards, either from uncertainty around policies or a reputation of not making good on open-ended promises, reduce the overall efficiency of contracting with MNEs. From the MNE's perspective, the state, with monopoly power, legal coercion, and an implicit presence in the background of every economic transaction, poses a threat or hazard. "Firms that perceive these contracting hazards will take hazard-mitigating actions. These actions should be designed to shift the decision calculus of the potential expropriating government either by raising their political and or economic cost to, or lowering their benefits from, the expropriation of assets (Henisz, 2000, p. 338). Williamson (1996) highlights this point with the illustration that Mikhail Gorbachev advised U.S. firms to invest immediately in the Soviet Union rather than wait, because the investing companies would have "good prospects," whereas those who postponed their investments would "remain observers for years to come." What Gorbachev inadvertently revealed through the above policy intention was that investing in the Soviet Union was hazardous, because politicians were not constrained by an independent judiciary to respect property rights. As a result, all investors, including those contemplating investing in the Soviet Union in the short run, faced the incentive to engage in easily redeployable investments.

The above TCE analysis of the shift toward Quadrant 4 has focused on the general trend toward harmonization of MNE-government relations, and the resulting economizing on bounded rationality and bounded reliability. TCE also offers insights into the specific changes associated with the institutional shift to Quadrant 4. For example, the trend toward increased dispersion of MNEs' FSAs and governments facing more symmetry in their nation's FDI position reduces transaction costs resulting from bounded reliability by aligning incentives. On the MNE side, highly asset-specific FDI is not footloose, but is embedded in specific locations: short-term relocation and negotiating with alternative partners (governments), to this effect, no longer applies. Thus, the relationship undergoes what Williamson calls a "fundamental transformation." When FDI is not only highly asset-specific but also associated with dispersed FSAs, a strategy of national responsiveness economizes on bounded rationality and bounded reliability in the MNE's interactions with governments. At the same time, a more symmetrical FDI position at the macro level provides an incentive for government agencies to not discriminate against foreign-owned MNEs in order to avoid reciprocal discrimination by other governments.

Another specific example of the shift in MNE-government relations that lends itself to TCE analysis is the preference by both MNEs and governments for supranational regulations. From a TCE perspective, supranational regulation reduces the monopolistic position of governments in the supply of regulation (Eden, Lenway and Schuler, 2004). It also provides mechanisms for ex-post recourse on contract enforcement, both of which reduce the transaction costs associated with a government propensity to renege on open-ended promises.

Finally, we can also apply the TCE lens to the MNE view that government policy can be influenced, that is the equivalent of an endogenous strategy variable. This view encourages the MNE to become involved in public policy formation and thus to engage the government and other stakeholders with an interest in public policy. Such actions decrease the institutional distance between the parties, and the reduction in institutional distance serves to lower transaction costs. Assuming the absence of practices such as coercion and corruption, the local partnerships created by such activities will also increase organizational legitimacy at the macro level (Eden, Lenway and Schuler, 2004), thus providing feedback to the level of goal consistency. To the extent that influencing government policy leads to higher "flexibility," in the sense of more custom-made regulatory solutions, a reduction in transaction costs for MNEs will result.

CONCLUSIONS

In this chapter we have analyzed changes in the relationship between MNEs and governments. This relationship has largely evolved in the past two decades from one based on goal conflict to one characterized by complementary goals. Such goal complementarity has been associated with a shift at the institutional level, in the sense that both MNEs and governments are now faced with a different set of incentives to guide their behavior as compared to a few decades ago. Specifically, an increasing number of MNEs have moved from low to high levels of FSA dispersion. At the same time, many countries have moved from an asymmetrical position, as being either exclusively an origin or a destination point of FDI, toward a more symmetrical position whereby both inward and outward FDI may be important simultaneously (though symmetry obviously does not imply that inward and outward FDI stocks and flows are necessarily of the same magnitude). In addition to this shift, we note a corresponding shift in the MNE's strategy toward government policy. This reflects the move from a view of government policy as exogenous, combined with a focus on benefits of integration, toward the view that government can be influenced and that the MNE must focus on benefits of national responsiveness.

In essence, the trend toward goal congruence, integrative negotiations, and national responsiveness can be seen as the foundation of strongly improved MNE-government relations over recent decades. Nevertheless, numerous examples of MNE-government conflict can still be observed. It has even been suggested that the 1990s, a decade of strongly improved MNE-government relationships, represented merely the eye of the hurricane and that an era of new conflicts may be ahead (Vernon, 1998; Eden and Lenway, 2001). However, most evidence still points to a trend toward Quadrant 4 in the MNE-government relations framework.

Our transaction cost analysis also suggests that this shift represents a comparatively efficient form of organizing MNE-government linkages, given the observed FSA dispersion at the micro level and symmetry between inward and outward FDI at the macro level. Thus, even if new goal conflicts arise, as exemplified by recent fears in developed countries, triggered by MNE outsourcing practices, transaction cost economizing considerations suggest it is still in the best interest of both MNEs and governments to seek common ground and harmonious relationships. These can build upon the reality of increased economic interdependence among nations, both at the macro level and inside the multinational enterprises themselves.

REFERENCES

Aliber, R. (1970). A theory of direct foreign investment. In Kindleberger, C. P., ed. *The international corporation*. Cambridge, MA: MIT Press, 17–34.

Argyres, N., and Liebeskind, J. (1999). Contractual commitments, bargaining power, and governance inseparability: Incorporating history into transaction cost theory. *Academy of Management Review, 24,* 49–64.

Bartlett, C., and Ghoshal, S. (1989). *Managing across borders: The transnational solution.* Boston: Harvard Business School Press.

Behrman, J., and Grosse, R. (1990). *International business and governments: Issues and institutions.* Columbia, SC: University of South Carolina Press.

Bergara, M., Henisz, W., and Spiller, P. (1998). Political institutions and electric utility investment: A cross-nation analysis. *California Management Review, 40,* 18–35.

Bergsten, C., Horst, F., and Moran, T. (1978). *American multinationals and American interests.* Washington, DC: Brookings Institution.

Blomstrom, M., and Kokko, A. (2003). The economics of foreign direct investment incentives. NBER Working Paper, No. w9489.

Boddewyn, J. (1988). Political aspects of MNE theory. *Journal of International Business Studies, 19,* 341–63.

Boddewyn, J., and Brewer, T. (1994). International business political behavior: New theoretical directions. *Academy of Management Review, 19*(1), 119–143.

Brander, J., and Spencer, B. (1985). Export subsidies and international market share rivalry. *Journal of International Economics, 18,* 85–100.

Brewer, T. (1983). The instability of controls on MNE's funds transfers and the instability of governments. *Journal of International Business Studies, 14*(3), 147–57.

Brewer, T., ed. (1985). *Political risks in international business: New directions for research, management, and public policy.* New York: Praeger.

Brewer, T., and Young, S. (1998). *Multinational investment rules and multinational enterprises.* Oxford: Oxford University Press.

Buckley, P., and Casson, M. (1976). *The future of the multinational enterprise.* London: Macmillan.

Buysse, K., and Verbeke, A. (2003). Proactive environmental strategies: A stakeholder management perspective. *Strategic Management Journal, 24*(5), 453–470.

Cantwell, J. (1989). *Technological innovation and multinational corporations.* Oxford: Basil Blackwell.

Cantwell, J. (1992). The theory of technological competence and its application to international production. In McFeteridge, D. G., ed. *Foreign investment, technology and economic growth.* Calgary: University of Calgary Press, 33–67.

Cantwell, J. (1995). The globalization of technology: What remains of the product cycle model? *Cambridge Journal of Economics, 19,* 1–27.

Casson, M. (1987). *The firm and the market.* Cambridge, MA: MIT Press.

Caves, R. E. (1996). *Multinational enterprise and economic analysis.* Cambridge: Cambridge University Press.

Coase, R. H. (1937). The nature of the firm. *Economica, 4,* 386–405.

Dowell G., Hart, S., and Yeung, B. (2000). Do corporate global environmental standards create or destroy market value? *Management Science, 46,* 1059–1074.

Doz, Y. (1986). *Strategic management in multinational companies.* Oxford: Pergamon Press.

Dunning, J. H. (1981). *International production and the multinational enterprise.* London: Allen and Unwin.

Dunning, J. H. (1993a). *Multinational enterprises and the global economy.* New York: Addison-Wesley.

Dunning, J. H. (1993b). Governments and multinational enterprises: From confrontation to cooperation? In Eden, L., and Potter, E., eds. *Multinationals in the global political economy*. London: MacMillan.

Dunning, J. H. (1994). Re-evaluating the benefits of foreign direct investment. *Transnational Corporations, 3*(1), 23–51.

Dunning, J. H. (1995). Reappraising the eclectic paradigm in an age of alliance capitalists. *Journal of International Business Studies, 26*(3), 461–492.

Dunning, J. H., ed. (1997). *Governments, globalization, and international business*. Oxford: Oxford University Press.

Dunning, J. H. (1998). Location and the multinational enterprise: A neglected factor? *Journal of International Business Studies, 29,* 45–66.

Eden L., and Lenway, S. (2001). Introduction to the symposium multinationals: The Janus face of globalization. *Journal of International Business Studies, 32,* 383–400.

Eden, L., Lenway, S., and Schuler, D. (2004). From the obsolescing bargain To the political bargaining model. Bush School working paper, #403.

Encarnation, D. J., and Wells, L. T. (1985, winter). Sovereignty en garde: Negotiating with foreign investors. *International Organization,* 147–171.

Eskeland, G., and Harrison, A. (2002). Moving to greener pastures? Multinational and the pollution haven hypothesis. NBER working paper, 8888.

Florida, R. (1997). The globalization of R&D: Results of a survey of foreign-affiliated R&D laboratories in the USA. *Research Policy, 26*(1), 85–103.

Ghadar, F. (1982). Political risk and the erosion of control: The case of the oil industry. *Columbia Journal of World Business, 13*(2), 47–51.

Gladwin, T. N., and Walter, I. (1980). *Multinationals under fire: Lessons in the management of conflict*. New York: John Wiley.

Globerman, S., and Shapiro, D. M. (1999). The impact of government policies on foreign direct investment: The Canadian experience. *Journal of International Business Studies, 30,* 513–532.

Goldberg, L. (2004). Financial-sector foreign direct investment and host countries: New and old lessons. *Federal Reserve Bank of New York Staff Reports,* 183.

Granovetter, M. (1985). Economic action and social structure: The problem of embeddedness. *American Journal of Sociology, 91,* 481–510.

Grosse, R. (1996). The bargaining relationship between foreign MNEs and host governments in Latin America. *International Trade Journal, 10,* 467–499.

Guisinger, S. E., and associates. (1985). *Investment incentives and performance requirements*. New York: Praeger.

Hart, S., and Christensen, C. (2002). The great leap: Driving innovation from the base of the pyramid. *Sloan Management Review, 44,* 51–56.

Henisz, W. J. (2000). The institutional environment for multinational investment. *Journal of Law Economics & Organization, 16,* 334–364.

Henisz, W. J., and Delios, A. (2001). Uncertainty, imitation, and plant location: Japanese multinational corporations, 1990–1996. *Administrative Science Quarterly, 46,* 443–478.

Hennart, J. (1982). *A theory of multinational enterprise*. Ann Arbor: University of Michigan Press.

Hennart, J. (1989). Can the "new forms of investment" substitute for the "Old forms"? A transaction cost perspective. *Journal of International Business Studies, 20*(2), 211–235.

Hennart, J. (2001). Theories of multinational enterprise. In Rugman, A. M., and Brewer T. L., eds. *The Oxford handbook of international business*. Oxford: Oxford University Press, 127–149.

Hobbes, T. (1651). *Leviathan or the matter, forme, & power of a common-wealth ecclesiasticall and civill*. Ed. Andrew Crooke. New York: Cambridge University Press, 1991.

Hufbauer, G. C., and Erb, J. (1984). *Subsidies in international trade*. Washington, DC: Institute for International Economics.

Hymer, S. H. (1976). *The international operations of national firms: A study of direct foreign investment*. Cambridge, MA: MIT Press (originally PhD dissertation, MIT, 1960).

Kobrin, S. J. (1982). *Managing political risk assessment*. Berkeley and Los Angeles: University of California Press.

Kobrin, S. J. (1984). Expropriation as an attempt to control foreign firms in LDCs: Trends from 1960–79. *International Studies Quarterly, 28*(3), 329–348.

Kojima, K. (1973). Macroeconomic approach to foreign direct investment. *Hitotsubashi Journal of Economics, 14*, 1–21.

Kojima, K. (1975). International trade and foreign investment: Substitutes or complements? *Hitotsubashi Journal of Economics, 16*, 1–12.

Kojima, K. (1978). *Direct foreign investment: A Japanese model of multinational business operations*. London: Croom-Helm.

Kojima, K. (1985). Japanese and American direct investment in Asia: A comparative analysis, *Hitotsubashi Journal of Economics, 26*, 1–35.

Krugman, P. R., ed. (1986). *Strategic trade policy and the new international economics*. Cambridge, MA: MIT Press.

Kuemmerle, W. (1999). The drivers of foreign direct investment into research and development: An empirical investigation. *Journal of International Business Studies, 30*(1), 1–24.

Liu, X., Silver, P., Wang, C., and Wei, Y. (2000). Productivity spillovers from foreign direct investment: Evidence from U.K. industry level panel data. *Journal of International Business Studies, 31*(3), 407–425.

London, T., and Hart, S. (2003). *Reinventing strategies for emerging markets: Beyond the transnational model*. Chapel Hill: University of North Carolina Working Paper.

Luo, Y. (2001). Toward a cooperative view of MNC-host government relations: Building blocks and performance implications. *Journal of International Business Studies, 32*, 401–420.

Meyer, K. E. (2004). Perspective on multinational enterprises in emerging economies. *Journal of International Business Studies, 35*, 259–276.

Nigh, D. (1985). The effect of political events on United States direct foreign investment. *Journal of International Business Studies, 16*, 1–17.

Oman, C. (2000). Policy competition for foreign direct investment: A study of competition among governments to attract FDI. Paris: OECD Development Center.

Organisation for Economic Co-operation and Development. (1986). *The OECD guidelines of multinational enterprises*. Paris: OECD.

Ostry, S. (1997). *The post cold war trading system: Who's on first?* Chicago: University of Chicago Press.

Peck, F. W. (1996). Regional development and the production of space: The role of infrastructure in the attraction of new inward investment. *Environment and Planning, 28,* 327–339.

Porter, M. G. (1990). *The competitive advantage of nations.* New York: Free Press.

Porter, M., and van der Linde. (1995). Green and competitive. *Harvard Business Review, 73*(5), 120–34.

Prahalad, C. K., and Doz, Y. L. (1987). *The multinational mission.* New York: Free Press.

Ramamurti, R. (2001). The obsolescing "bargaining model" MNC-host developing country relations revisited. *Journal of International Business Studies, 32,* 23–39.

Reinicke, W. (2000). The other world wide web: Global public policy networks. *Foreign Policy, 117,* 44–57.

Rugman, A. M. (1980). *Multinationals in Canada: Theory, performance and economic impact.* Boston: Martinus Nijhoff.

Rugman, A. M. (1981). *Inside the multinationals: The economics of internal markets.* New York: Columbia University Press.

Rugman, A. M. (2000). *The end of globalization.* New York: Random House.

Rugman, A. M., and D'Cruz, J. R. (2000). *Multinationals as flagship firms: A new theory of regional business networks.* Oxford: Oxford University Press.

Rugman A. M., and Verbeke, A. (1990). *Global corporate strategy and trade policy.* London: Routledge.

Rugman, A. M., and Verbeke, A. (1998a). Multinational enterprises and public policy. *Journal of International Business Studies, 29,* 115–136.

Rugman, A. M., and Verbeke, A. (1998b). Corporate strategies and environmental regulations: An organizing framework. *Strategic Management Journal, 19,* 363–375.

Rugman, A. M., and Verbeke, A. (2001a). Multinational enterprises and public policy. In Rugman, A. M., and Brewer, T. L., eds. *The Oxford handbook of international business.* Oxford: Oxford University Press, 818–842.

Rugman, A. M., and Verbeke, A. (2001b). Subsidiary specific advantages in multinational enterprises. *Strategic Management Journal, 22,* 237–250.

Rugman, A. M., and Verbeke, A. (2003). Extending the theory of the multinational enterprise: Internalization and strategic management perspectives. *Journal of International Business Studies, 34,* 125–137.

Safarian, E. A. (1966). *Foreign ownership of Canadian industry.* Toronto: McGraw-Hill.

Safarian, E. (1993). *Multinational enterprises and public policy.* Aldershot, UK: Elgar.

Scherer, A. G., and Smid, M. (2000). The downward spiral and the U.S. model business principles: Why MNEs should take responsibility for the improvement of worldwide social and environmental conditions. *Management International Review, 40,* 351–371.

Shan, W., and Song, J. (1997). Foreign direct investment and the sourcing of technological advantage: Evidence from the biotechnology industry. *Journal of International Business Studies, 28*(2), 267–284.

Stopford, J. M. (1994). The growing interdependence between transnational corporations and governments. *Transnational Corporations, 3,* 53–76.

Strange, S. (1988). *States and markets: An introduction to international political economy.* London: Pinter.

UNCTAD. (1998). *World investment report, 1998: Trends and Determinants.* New York: United Nations.

UNCTAD. (1999). *World investment report, 1999: FDI and the challenge of development.* New York: United Nations.

UNCTAD. (2001). *World investment report, 2001: Promoting linkages.* New York: United Nations.

UNCTAD. (2003). *World investment report, 2003: FDI policies for development, national and international perspectives.* New York: United Nations.

United Nations Department of Economic and Social Development. (1992). *Transnational corporations as engines of growth.* New York: United Nations.

Vernon, R. (1966). International investment and international trade in the product cycle. *Quarterly Journal of Economics, 80,* 190–207.

Vernon, R. (1971). *Sovereignty at bay: The multinational spread of U.S. enterprises.* New York: Basic Books.

Vernon R. (1991). Sovereignty at bay: Twenty years after. *Millennium Journal of International Studies, 20*(2), 191–195.

Vernon, R. (1998). *In the hurricane's eye: The troubled prospects of multinational enterprises.* Cambridge: Harvard University Press.

Williamson, O. (1975). *Markets and hierarchies.* New York: Free Press.

Williamson, O. (1985). *The economic institutions of capitalism: Firms, markets, and relational contracting.* New York: Free Press.

Williamson, O. (1996). *The mechanisms of governance.* Oxford: Oxford University Press, 1996.

Yarbrough, B. V., and Yarbrough, R. M. (1990). International institutions and the new economics of organization. *International Organization, 44,* 235–259.

_____ 8 _____

Values-Based Leadership: Building Trust in the New Tyco

FRUZSINA M. HARSANYI

Since the 1970s, I've represented my companies' issues to governments at the state, federal, and international levels. I have learned that values-based leadership contributes greatly to business success and to the success of public affairs initiatives.

What I would like to offer is the perspective of a practitioner. Because I'm a businessperson, I will focus primarily on value-based *business* leadership and try to describe to you from inside the corporation what good leadership feels like. I will comment on what my discipline of public affairs can contribute to values-based leadership—and what values-based leadership can contribute to the effective implementation of a public affairs strategy.

I have been fascinated with the subject of leadership and public affairs from the time I got my first corporate job in 1978. I went to work for the $5 billion Continental Group, whose chairman, Bob Hatfield, was active in the Business Roundtable. It was a time when the chairmen and CEOs of America's corporations found their collective voice and spoke out on public policy issues of importance to their businesses, but also to the community and the country. Hatfield and others were business pioneers in defining the nexus between the economic, political, and social issues that affect the bottom line—and the national interest. They were leaders in redefining the role of the chief executive.

I also learned about leadership as a corporate officer for thirteen years at ABB. For much of that time ABB's leadership philosophy kept business case study writers very busy indeed. I worked with the legendary Percy Barnevik, the genius who forged the merger between Asea and Brown Boveri to create ABB. I saw his fame rise throughout the nineties as he was repeatedly voted Europe's most respected business leader by his peers. I witnessed his fall in 2001, when it was learned that he took a lump-sum retirement payout without the full knowledge of the board and at a time when ABB was posting its first major loss. Was what he did illegal? No. Was it a failure of corporate governance? Yes. Was it a failure of leadership? Absolutely.

I've met some great leaders—from both the public and private sectors. And I've seen some great leaders stumble. I have never forgotten the parting words of my mentor in graduate school, Professor Sam Sharp, who reminded me during my most heady moments as a new PhD that it's never too late to "screw up." I have often reflected on what it takes for leaders to do the right thing. And why some go wrong.

Let me begin with some comments on life inside the corporation, any large corporation, but in my case specifically Tyco. A company is not a monolithic entity. It's made up of businesses of different sizes, making a variety of products and services, managed by people from a variety of backgrounds, connected by an organizational framework that divides them or unites them according to criteria defined by the business leadership. The day-to-day life of almost all the employees is far removed from the corporate suite. Employees care about their local workplace and about their supervisor. It's a truism, but worth repeating: Companies are run by human beings, who work with more or less imperfect information and take risks every day with the decisions they make.

Tyco was a company that grew from $4 billion in revenues to $36 billion in just ten years, primarily through acquisition. Driven by growth for the sake of growth, hundreds of companies were brought under the Tyco umbrella. Bonuses were tied to how many deals you made. Companies that were acquired were not integrated, but left to themselves as long as they made money.

A *Business Week* article from January 2001 named Dennis Kozlowski one of the twenty-five top managers to watch. They sure were right—but for the wrong reasons. It's not that he wasn't smart or didn't know how to buy good companies. But he got lost along the way. His moral compass couldn't find true north.

The *Business Week* article quoted Kozlowski as saying he preferred managers who were "smart, poor, and want to be rich." He would give these managers tremendous autonomy, as long as they made money.[1]

Back then, Tyco was managed as a holding company, which meant autonomy for the businesses to operate on their own with minimal control from corporate headquarters. Tyco didn't have common processes across these businesses. There were also no common financial controls, no common payroll or IT systems. There were no common values. Tyco was a collection of brand names, some well known like AMP in electronics, ADT in security, or Mallinckrodt in health care; some were not so well known. Each had a distinct set of values, culture, and creative ways of doing things.

The good times came to an end, both figuratively and literally, in June 2002, when the Manhattan district attorney charged Kozlowski with avoiding more than $1 million in sales tax on some expensive paintings he bought.

I'm sure you all remember what happened next. The sales tax was the tip of the iceberg. Next we heard stories about a $2,000 wastebasket, a $6,000 shower curtain, and a $15,000 umbrella stand. Then we heard about the now infamous $1 million birthday party Kozlowski gave his wife. When accountants finished running the numbers, Kozlowski and two other executives were charged with stealing $600 million of Tyco's money. A corruption trial followed, and the judge in the 2004 case declared a mistrial. A second trial began early in 2005.

When a crisis strikes, people in organizations like Tyco often experience something I call "the wave" phenomenon. When I'm at the beach and I see a wave heading toward shore, I notice that the wave first gently bounces the boat off in the distance. As it gets closer to shore, swimmers have to fight through it. Finally, the wave crashes violently against the beach and destroys someone's sandcastle.

A scandal involving the executives in a corporation is similar to the experience created by the wave. It hits different levels of the corporation at different times. The scandal hits the executive suite first, and there is a lot of bouncing around. If the scandal is so big it draws media attention, it affects the larger employee base and the company's reputation. And if the scandal ends up in court, it often destroys someone's castle or creation. In Tyco's case, it damaged the entire beach. The Tyco scandal, which, unlike Enron, was not a systemic failure but an ethics failure by a few guys at the top, brought shame to thousands of workers who had nothing to do with what happened. It damaged the reputation of a company that had created jobs for 260,000 employees. Tyco's employees had to live with the results. For example, the scandal affected the ability of our salespeople to compete for business because Tyco was perceived as a bad company. Why would a major public customer want to award Tyco a project? It affected the company's public affairs activity, including the ability to lobby on legislation affecting the company. Why would a legislator want to listen to our issues when we had violated the public trust?

At the height of the media frenzy around Tyco, one employee said he was so embarrassed to work for Tyco he wouldn't even wear his Tyco T-shirt when he mowed the lawn.

Today, life inside Tyco is dramatically different as a result of changes brought about by new leadership—values-based leadership. This has also affected the ability of Tyco to do good public affairs.

First, we need a definition of values-based leadership. In 1942, eleven thousand U.S. Marines landed at Guadalcanal in the South Pacific. Adm. Chester Nimitz commanded the officers and enlisted men who went ashore at

Guadalcanal. What kind of leadership values did Nimitz and the commanding officer under him possess? What values enable officers to lead young men and women into battle then and now? The values were duty, honor, service, love of country.

Today, most Americans believe that the military, one of the most respected institutions according to most surveys, still lives up to these values. The news about Abu Ghraib prison shocked us precisely because we have such high expectations of the values embodied by our men and women in uniform. The corporate scandals also shocked us, but, polls suggest, didn't surprise us. What else could we expect from greedy businesspeople? They have no real values, many believe.

Thirty years ago, Gerald Ford succeeded Richard Nixon as president of United States. What values did Gerald Ford bring to his presidency? The Presidential Medal of Freedom President Clinton presented Ford in 1999 cited his character, courage, decency, and integrity. These were values the nation needed so badly at that moment in our history.

In business it is easy to point to the former Tyco executives, Enron, or Martha Stewart as examples of what values we don't want as part of our leadership model. But what values we do want? And where do these values come from?

Walt Disney's core personal values focused on imagination, learning, and making people feel good. Bill Marriott's core personal values focused on service and hard work. Marriott believed service contributes to society. And when someone asked him why he traveled two hundred thousand miles a year to visit company locations, he responded, "If I sit back and relax, a lot of other people will sit back and relax."

Both Disney and Marriott believed in something greater than making money. Yes, money was their business goal. But how they went about creating organizations that made money was defined by values that gave importance to the aspirations of employees and the welfare of society. They, like many others, have proven that values can dictate *how* a company makes a profit.

GE's Jack Welch credits his mother's influence on his values. He laid out a standard for his company, which says that it's not enough for managers just to *achieve* results; it also matters *how* they achieve those results.

When Juergen Dormann took the helm of the battered ABB, he wrote weekly letters to employees, as did Lou Gerstner when he took over IBM, telling them the truth about the state of their company, earning their trust. Transparency, integrity, steadfastness in pursuit of a goal.

There are at least two reasons why it's harder to define values-based leadership in business than in other areas. One is that business *is* about making money. That's what the shareholder pays us to do. That's what creates jobs; pays taxes. The other reason is that, in America at least, Wall Street dictates corporate success. The quarterly scorecard rewards short-term behavior narrowly defined as improvement in the economic bottom line. Recently, when I visited one of our businesses, I tried to persuade them to spend some money on building the company's reputation. You don't understand, I was told. I'd like to do what is right, but I just don't have the money. I have to make $21 million EBIT. If I spend a million on what you're asking me to do, that's fine; but then I'll have to make $22 million. In this scenario, the only stakeholder that matters is the shareholder. Managers have a very short runway to do the right thing. It takes enlightened leadership to create an environment that recognizes the claims of all stakeholders, factors them into the bottom-line equation, and rewards behavior consistent with that philosophy.

I believe I have learned four lessons about the nature of leadership in the organizations I have served.

Lesson One: Business leadership must be values-based to be true leadership. This starts with having the right people and being committed to a specific set of values. The October 25, 2003, issue of *The Economist* had a ten-point checklist of the necessary qualities for successful leaders. Number one on the list was "a sound ethical compass." The article said, "If the boss's values are undemanding, the company's will also be wobbly. That may not put it out of business, but it means the company will have to pay a premium for talent. Good people do not like working for organizations whose values they mistrust."[2]

Based on my thirty years of observing business leaders, I believe that for leadership to be leadership, it must to be values-based. There is a difference between a manager and a leader. A manager gets things done; a leader motivates employees to get things done the right way. The difference is that a leader's actions are connected to something larger than the task at hand, and that something larger is the value system of the organization as embodied by the leader. This can never be translated into numerical measures alone. I am told that Tyco's former CEO was interested only in financial results. One executive told me "Under Dennis, the standard was if the numbers were good, the company was good." This was management, not leadership.

The best business leaders have learned that you can't be successful if making money is the only thing holding the organization together. Tyco had no credit to draw on when the good times ended because it was nothing more than a moneymaking machine. While shareholders were happy with the share price, the community didn't even know who we were. Once we were in the news, we had one image. When one of our executives attended a meeting with a U.S. senator, he was greeted with the question: "Tyco. Are you the toy company or the crooks?"

Ed Breen joined Tyco in July 2002 as chairman and CEO. His first decision was to change the leadership of the company, the senior management. We've learned from Jim Collins in his book *Good To Great* that to build a great company, you have to begin with people. Jim said, "First get the right people on the bus and then figure out where to drive it." Ed didn't know who had been involved in the scandal, but he couldn't take a chance. So he fired everybody and put in place an entirely new management.

This took courage. Breen was running a $36 billion company without anyone to talk to. He sought out the best people from wherever they were: the CFO from UTC, the general counsel from International Paper, the HR head from Honeywell, communications from GE. The biggest housecleaning had to do with the board. Ed Breen changed out the entire board of directors. This had never been done before in an American company.

The new leadership team had to agree on one thing: Though they came from different corporate backgrounds, they had to be of one mind in their commitment to the highest standards of corporate governance and values. Given this mandate, one of Breen's first hires was probably the most important. Breen picked Eric Pillmore to fill a new position: senior VP of corporate governance. Pillmore, together with the corporate ombudsman and the vice president for corporate audit, reports directly to the board. It sent a strong message to investors.

Lesson Two: The values of leaders must be aligned with the values of stakeholders, and the organization must be structured so as to make the values operational. The concept of the "stakeholder corporation" has been one of my "eureka learnings" of the past ten years, and I owe a lot to my colleagues Jim Post of Boston University, who has written extremely on public affairs, and Charles Fombrun of Columbia, whose ideas on reputation I have applied in my own work. Jim writes, in his book *Redefining the Corporation: Stakeholder Management and Organizational Wealth*, that "stakeholders . . . are the key to organizational wealth and success. . . . Organizational wealth is increasingly attributable to 'soft forms' of capital—reputation, trust, credibility, good will, image, relationships. . . . Intangible assets are intrinsically connected to an organization's stakeholders. Respect the stakeholders and you protect your assets. Disrespect your stakeholders, and your intangible assets are placed at risk."[3]

Values-based leadership, then, is leadership that links the company's values with the expectations of its key constituencies. The most fundamental of these values, according to Margery Kraus, CEO of APCO Worldwide, is transparency. It includes honesty and ethical behavior, which are elements of good corporate governance and critical to a positive reputation.

In Tyco today there are four corporate values: integrity, teamwork, excellence, and accountability. Arriving at these values was not a bottom-up process. There was no time for that. But neither was it created at the top in a vacuum. These values were distilled from the personal values of the leaders, the experience from the company's past, and the leadership's vision for the future. Tyco wanted to be a company whose foundation values would be integrity, working as a team, instilling excellence, and accountability.

While bottom-up may be better in terms of ultimate buy-in, what really matters is whether the values resonate with employees and whether the organization is structured to implement them.

With respect to organizational implementation, here are the learnings from Tyco:

1. The holding company form of organization stood in the way of implementing strong corporate governance values. Breen made the decision to run Tyco as an operating company. Without this there could be no common values, no common controls, no common processes, and no accountability.

2. Finance must be separated from operations. When we looked at the companies that had suffered governance breakdowns, one factor stood out. There were no clear delineations between finance and operations management. Finance was no longer a check on operations; they had become partners. The new organization had them all report directly to the CFO. Similarly, the legal counsels of the various businesses now report to the corporate general counsel.

3. A third major area of organizational change was in HR. The failure of leadership in the 1990s was a failure to teach leaders the behaviors required of them. There was no succession planning and no mentoring. To remedy this, Tyco instituted a system of organizational and leadership reviews that would evaluate managers on the basis of their performance and the behaviors associated with Tyco's four values.

Lesson Three: The values of the corporation must be communicated values to the company's stakeholders. *The Economist* article referred to earlier also includes effective communication skills among its list of top ten commandments. "Motivating a large workforce requires a gift to present a clear vision persuasively." A leader must be able to "inspire trust and convey authenticity."[4]

I know many businesspeople who think they're leaders, but lack the one competence that would enable them to lead: the ability to communicate. Communicate by words and by behavior; walk the walk; be consistent in what you say and do; connect the dots of your actions; tap into the needs and interests of your constituencies; seek out your stakeholders and tell them what you are doing.

During my first months at Tyco, I commissioned a stakeholder perception survey as part of a reputation audit. I wanted the perception survey because I wanted to know what our important stakeholders—government decision-makers and opinion leaders—thought about Tyco and what we had to do to win back their trust. One of the things they told us was "don't expect us to keep up with what is happening inside Tyco. Find us and tell us." This was an important finding. We had in fact been making dramatic changes, but we did not communicate it to our Washington stakeholders.

The learning here is that public affairs is about both issue management and reputation management: the message and the messenger. If the messenger's integrity has been compromised, no one will believe the message. So we embarked on a program to build trust. We deployed staff and executive management for one-on-one meetings with a selected list of legislators. We designated a Tyco manager to be our public affairs representative in every congressional district where we have more than 500 employees. We have 50 of these. This proved to be a tremendous resource for rebuilding the company's reputation by establishing constituency relationships with our elected officials.

The survey also told us that while it was good to have made changes at the top, we had to demonstrate that the new values penetrated the entire organization. So we began to communicate to Washington audiences about the company's program to educate all our employees on the new Tyco values, beginning especially with integrity. Tyco created a *Guide To Ethical Conduct*, a booklet and an online course—with exam—that answers the question of what is the right way to do things. Every new executive has to take the course and pass the tests.

As a new employee, I went through this program. I had to complete six modules, and it took me about forty-five minutes to finish each one. After each module I had to pass a test. If I didn't pass, my failing grade would become part of my performance appraisal. In the past year we have pushed the ethics program down throughout the organization, first by training trainers and then educating all employees. The theme was "Integrity Matters!"

Tyco is taking significant steps to regain trust, but the job isn't complete. During my professional life I have seen my share of corporate programs that are announced with a bang and go out with a whimper. Top management is inconsistent or gives up, middle management stonewalls, employees don't see behavior that models the new values, and the commitment collapses.

Lesson Four: Execution is everything. I call this the "rule of half done." On their new initiatives a corporation will usually complete half of what needs to be done, then move on to something else before the job is finished. Employees complain of too many new initiatives, flavor-of-the-month management, of not seeing a job done. Great leadership focuses on getting things fully done. I have worked for thirteen CEOs in thirteen years. I have known so-called charismatic leaders and others who quietly and methodically got the job done.

The leadership team at the new Tyco says integrity matters. There is an article on that subject in every issue of the company publication, a series of continuous employee meetings, and real senior management commitment and follow-up. People at Tyco recognize that in order to regain stakeholder trust, they must commit 100 percent to this project and see it 100 percent through until everyone is 100 percent on board. Not halfway. Not this time. Not this company.

Tyco is not a paragon of virtue. And it may never be one. We're a company of 260,000 people. There is a lot going on at a lot of different levels. But if we are going to be the kind of company that our stakeholders can trust, everyone at Tyco needs to think of him or herself as an ethical leader—a leader who shares a set of core values with other Tyco employees, core values based on ethical behavior and integrity.

This concept isn't always an easy sell. When Tyco rolled out the ethics program, some managers grumbled, "Why are we being punished? Why are you laying this stuff on us? We didn't do anything wrong." No, they didn't do anything wrong. But if we expect leadership only from the top and don't create an environment where everyone can lead by example, what do we really hope to accomplish?

The higher up one goes in our respective organizations, the more people there are taking their cues from us. Leaders at the top are responsible for modeling organizational values by their behavior and for creating the environment where those values can flourish. But employees at every level are responsible for the cues their behavior sends to other people. There may be 260,000 people taking their cues from you, there may be three people taking cues from you. Either way your example is important.

I don't worry whether new employees already have good values. If Mom instilled good values in you at an early age, great! If Ed Breen forced them on you at an older age, that's okay, too. And if you have to take a course to figure out that business and ethics are not conflicting values, then enroll now. The important thing is that we all come to share the same values.

Tyco experienced firsthand what many of us, thankfully, only read about: It takes years to build a good corporate reputation, but only a few minutes to destroy one. One's reputation can be destroyed as quickly as a sandcastle disappears under a wave. In the final analysis, it would have been easier for Tyco's management to have done things the right way the first time. But they didn't, so the new management team must make sure they get it right the second time. Baseball players get three strikes. Organizations don't.

HOW VALUES-BASED LEADERSHIP SERVES CORPORATE PUBLIC AFFAIRS

Now let me come back to the theme I began with: how public affairs can contribute to values-based leadership, and how values-based leadership can contribute to the effective implementation of a public affairs strategy.

Repeatedly throughout this article I have emphasized that leadership must be about more than just making money. It's about how you achieve *all* your goals. Values-based leadership is an expansive concept. It presumes a role serving others in society.

Public affairs is the discipline that provides the bridge between the world inside the corporation and the world outside. I believe that a corporation, especially a large one, cannot be successful by just sticking to its own internal affairs. It cannot compete successfully if it focuses only on price and quality. It has to be engaged with its major stakeholders, and it has to be involved in making the policies that shape the business environment. Companies that chose to ignore this larger mandate pay a substantial price.

The best business leaders I have known over the years have been the ones who understood the value of public affairs as a key way to communicate with the broader society. They were willing to fund the staff and the programs associated with it. They saw public affairs as an investment, not a cost, because it gave them the tools to anticipate change, to manage issues, and to connect to their stakeholders. Public affairs is the voice of the stakeholder in the board-room, and of the company in the broader society.

How then does values-based leadership serve corporate public affairs? Ef-fectiveness in public affairs is measured in terms of a company's ability to persuade government officials to make decisions that are consistent with the company's interests, or at least not adverse to them. This ability is comprised of many ingredients, but certainly one of the most important is a good reputation. The absence of a bad reputation helps, but is not enough.

Tyco's problems in the public arena began with not being known until the scandal hit. There was nothing to counter the bad news and so the downward cycle began. Most lawmakers didn't know who Tyco was. When they criticized Tyco, they were often not aware that they had Tyco employees in their state or congressional district. To be effective depends not just on the absence of negatives, but on having a positive image and reputation. Values-based lead-ership makes this reputation possible.

In business-government relations, integrity is the coin of the realm. With 4,697 registered lobbyists who are active on behalf of 19,658 clients, spending hundreds of millions of dollars to get their message across to elected and ap-pointed officials, the competition is intense. How does a corporate public affairs representative break through the clutter? What kinds of credentials are nec-essary? How does one get access to decision-makers? While the full answer to this is a whole course in public affairs, the short answer is that a good reputation and public trust in the company are critical to credible communication in the public affairs role. Without values-based leadership inside the company, the public affairs professional is working with one hand tied behind her back.

Having values-based leadership has enabled Tyco to recover its voice in the public arena. Corporate leadership is the most visible representative of the company, and therefore, potentially the most credible messenger. When Tyco announced that it had an entirely new management team, it sent a signal that it was not doing business as usual. While there was a press release about the new team, the change had to be communicated using a variety of communications vehicles, most important by way of face-to-face encounters between the new management team and lawmakers. Lawmakers could test for themselves, ask questions of the CEO or the CFO, push back until they were satisfied. Values-based leadership had a face. It was not a disembodied message or a public relations innovation. It was a person who could project that he or she stands for something.

But trust is not a wholesale commodity. It has to be built over time, one person at a time. Every employee becomes an ambassador. A grassroots net-work at the local level made up of the company's managers building rela-tionships with their elected officials becomes an asset to effective public affairs if the message is consistent with the company's values. Values-based leadership at all levels in the organization is necessary for effective public affairs.

Reputation is the sum of everything a company says and does. The individuals who speak for the company at the highest level or at the local level, in Washington, in state capitals, and around the world, all have the potential of enhancing or hurting the company's reputation. This is why their personal reputation and their personal integrity is so important. And this is what hurt Tyco so badly in 2002. Tyco's public affairs professionals all know that they too must exhibit the highest ethical standards in their work. Having broken the public trust, Tyco must now be better than the best to win it back. Even our outside consultants have to meet this standard. We tell them they are an extension of Tyco, which means that their values have to align with ours.

The headlines in Washington these days suggest that "the right thing" is an elusive concept. Is the right thing in public affairs to pursue whatever you can get away with? Is the right thing the same as generally accepted behavior? Do you lose competitive advantage if you play by stricter rules than the generally accepted standard? I don't think so. This is where values-based leadership informs behavior and becomes a guide to the choices we make in influencing public policy. What was generally accepted in the past may not be valid in the future. The only thing we can count on to give us credibility in the future is integrity, transparency, and accountability. Applied consistently, leaders who live by these values build public trust, making the messenger, and the message, credible.

NOTES

This chapter is an adaptation of a speech presented to the Academy of Management, August 2004, which also appeared in the newsletter of the Centre for Corporate Public Affairs, Australia, January 2005.

1. Top 25 managers: Managers to watch, *Business Week* (2001, January 8).
2. How to run a company well, *The Economist* (2003, October 25).
3. James E. Post, Lee E. Preston, and Sybille Sachs, *Redefining the corporation: Stakeholder management and organizational wealth.* Stanford University Press, 2002, 244–256.
4. *The Economist,* cited above.

9

Public Affairs and Game Theory

JOHN F. MAHON

During the past decade, one of the more interesting developments in the evolution of strategic management literature has been the introduction of the Game Theory. A series of Nobel awards (John von Neumann, a mathematician; Oskar Morgenstern, an economist; and John Nash of *A Beautiful Mind* fame) in mathematics and economics have been given to the founders of Game Theory. So while these purveyors of Game Theory have impressive credentials, the introduction of the rather esoteric concepts of Game Theory would at first seem to run contrary to the tradition of Strategic Management's stress of being useful to the "practicing" management and have no relevance to public affairs and political strategy. In fact, I believe game theory will make a significant contribution to Strategic Management and corporate public affairs in the twenty-first century.

In the Strategic Management context, Game Theory has been utilized to describe how managers need to think about how their competitors will respond to actions they take. In other words, there is a strategic interdependence among the various participants or stakeholders. In traditional economic theory, each individual makes choices in isolation, unaware of what other competitors are doing. However, in Game Theory, two or more participants try to maximize their utility, well aware that competitors are aware of what they are doing.

But what makes Game Theory even more revolutionary in the development of economic theory (and in turn strategic management) is that it takes into account the risk preferences of the various participants. No longer is it assumed that every competitor would want to maximize profits or have perfect information about the market, but rather competitors will act to bring about the most preferred of possible outcomes for themselves and other players. In this environment, strategy is important, but perhaps more important is the signaling of intentions and behavior to other players in the game if the goal is to achieve the most preferred outcomes. In the realm of public affairs, signaling and the "correct" interpretation of those signals is a crucial but oft undeveloped skill.

Information for Game Theory decisions is probabilistic in nature and every participant has a different risk preference. The source of uncertainty in Game Theory is the intentions of other players. Risk structures and the use of the mean and variance (in order to determine probabilities) help identify how participants in the game will respond to uncertain prospects. By doing this, participants use marginal analysis to make optimal decisions given the constraint that other players are acting in the same manner.

But while Game Theory has been become an integral part of the business strategy classes, we find it curious that it is almost totally neglected in the business and society literature and in the boardrooms of corporate America and beyond. This chapter is a first step to remedy this deficiency in the business and society field, and especially in the field of political strategy. Just as Game Theory has redefined what the "rational" actor is in a microeconomic setting, it might provide the opportunity for business and society scholars/managers to reevaluate how firms and various stakeholders deal with political economy questions.

In order to accomplish this introductory task, this chapter will be divided into three parts. First, the characteristics of "game" need to be delineated. The emphasis will be on the those features of a "game" that have to do with "fairness" since this is the characteristic of a "game" that has the greatest influence in the outcome of political economy dilemmas. The second part of the analysis will develop a model entitled "The Arena for Business and Societal Games." This model will attempt to provide managers a framework that will allow them to catalog the various types of "games" that they could encounter as part of the "Business and Societal" process. The third section will apply this model to develop possible strategies in dealing with various dilemmas that managers might confront, using illustrative examples to apply the model in practice.

CHARACTERISTICS OF GAMES

How many times as a child did we hear the phrase "It's only a game!" Usually it was reserved for someone who was taking the game "too seriously" or taking a loss too personally. Every summer there are numerous reports of parents who have interfered with Little League baseball games. A recent example occurred in the suburb of Philadelphia. In this incident, the manager of a Little League team (a policeman!) paid his pitcher to hit the best hitter of an opposing team in the head. Unfortunately, the pitcher was successful and resulted in the hospitalization of the hitter. However, the pitcher felt such remorse over the incident that he told authorities about how he had been paid by his manager to aim at the head of the opposing player. The reaction to the previous example is summed up in the phrase "Isn't it a shame that adults can't just let the kids play the game." The emphasis on "winning" at all costs is decried, and there is a nostalgic yearning for simpler times when adults would not interfere in "kids' games." So what have these adults done that has violated our sense of a "game"? Adults certainly regulate every other aspect of a child's life, so why shouldn't adults interfere in a child's game?

The objection to adult interference in games is that games are a special world where children are protected against the reality of the adult world. In fact, all games are construed to be occasions that operate outside the "normal" world. What makes the world of a game so unique? It has been proposed by the French sociologist Roger Caillois that the following three characteristics of a game are what separate games from "reality." These characteristics are: (1) a game must be voluntary; (2) a game must have boundaries; and (3) a game must have uncertain outcomes.[1]

Game: A Voluntary Activity

A game certainly must be defined as a free and voluntary activity (otherwise the dynamics of the game and its outcomes are very different—as an example, consider the ancient Roman Colosseum and its "games." When a game begins, it is presumed that the game will be a source of fun and rewards for the players, the "coaches," and the audience. If any of the participants were forced to play a game, it would no longer be "fun," nor could there be any reward. The entertainment value of the game for all would be lost. Participants play a game only if and when they wish to. In this sense, a game is a free or voluntary activity. Unfortunately, over time the participants sometimes "forget" that the game is a free and voluntary activity (thereby forfeiting the ability to exit or withdraw from the game—and such a choice can be made without conscious consideration). Certainly stakeholders have the option to play or sit out any issue contest and political game.

This desire to play a game is what makes the game entertaining as well as rewarding. The quality of a game is judged by its ability to provide excitement, escape from the routine, and hold the attention of the audience and the participants. The chief reward of playing a game is to be recognized for the skill in playing the game—and in any game there are various skill sets that are desired and admired by the players. This sense of freedom also extends to "exiting" the game. A person playing a game has to be free to say, "I am not playing this game anymore." Finally, a game is something that creates neither goods nor wealth. It is unproductive activity where participants play the game for the "love of the game." The "thrill" of victory and the "agony" of defeat are the chief emotions that describe participation in a game. That is the reason why "sports purists" dismiss professional athletics where the contest is played by paid profess-sionals who no longer play for the "love of the game."

In the previous example concerning Little League, the manager is willing to do anything to "win the game." He was not allowing his players "to be kids." His players were not having "fun" or, even more damming, were not playing for the "love of the game."

Game: Governed by Rules

A game is also an activity that is separate from the "real" world. Games are isolated from the rest of life. Critics often disparage professional sports as "men playing boy's games." For what makes games different from the real world is that all games have precise limits of place and time. Players need a board for checkers and chess, a racetrack, a field, a ring, a stadium, and so on. To leave the "place" where the game is to be played is a way to disqualify the player of the game.

There are also boundaries placed on the time in which the game needs to be played. A *specific* game has definite starts and conclusions to it, as does a season (the distinction being that a season encompasses a series of games, and that the outcome of one game has spillover impacts on the team's performance during the season). Think of this in terms of an unfolding legislative term—each bill is a game, and the season is the legislative cycle encompassing all bills introduced and acted upon. The same is true for an issue, except that with many issue contests the length of time the issue unfolds is uncertain. Indeed, both the start of the issue "game" and the conclusion may be somewhat vague. Everyone playing the game has to follow the rules or at least pretend that they are fol-lowing the rules. In order to move the "play" of a game along, all players agree to abide by the decisions of an umpire or referee, who generally interprets events according to pre-established rules of play. Every game is a restricted, closed, and protected environment, very unlike the "real" world. Games provide their participants a certainty that the real world can never provide. To employ a person or thing that comes in from outside the ring or stadium is con-sidered "bad" sportsmanship and usually disqualifies the player who brought in the outside influence. However, a key consideration is that the player brought in from outside the ring has to be recognized as an outsider by all of the players.

Clearly, the manager who paid to have an opposing player hurt violated the rules of the game. Adults who inject themselves into a "Little League" game violate the "enclosed" and "protected" atmosphere that ought to characterize a game. Parents' behavior toward umpires by constantly challenging the um-pire's calls and even threatening the umpires with violence, destroy the "safe" and contained world that a game is designed to provide the participants. Similarly, when parents badger the coach of a Little League team to win at all costs or play their son or daughter at various times, this is also an occasion when the "sanctity" of the rules by which the game is operated are violated.

Game: As an Uncertain Activity

The characteristic that keeps a player playing a game is the uncertainty of results. The old baseball maxim of "you never know until the last out" explains this facet of a game. Games are stopped once the outcome is no longer in doubt, or upon pre-established conditions. Every game of "skill" involves the risk for the player to miss a shot or make a poor throw. The old adage of "the thrill of victory and the agony of defeat" is what keeps a game exciting and absolutely uncertain. If teams are unfairly matched, the game between these teams is boring and both players and the audience lose interest. Issue management, stakeholder management, and political strategy share the same degree of uncertainty.

Even for "unskilled" games such as lotteries or roulette, a player has to be assured that there is a possibility that the player can win or not win. The entertainment value of a lottery game or a card game rests with the ability of the player to believe or dream that every player has an equal chance of winning the game. Hence, there is a certain amount of "trust" that the player of an unskilled game places in the operators of the game. If that "trust" is violated, then the game ceases to be played, or charges of unfairness in the game are raised and the results might be challenged in a different arena (recall the appeals arising out of issues in the last summer Olympics in Greece).[2]

Once again, the manager in our "Little League" example violated this fundamental gaming principle. Clearly, the manager's wish to win at all costs is trying to remove "uncertainty" for his players. When adults are accused of taking the fun out of the game, it is precisely because the adults want to rig the results. If there is no doubt to the outcome of a game, then there is no joy or fun in playing the game; indeed, we could argue that no game truly exists in these circumstances (one could argue, for example, that monopolies can not play the traditional "market" game as there are no players [just one] and the outcomes are not unpredictable in the long run). The child is also not free to enter or leave the game if he or she wishes.

While there are other characteristics of games, these three characteristics seem to be universally a part of every game. They also correspond to a player's conception of a "fair" game. In other words, a game is considered "fair" if following conditions are maintained: (1) the player is free to enter or leave a game; (2) the rules that govern the game apply to all players at all times (but "interpretations" of the rules by the umpires or referee can vary and impose an element of unpredictability not under the control of the players); and (3) the results of a game cannot be rigged beforehand.

The rules for "fairness" will form the basis of a model that will be developed in the next section. This model is intended to be a "first look" at the various issues that confront a manager of a firm, a leader of a public interest group, or a nongovernmental organization as they play the "game" of public policy.

THE ARENA FOR BUSINESS AND SOCIETAL "GAMES"

We have articulated the essential aspects of a "game" in general and now wish to move to a more specific analysis of what we will term the public policy game. To recap, essential aspects of a game are that it is free and voluntary, that it is governed by rules, and that the results or outcomes are uncertain at the time the game is entered into (clearly as the game unfolds, elements of uncertainty can be removed, and the outcome can become more "certain"). There is also some agreement among the players of the game as to what constitutes "winning the game." We offer Figure 9.1 for your thoughtful consideration.

The model or "arena" described in Figure 9.1 (The Arena for Business and Societal "Games") has three distinct parts. The first part is "The Ring or Field." This is where the contest is played and includes the rules of engagement (specific procedures, processes, and the like) as well as the generally accepted rules of behavior (which are not necessarily written down but which every player knows). Players can be individuals, organizations of every kind and variety, networked organizations, public interest groups, and the government (which can also play the curious role of "referee" here). This ring is the place in which the game is played—and is entered voluntarily, has rules, and outcomes are uncertain. There are, of course, players that are not part of the game as it is initiated, but get drawn in as the game unfolds. We do not wish to make this to much of a sporting example, but the notion of substitute players, relievers, and the like are examples of players drawn into the game at a later point. These "players" reflect the changing circumstances and uncertainty that has unfolded as the game is engaged.

The second part is the area of "the audience and/or the contestants." The "and/or" choice is important here as it reflects two key aspects of the game. The first is that, as in every game, there is an audience. The audience has the power to influence the outcome of the game by the nature and extent of their involvement.[3] This does not mean that they become actively involved as a "player or contestant," but that they can exercise influence by whom and to what degree they support a player in the game (in a sports game, the value of the "home advantage" is considered important as the audience can support the team by cheering them on and booing the opposition or intimidating the opposition by their size and aggressive support of the home team; in any game the audience can provide resources to the players that enable them to compete). The second aspect of the audience is that they can become "contestants" and enter the ring or field as a player. For organizations, the process and motivations for actual involvement of audience members as they become contestants is an important one and can provide clues as to how to prevent this process from unfolding or to accelerate it if it is to the advantage of the organization.

FIGURE 9.1. The Arena for Business and Societal "Games"

The third part of this model is the larger environment. Note carefully that the "game" area is separated from the larger environment by a permeable line. That is, it is very possible that other actors (for want of a better term) can either enter as part of the audience or move directly into the field or ring of the game. The analysis to follow will give managers/firms a sense of the various business and societal "games" they might encounter; suggest strategies to deal with audience members who are not contestants; and strategies to deal with contestants in the ring or field. We begin our discussion by focusing more clearly on the ring, or field of engagement.

Ring or Field

In dealing with a business and societal problem or "game," the players need to decide where and *under what rules* the game is to be played. In other words, where is the "action" to take place and under what "rules" is the game to be governed. The players need to agree on these conditions that also mark the beginning of "game" play. One important difference is that one player can determine initially "where" the game is to be played, and tactics open to other players are to move the game to another arena. In essence, three questions need to be answered in order to determine the "ring" or "field":

1. What "level" will the game be played at?
2. "Where" will the game be initiated?
3. Who will serve as referee?

The Level of the Game

There are at least six levels where the game can be played. The local, state, regional, national, transnational (but regionally based), and global afford different levels of engagement for organizations to consider. In general, if the game involves contentious issues or "high" stakes, it will most likely be played at the federal level. Clearly, each player will try to pick that level where they would feel "at home," for example, wield the greatest power or have the greatest advantage over other competitors, or where the "rules of the game" are more favorable. But picking a level is not without risk. One can overestimate one's strength at a particular level, underestimate the strength of competitors at that level, or misread the sheer number and level of audience involvement and potential participation in the game itself. Not to overstate the analogy, but in baseball, the level of competition at Single A, Double A, Triple A, and the major leagues is quite different.

Where Will the Game be Played?

Once the level of the game has been determined, the next question is where the game will be played. We offer alternative "playing fields" wherein the game can be played, and each of these fields has its own rules and procedures, audiences, referees, and appeal processes. The potential fields are (at all levels noted above): (1) the legislative branch of government; (2) the judiciary branch (and we would include here such areas as mediation and arbitration); (3) the regulatory branch; and (4) what is euphemistically referred to as the "court of public opinion."

Who Will Serve as "Referee"?

In all games and in many ways the ultimate referee is the audience— especially where issues of fairness and equitability are raised. However, for the normal operation of the game, the selection of the ring presumes the existence of a referee that is acceptable to the players of the game. What makes games in the public policy arena such an interesting challenge is that government can simultaneously serve as a "player" and a referee in the game—an interesting way of looking at a conflict of interest.

In the legislative game, the referee can be either the executive branch (in the form of a veto) or the committee system and leadership of the legislative bodies. The leadership plays a key role in the selection of issues (or the agenda), how the issues will be brought forth, and what committees will consider the issue.[4] The committee system invests enormous power in the chair and in the individual members with regard to the consideration of issues and the form and manner in which they will be delivered (if at all) to the legislative body for consideration. There are also clear rules regarding the what, whom, and how a piece of legislation can be introduced, considered, and processed. If players are unhappy with the outcome of the game or a decision made in the game, they can appeal the referee's decision to the judiciary (shifting the playing field).

In the judicial game, the referee can be the jury, the presiding judge, or the appeals court(s). It is the jury or the judge that makes the ultimate ruling on guilt or innocence and/or on the amount of damages/punishment to be awarded to the defendant(s). Curiously enough, appeals of these referee's decisions stay at least initially within the judiciary and move through a clear appeals/appellate process. Ultimately, an appeal of a decision can be taken to the legislature, but this is usually in the most extreme of circumstances. Like the legislature, the judiciary has a clear set of rules and processes for consideration of issues that come before it. Unlike the legislature, the judiciary is a reactionary game field—that is, the judicial system awaits players to bring the game into this playing area. The legislature can select the game (issue) that is to be played in a more activist manner.

In the regulatory game, the referee consists of the members of regulatory agency themselves. The sitting commissioners (or whatever term is used) are the ones that make the final decision/judgment. However, regulatory staff members have enormous unseen influence on the thinking of the commissioners and the framing of the issues brought before them. Regulatory agencies lie in the middle in terms of games between the legislature and the judiciary. That is, regulatory agencies can wait for issues to be brought to them or seek out issues on their own. Regulatory agencies have their own rules and processes. Because of the nature of regulatory games, they receive far less publicity than issues in the legislative or judicial ring and have smaller audiences. However, the audience is usually very interested and knowledgeable about the game being played and often quite eager and willing to be involved. Decisions of regulatory agencies can be appealed to the judiciary or the legislature.

In the "court of public opinion" it is the people who serve as referee, and the majority (or the illusion of a majority) rules. Therefore, an organization that can show (either substantively and/or perceptually) that the larger audience supports their position "wins." Of course, such decisions can be appealed to the legislature, judiciary, or regulatory agency (depending on the specific nature of the issue contest).

It is our opinion (based upon significant empirical, practical, and theoretical experience) that from a strict "rules" perspective there are clear choices for organizations to consider when playing the game. The "best" set of rules (in terms of clarity, consistent enforcement, interpretability) lie in the regulatory arena. That is, from a probability or uncertainty standpoint, engaging in regulatory game is more predictable (note we did not say certain) than in any other arena. Then, in order of increasing uncertainty, we would suggest that judicial games are next, followed by legislative games, and finally the most uncertain outcome of all is found in the court of public opinion. Part of the reasoning here also rests in where decisions in the game can be appealed and under what "rules" such decisions can be appealed. In the court of public opinion, appeals can be taken to any of the other game fields; in the legislative game, appeals can be taken to the judicial game (but only a limited number of decisions can be appealed) or executive branch (but with the potential override of a veto always a possibility).

Now that the framework for the game has been addressed, and the elements of the game of public policy explicated, we can turn to broad strategies that organizations can use to play the game.

STRATEGIES FOR PLAYING THE GAME

As with any game, an understanding of the rules of the game and experience with the game is important to success. Microsoft over the last few years has learned this lesson the hard way. Microsoft had not invested any serious resources or time in working with Congress or building bridges with legislators in Washington. When the antitrust suits (clearly a judicial game) arose, Microsoft found itself in the onerous position of having to compete in that game ring and not being able to shift to any other field to play the game.

Space precludes a full discussion and analysis of the strategies available to organizations in playing the game of public policy. We would like to concentrate on two important strategies—strategies of obstruction and strategies of engagement. There is another set of strategies—strategies of compliance and exit that we simply will not address here.

Strategies of Obstruction

Take a close look at Figure 9.1 once again. There are several "potential" entrants into the field or ring in which the game will be played. In strategies of obstruction, there are three potential major foci of action—a set of strategies to prevent an issue or situation from arising at all (and therefore needing no field in which to be resolved); a set of strategies to prevent players from entering into the game; and a set of strategies to prevent coalitions from forming across players and audience members to thwart the organization's objectives and goals.

Cobb and Ross identify a set of strategies (and their associated tactics) for dealing with denying access to what we have termed the field or ring in which the game is to be played.[5] The notion here is how can a group or an individual deny access of other groups (and issues/problems) to the game? Cobb and Ross identify several categories of strategies, but the ones of most interest here are what they term low-cost strategies and medium-cost attack strategies.

Low-cost strategies are usually the first choice of organizations as they involve the minimal commitment of time and resources. As Stone observed: "Keeping an alternative from explicit consideration is even better than defeating it.[6] The idea here is to keep a problem from being considered (if it cannot be named and blame cannot be assigned, then the problem does not exist in the public's conscious and needs no action). They offer several useful strategies and tactics here.

The first tactic is to simply refuse to recognize that a problem exists. This is exactly the strategy that President Bush took initially with regard to ozone layer depletion. He simply argued that he did not see the problem and could not agree to international accords that were being developed to improve air quality. The same is true of the battle between Northeastern and Midwestern states over acid rain. The operators of power plants have refused to acknowledge the existence of acid rain. Ford argued that there was no real problem with the Explorer, and Firestone made the same arguments with regard to its tires.

The second approach is to recognize that there is a situation, but it is not a real problem, so it is unworthy of action. Cigarette manufacturers denied that there was a problem with secondhand smoke. These firms still deny today that there are any health effects associated with smoking.

Ibara and Kitsuse offer another approach, which they term antipatterning.[7] In antipatterning the argument is that the problem exists, but it is an isolated incident or does not apply broadly. When AIDS was first discovered, the argument was that it was isolated to drug users and homosexuals and therefore not of sufficient concern to the general populace. This is a clear attempt at antipatterning. When it was discovered that AIDS could be transmitted through the blood supply or through sexual contact between nonhomosexuals, the "isolated" nature of the problem evaporated and significant increases in funding of AIDS research occurred.

Another alternative is to refuse to recognize the existence of any group that is advocating the problem. Cobb and Ross observe that this occurred with the civil rights movement in the 1960s, when government leaders refused to recognize the existence of civil rights groups. Some would argue that the Israeli refusal to recognize the Palestinians is a similar tactic.

The theme in all of these approaches is to avoid confrontation with either the problem or those advancing the problem. If we do not agree that a problem exists or we do not deal with the advocates of a problem, we do not make the publicity of the problem easy, the naming or blaming of the problem easy, and therefore retard any solution to the problem. Unfortunately, while these strategies and tactics can eliminate some of the nuisance groups, they do not always succeed, so the organization needs to pursue more aggressive strategies and actions.

These strategies are termed medium-cost attack strategies by Cobb and Ross (1997), and their major purpose is to buy additional time for the organization to deal with the problem. Sometimes, delay is the best tactic to use.

The first set of actions that can be used here are centered on discrediting the issue stance of the group or the group itself. The latter approach, attempting to discredit the group, can have serious repercussions for the organization. It can turn the situation into a "David versus Goliath" battle, where the audience has sympathy for the party being attacked. The issue of sex-education in public schools is illustrative here. The problem is a legitimate one, and the advocates for sex education in schools were and are highly respected. Attacking them would not be a smart tactic. However, arguments to discredit the issue—along the lines that it is and should not be a public concern but a private, familial one has carried a lot of weight in the debate. It is a clever approach to essentially discredit the issue stance of the advocates—we agree that sex education is important, but it should be done in the home. It places opposition advocates in an awkward position, the issue is recognized, but the treatment of the issue is not what the advocates support and is itself reasonable.

The next set of tactics is to argue on the facts and the analysis used in looking at or developing the problem. The tobacco industry has argued for some time that the statistics and analysis of smoking are seriously flawed and that no conclusion can be reached from this analysis. This is a favorite tactic as it sounds reasonable on its face and can involve significant amounts of time to redo studies and relook at problems and issues. A current example of such a debate is over the Social Security fund at the national level and its solvency. The issue is very technical and can be subjected to a great deal of analysis and follow-on questions about that analysis.

Another approach is to use symbolic measures to deal with the problem—of which a consistent approach is to appoint a blue ribbon panel to deal with the problem. Then any inaction can be blamed on the lack of consensus or action by the panel. Any results can either be discounted based on faulty analysis or on changed circumstances. It is a near-perfect tactic to buy time. The symbolic actions that can be utilized here are addressed in more detail in Mahon, 1989, and in Mahon and McGowan, 1996.[8]

All of the aforementioned strategies and tactics can be used to prevent a coalition of players opposed to the organization's position from forming. They can be used, however, only if the organization is even aware of coalition-forming in the past among players. But most organizations are near-ignorant of the coalitions that are formed against their interests *and* with what success these coalitions have opposed their interests. Unfortunately, these strategies and tactics are not always successful, so an organization needs to have a set of strategies for engagement in their response toolkit.

Strategies of Engagement

If an organization is unsuccessful in preventing an issue and/or player from entering the game, then strategies of engagement must be implemented. Some of the aforementioned strategies of obstruction can be continued into this stage of the game, but the focus or theme of strategies at this time are centered on (1) choice or altering the field by shaping the field or by tilting the field; (2) framing the issue or problem in distinctive ways; and (3) forming coalitions and using agents to play the game for the organization.[9]

Altering the Field

The purpose of altering the field or ring where the game is played is to change the performance of the field or ring itself. Obviously, strategies to alter the field in this manner are aimed at improving the probabilities that the organization's position will win out.

Field-shaping strategies and tactics are modification of the tools or rules so that the players in the game are subjected to different incentives or instructions. For example, one could change the threshold level of damages before an issue could enter the judiciary or change or institute a rule requiring a certain level of support from the referees in the game before an issue will be admitted, require licensing/certification of players, or require players to post a bond in order to enter the game. In this manner, an organization can shape how the game is engaged in initially and raise the stakes for individual players to enter (or exit) the game.

In addition, actions can be undertaken to insure that the players within the shaped field feel (either in actuality or perceptually) that their behaviors are now constrained. The former is an attempt to change the rules as noted, while the latter is an attempt to alter the discretionary behavior of the players in the game itself in ways favorable to the organization. An example of this field-tilting offered by Mitnick is the use of regulatory and judicial appointments to select officials more or less in tune with the organization or industry interests. Note carefully that no rules or tools are impacted in any way, but that the likely exercise of discretion by the individuals (in our case the referees) can alter outcomes in major ways.

Framing the Issue/Problem

We understand issues and problems by use of frames and analogies.[10] The use of framing has dramatic impact on the nature of the game, where it is played, and who the players are in the game. As a brief example consider the unfolding fallout from the Enron scandal and focus on Arthur Andersen. What exactly is the frame to be used for this issue? Andersen would have liked it to be any of the following. One frame could be that this is simply a problem of criminal activity by the officers of Enron, and is therefore not the responsibility of Arthur Andersen. Notice that this suggests that the field for the game will be the judiciary. Another frame could be that this is a failure of SEC oversight and not of Arthur Andersen or accounting in general. Again, this frame suggests that the field for the game will be the regulatory or legislative area. A final frame would be that this is reflective of a problem with the accounting profession overall, and therefore a solution should be pursued that impacts all firms in this area. This would suggest a legislative, regulatory, or self-regulatory game. Note that the focus of the aforementioned frames is to remove Arthur Andersen as the focus of activity and involvement and shift the issue to others. In addition, the final game that is selected among the three offered will have different rules and players engaged and offer different outcomes.

Forming Coalitions/Agents

Sometimes the best strategy in contests like these is to form coalitions. The coalitions extend the reach and impact of the organization and can improve the chances for victory. As an analogy, think of bicycle races like the Tour de France. Teams enter the race, but the real goal is to have one member of the team win. The rest of the team engages in tactics and strategies to insure that their best rider is positioned to win. So to in public policy games, coalitions (or teams if you prefer) can be formed to position one of the members of the coalition to win "more" than the other members (clearly there has to be some incentives for the other members to join the coalition—but in some cases they can be promises of support in other games).

There may be situations where coalitions cannot be formed, but where the use of an agent to act on the organization's behalf is the preferred approach. For example, when a business enters a foreign country, it is not unusual for the organization to hire a "local" to act as its agent and conduct business for them. The agent affords many advantages (knowledge of the game, the referees, independent reputation) to the organization but also brings some potentially negative baggage (agent's past ties, reputation, may not act in accordance with instructions, etc.).

CONCLUSION

We believe that considerations of Game Theory as it applies to issues management, stakeholder management, and political strategy have great potential for the organization. An understanding of Game Theory in the context of an arena and ring as developed herein can sharpen organizational tactics and strategies in such political contests and lead to increased success or, at a minimum, better shaping of acceptable outcomes. In a very practical sense, such attention can help reduce uncertainties and allow for the integration of strategies and tactics across issues, stakeholders, and arenas and rings.

Organizations often miss this coordinating aspect of multiple issues/stake-holders/arenas/rings and end up reducing their effectiveness overall.[11]

NOTES

1. R. Caillois (1979), *Man, play and games,* New York: Schocken Books.

2. R. McGowan (1994), *States lotteries and legalized gambling: Painless revenue or painful mirage,* Westport, CT: Quorum Books.

3. E. E. Schattschneider (1960), *The semi-sovereign people: A realist's guide to democracy in America,* New York: Holt.

4. R. W. Cobb and C. D. Elder (1981), *Participation in American politics: The dynamics of agenda-building.* Baltimore: Johns Hopkins University Press; J. F. Mahon and R. A. McGowan (1996), *Industry as a player in the political and social arena: Defining the competitive environment,* Greenwich, CT: Quorum Books; J. F. Mahon and R. A. McGowan (1998), Modeling industry political dynamics, *Business and Society, 37*(4), 390–413; J. F. Mahon and R. A. McGowan (1999), How legislation, regulation, and society change competition, in P. Goett, ed., *1999 handbook of business strategy,* New York: Faulkner and Gray, 211–222; R. A. McGowan and J. F. Mahon (2000), Corporate political competitive analysis, in P. Goett, ed., *2000 handbook of business strategy,* New York: Faulkner and Gray, 189–203.

5. R. W. Cobb and M. H. Ross, eds. (1997), *Cultural strategies of agenda denial; Avoidance, attack, and redefinition,* Lawrence: University Press of Kansas. A significant portion of the discussion that follows draws heavily on their work and ideas.

6. D. Stone (1988), *Policy paradox and political reason,* Glenview, IL: Scott, Foresman, 196.

7. P. R. Ibarra and J. I. Kitsuse (1993), Vernacular constituents and moral discourse: An interactionist proposal for the study of social problems, in G. Miller and J. A. Holstein, eds., *Constructionist controversies: Issues in social problems theory,* New York: Aldine de Gruyter.

8. J. F. Mahon (1989), Corporate political strategy, *Business in the Contemporary World, 2*(1): 50–63; Mahon and McGowan (1996), cited above.

9. B. M. Mitnick (2001, August), The uses of political markets, paper presented at the national meetings of the Academy of Management, Washington, DC.

10. For a more detailed discussion of the power of framing an issue see J. F. Mahon and S. L. Wartick (2003, Spring), Dealing with stakeholders: How reputation, credibility, and framing influence the game, *Corporate Reputation Review, 6*(1), 19–35.

IV
CRITICAL ISSUES IN BUSINESS-GOVERNMENT RELATIONS

—————— 10 ——————

Understanding Whistle-Blowing Effectiveness: How Can One Person Make a Difference?

MARCIA P. MICELI and JANET P. NEAR

Shocking photos of abuses at the Abu Ghraib prison in Iraq were revealed after U.S. Army specialist Joseph Darby and at least two other soldiers blew the whistle.[1] After looking at the graphic images, Darby said that he felt "very bad" about what was going on in the prison and that he "thought it was very wrong."[2] So he slipped an anonymous note under a division officer's door and later identified himself, in a sworn statement, reporting the problems.[3] The world's attention was drawn to the scandal when the *New Yorker* magazine published a series of articles about the prisoner abuse.[4]

While this is a dramatic and recent example, there are many instances of organizational wrongdoing that might go uncorrected but for a courageous insider's willingness to speak up. Recent U.S. scandals and allegations of illegal practices involve diverse industries.[5] Such cases demonstrate that authorities and the general public often are unaware of organizational wrongdoing until considerable damage is done.[6] Insiders can help the organization take corrective steps if top management is inclined to do so; but if it is not, the public depends on insiders to alert a powerful outsider. Unfortunately, research consistently shows that the vast majority of employees who believe they have observed wrongdoing do not report it to any authority.[7]

One reason why employees do not report wrongdoing is that they believe they will get a poor response from the organization; they could be ignored, or penalized, and the wrongdoing would continue.[8] Because this suggests inadequate legal protection for whistle-blowers or inadequate incentive to organizations to respond appropriately, legislation is increasingly turning to whistle-blowing as the solution to fraud and misbehavior. As a result, greater attention is being focused on the critical concern of how to make whistle-blowing more effective.

Research on the effectiveness of whistle-blowing in getting wrongdoing stopped could be useful, in at least four ways. First, some top managers are sincere about wanting to correct and prevent wrongdoing, for ethical reasons, or because they are wise enough to realize that allowing wrongdoing ultimately hurts their organizations. If these managers respond poorly to valid whistle-blowing, research can suggest ways to improve their responses. For example, if whistle-blowers are more effective when wrongdoing is easy to change, then organizations whose leaders are sincere can look hard at internal operations to find ways of: (a) dealing with more challenging or entrenched problems, and (b) encouraging employees who take on these challenges.[9]

Second, for those top managers who need more encouragement, research can help inform the work of legislators or legal scholars who are investigating ways in which legislators can write better laws, giving organizations more incentive to act appropriately.[10] Legislators in the United States and elsewhere have traditionally focused primarily on providing protection from retaliation rather than encouraging organizations to respond effectively to whistle-blowing complaints, with disappointing results.[11]

Third, research on effectiveness may help observers of perceived wrong-doing to assess the likelihood of change and may suggest strategies for increasing that likelihood. Over the past twenty years, research findings have identified many factors predicting the decision to blow the whistle.[12] One important factor is expected effectiveness. Research has demonstrated consistently that observers of perceived wrongdoing are more strongly influenced to blow the whistle by their perception that they will be successful in getting the wrongdoing stopped than by expected retaliation.[13] But factors that affect the actual probability of terminating the wrongdoing have less frequently been explored.[14]

A fourth reason why whistle-blowing effectiveness is important is that it can improve the functioning of capital markets. At a meeting of a White House task force charged with responding to corporate accounting scandals, Federal Reserve chairman Alan Greenspan argued that wrongdoing by corporate executives had "undermined the system by which free markets allocate capital to the highest and best use." Further, in a follow-up memo, Greenspan "acknowledged that Wall Street was implicated in the accounting shenanigans. Wall Street analysts and money managers, "he wrote," put executives under increasing pressure to meet elevated and unrealistic earnings expectations. And it was Wall Street bankers who lent their good names to misleading corporate bond offerings while structuring complex financial transactions whose purpose could only have been to inflate their clients' reported income while camouflaging liabilities."[15] Subsequently, the Sarbanes-Oxley Act was passed in response to these and related concerns; some of its provisions were designed to protect and encourage valid whistle-blowing.[16]

Therefore, the purpose of this chapter is to encourage research that can ultimately identify conditions that enhance the effectiveness of whistle-blowing. In this chapter, we review theory and empirical research on the effectiveness of whistle-blowing. We discuss the implications of this work, and offer propositions for future research.

DEFINITIONS

In 1985 we defined whistle-blowing as "the disclosure by organization members (former or current) of illegal, immoral or illegitimate practices (including omissions) under the control of their employers, to persons or organizations that may be able effect action."[17] This is the most commonly used definition in the empirical literature.[18] The "disclosure" can refer to (a) an incident—the act of reporting—or (b) a process, which would include the precursors to reporting, deciding to report, reporting, and its consequences. Whistle-blowers often report problems to multiple parties, sometimes sequentially, as when internal reports are ineffective and the wrongdoing continues or worsens. Organizational change scholars have urged scholars to study changes as "continuous processes and not just detached episodes"[19] and we believe that whistle-blowing is, in most cases, an organizational change process.

We define whistle-blowing effectiveness as "the extent to which the questionable or wrongful practice (or omission) is terminated at least partly because of whistle-blowing and within a reasonable time frame."[20] This definition was derived from one of the earliest empirical findings on this question: that whistle-blowers themselves perceived the process to have been effective if they were successful in changing management's views about the wrongdoing,[21] but goes a step further; it requires corrective action on the wrongdoing itself. Similarly, the definition of effectiveness cited here differs somewhat from James Perry's definition of the related construct of "resolution." Resolution "involves whether the controversy reaches closure," which may occur "when an authoritative source inside or outside the organization vindicates the whistleblower's position and punishes wrongdoers. A variety of other scenarios are possible as well, among them that the controversy continues and the issue dissipates without any formal resolution."[22] Perry's definition seems to allow for resolution of some sort to take place (for example, if the whistle-blower agrees to stop complaining), yet wrongdoing continues. Another difference between it and our definition is that we believe that wrongdoer punishment is not central to the question of effectiveness. Rather, we are interested in consequential change of the bad practice or omission—although wrongdoer punishment could in some cases go hand-in-hand with that change.

It is important to recognize that whistle-blowing is not merely an American phenomenon; it has been documented in many cultures, including Australia,

China, Great Britain, and Japan.[23] Unfortunately, however, studies of whistle-blowing in cultures outside the United States have focused on the conditions leading to the reporting of wrongdoing; we know of no published international studies investigating the effectiveness of whistle-blowing. Therefore, we cannot say to what extent theorizing about, and empirical research examining, effectiveness based primarily on U.S. organizations and employees would be generalizable to other cultures.

The definitions of whistle-blowing and its effectiveness imply that, if organizational members believed they had sufficient power to stop perceived wrongdoing, they would not require intervention of others with this power. Therefore, whistle-blowers' effectiveness depends on their ability to influence parties who are powerful.[24] Consequently, power relationships, and whistle-blowers' views of them, are critical. In the next section we discuss how power theories can facilitate understanding of whistle-blowing effectiveness.

POWER THEORIES AND WHISTLE-BLOWING EFFECTIVENESS

A series of incidents occurring in 2003 at the public radio station WAMU in Washington, DC, provides an excellent example of the role of power in whistle-blowing and its effectiveness. WAMU, at American University, has been a Washington "institution" for more than forty years. It is the home to several programs heard all over the nation or with a strong regional following, such as *The Diane Rehm Show*, which has for years featured issues-oriented interviews and listener call-in opportunities. In late 2003, by all outward appearances, WAMU was extremely successful; a recent fund-raising drive had raised nearly $1 million, listenership was at an all-time high, and the station's executive director, Susan Clampitt, had been honored by a business magazine for her work there.[25]

But appearances were deceiving: An October 2003 story in the *Washington Post* revealed that the prior February, Rehm had conveyed employee concerns about station mismanagement, including perceived inadequate communication, questionable hiring decisions, abrasiveness in dealing with staff, and financial irregularities, to top management at the university. Yet problems continued, and employees considered escalating the concerns. Unfortunately for them, Clampitt had insisted that staff members sign confidentiality agreements to not reveal information about the station to outside parties. But Rehm had refused to sign one.[26] Obviously the popularity of her program and the respect of her audience gave her power that others did not have; the station was not about to risk losing her by forcing her to sign. But her power may not have been great enough to get top management to respond fully to all the employee concerns.

So, Rehm went on record in public to call attention to the problems and get them resolved; other employees, out of fear for their jobs, could support her only anonymously. Listeners, donors, and others were then made aware of what was happening behind the scenes, and they began to pressure the university to take action, increasing the power Rehm had. As noted in the *Washington Post*, under Clampitt, WAMU "ran large operating deficits in each of the past three fiscal years, depleting more than $4 million in cash reserves in the process. Public scrutiny of those numbers, as well as expressions of disgruntlement by WAMU staff members, led to the firing of executive director Susan Clampitt on Oct. 30."[27]

The experiences of the employees at WAMU show clearly how critical power can be to whistle-blowing effectiveness. Therefore, research on power can be helpful in understanding whistle-blowing effectiveness. Power is a property of relationships between one person and another, or one subunit of an organization and another.[28] Power is the opposite of dependency;[29] that is, if one social actor depends on a second for some resource, then the second social actor has power over the first. Various theories of power have been tested as bases for predictions about who blows the whistle and which whistle-blowers are likely to suffer retaliation.[30] The resource dependence theory of power, in particular, has been examined in past research on whistle-blowing in general and on the effectiveness of whistle-blowing specifically.[31]

Resource dependence theory holds that a social actor (such as an organization or an employee) who possesses or controls a resource needed by another social actor, has power over him or her.[32] Although power derives from situations, it depends upon people, because people control activities, have followers or subordinates, and may be members of multiple coalitions.[33] The unit of analysis can be any social actor—an individual, a group, an organization, or a larger collectivity,[34] although much of the empirical research focuses on relationships between organizations.[35]

The Power of the Whistle-Blower

Resource dependence theory posits that three key factors differentiate the power of organizational members. These three factors are (1) the hierarchical structure of organizations, (2) the specialization of labor, and (3) differences in the supply and demand for specific knowledge, skills, and abilities.[36]

The first factor emanates from the hierarchy. The hierarchical structure of organizations conveys power because greater resources are controlled at higher levels. For example, compared to a first-level supervisor, a top manager controls larger budgets, can hire and fire more important employees, and makes more strategic decisions. Therefore, power is a function of structure.[37]

The second factor is the specialization of labor. Organizations depend on certain employees who have specialized knowledge and skills that are not easily replaced,[38] rendering them influential, relative to employees with less critical human capital. These key employees have greater latitude in how they accomplish their goals, how they interact with others, and how they use resources; also, their activities are harder to monitor.[39]

The third factor is the differentiation of supply and demand. Employees supplying demanded resources are better able to benefit the organization and are therefore more powerful than those holding jobs where qualified applicants are plentiful or few openings exist.

If employees are powerful because of these three factors, they will be more powerful as whistle-blowers, and sometimes, as complaint recipients such as senior audit staff, managers, or attorneys. Further, according to agency theory, good agents, in this case top managers, are motivated primarily out of concern for the organization's welfare rather than for personal enrichment, career advancement, or some other motive that conflicts with that concern.[40] Thus, top managers who are good rather than poor agents strive to avoid alienating employees on whom the organization depends, because doing so would hurt the ability of the organization to meet its goals. Therefore, agents who hear the concerns of powerful employees may be inclined to do what they want, suggesting that more powerful employees would be more effective whistle-blowers.

Despite the theoretical support, the limited extant research shows no relationship between measures of the position power of whistle-blowers (supervisory positions, and those with higher levels of education, pay, or tenure), and whistle-blowing effectiveness.[41] This may be true because resource dependence theory also proposes that organizational power is not absolute; power normally is limited to specific types of actions and decisions in specific situations.[42] Power relationships are dynamic; dependencies are determined by interactions and the flow of information and processes.[43] Therefore, resources that have utility in one situation will not have the same utility in all situations.

The problem with any list of power resources is that it assumes the same resources have utility in all situations, and it assumes that people are able to judge the utility of all resources in all situations. If so, more effective whistle-blowers will be those who possess *relevant* power, that is, power in the specific situation surrounding the wrongdoing and whistle-blowing. For example, consider two lower-level employees for the CIA, both of whom are equally skilled in a language other than English. In the 1970s, the employee who was fluent in Russian was likely to have greater power than the employee who was fluent in Arabic; today the reverse is true. Both employees might hold the same rank and tenure with the organization, and both be equally proficient at their jobs, but the skills of one are in greater demand just now than the skills of the other, thereby giving one greater power than the other within the organization. This analysis and review of insights from research suggest the following conclusion, which needs to be tested by further research. We will call this tentative conclusion, and those that follow, "propositions."

Proposition 1: Whistle-blowers who possess greater stocks of relevant or situation-specific power will be more effective than other whistle-blowers.

Some Bases of Situation-Specific Power

Whistle-blowers may also have power because of characteristics of the specific situation, including both the wrongdoing and the nature of the organization itself. Situation-specific bases of power that we consider below include:

(a) whether whistle-blowing is role-prescribed; (b) whether the complaint is viewed as valid or meritorious; (c) whether the whistle-blower feels self-efficacious in the context of the situation; and (d) whether the whistle-blower has leverage over the wrongdoer or complaint recipient.

Role-Prescribed Whistle-Blowing

One basis of situation-specific power is the extent to which whistle-blowing is supported by the organization.[44] By definition, whistle-blowing ought to be organizationally supported when whistle-blowing is specified by the organization as being part of one's job (for example, internal auditors may be required to report financial wrongdoing). But as many whistle-blowers have learned through difficult experience, what is said and what is done is not always consistent.

A recent study showed that, in two samples, role-prescribed whistle-blowers were more effective than were non–role prescribed whistle-blowers;[45] the variable was not included in the third sample. One of these samples focused on federal employees, and the other on directors of internal auditing in a wide variety of North American organizations. In a later study of employees at a large military base,[46] role prescriptions were not significantly related to effectiveness. Therefore, future research is needed to determine whether role prescriptions matter across a wide variety of organizations and occupations or whether they are important only in certain situations, and if so, why. One possibility is as follows:

Proposition 2: Role prescriptions supporting whistle-blowing will be more strongly associated with effectiveness when they are consistent with organizational actions as well as verbalized policies, and other members of the organization agree with whistle-blowers that whistle-blowing in the situation is role-prescribed.

Valid Whistle-Blowing

Another related basis of situation-specific power is the extent to which whistle-blowing on the particular wrongdoing observed is viewed as credible or legitimate by other members of the organization. Others judge both: (a) the content or validity of the allegation itself, and (b) the process of blowing the whistle. For example, a coworker may agree with the whistle-blower that wrongdoing has occurred (that is, the content of the complaint is seen as credible, legitimate, or valid), but may believe the whistle-blower was wrong in going over his or her boss's head to complain about it. In an organization where dissent and innovation are encouraged, whistle-blowing may be viewed with less concern than in an organization where the chain of command is viewed as inviolate.

Managers who want to respond appropriately will focus primarily on the content. "Although the authenticity of a whistle-blower's complaint may be irrelevant for the organization that chooses to ignore it or to retaliate against the whistle-blower, it is clearly relevant to the organization that wishes to respond appropriately. Responsive organizations are faced with investigating the complaint to identify whether it is authentic or inauthentic."[47]

One indication of validity (albeit imperfect) is the extent to which the complaint recipient is convinced of a problem. There is little controlled research on the proportion of whistle-blowing complaints that are judged by authorities to be valid, and estimates from anecdotal sources reveal wide variations in estimates. In one study, the authors reported that "a survey[48] of more than 125 chief internal auditors concluded that 76% of employee whistleblowing complaints were found to be true."[49]

Studies of complaints filed with federal agencies reveal much lower percentages. "New federal and state legislation, such as the Truth in Lending laws, the Fair Credit Reporting Act, and the Environmental Protection Act, protected the public from illegal or unethical business practices. Many of these laws also contained provisions against reprisal for reporting violations. Although these laws appear to protect whistleblowers, a 1976 study of OSHA showed only 20 percent of the complaints filed that year were considered valid. About half of these claims were settled out of court, and of the 60 claims taken to court, only one was won."[50] The Equal Employment Opportunity Commission dismisses 90 percent of employees' charges.[51]

Such numbers are far out of line with the perceptions of employees in general, when surveyed anonymously; they may sometimes be in error, but presumably have no incentive to inflate such perceptions. For example, approximately 33 percent of 1,500 public and private sector workers surveyed by the Ethics Resource Center said they had witnessed misconduct within the past year, and nearly 75 percent of 3,075 workers surveyed by KPMG said they had seen violations of the law or company standards within the previous six months.[52] These higher percentages are consistent with estimates from large surveys of federal employees conducted by the U.S. Merit Systems Protection Board over many years,[53] and with the findings from internal auditors reported above. But they still vary widely, and there is no independent corroboration.

Taken together, these findings suggest that the validity estimates offered by some complaint recipients are low, which could be caused by many factors. Some of these are understaffing or inadequate budget in the complaint recipient's office, a wish to appear effective at preventing wrongdoing, or an unwillingness on the part of management to take complaints seriously or understand what is wrong (that is, using a "window dressing" approach rather than vigorous policies), or worse, a wish to continue to engage in wrongdoing. Obviously, rigorous research is needed to settle these questions.

One implication is that, if perceived validity varies widely, effectiveness will also vary widely because there is no need to take action if the authority does not believe wrongdoing has taken place. Where it has, if organizations are led by good agents who wish to act in the best interests of the organization, they will want to eliminate wrongdoing quickly, because it is quite costly (if for no other reasons); for example, $5 billion per year is lost due to employee theft, as is $200 to $300 billion per year in tax fraud.[54] This suggests that, the greater the agreement between complaint recipients and whistle-blowers about the wrongdoing, the more effective will be the whistle-blowing in getting it stopped. Consistent with this hypothesis, third-party verification of the complaint was related to issue resolution.[55] We would expect that this effect would be stronger when there is independent evidence of good management and maintenance of high ethical standards as part of organizational operations.

Proposition 3: In well-managed organizations and those behaviorally committed to maintaining high ethical standards, whistle-blowers will be more effective when the internal authority to whom the wrongdoing is reported agrees that the complaint's content is meritorious or valid.

The support of other third parties, such as coworkers or managers, may be important in the complaint recipient's judgment about whether the complaint is meritorious. This support may suggest legitimacy in the content of the complaint or in the process of complaining.

One factor that both persons who are not the complaint recipient and complaint recipients may use to judge this legitimacy is perceived motive. Appearing to have lofty motives may make the whistle-blower seem more credible or admirable. Unfortunately, the focus should be primarily on the evidence, because persons with bad motives may have identified wrongdoing that needs to be corrected, yet these perceived motives might obscure the validity, or others may use this as an excuse to ignore the message. Whistle-blowers who are not the target of the wrongdoing may be viewed as more credible, because their actions may be seen as less self-serving; for example, male whistle-blowers who object to discrimination or harassment against women may be respected more than if they complained on their own behalf. Even an etiquette columnist has noted that social disapproval of whistle-blowers depends on others' perceptions of motives: "[Miss Manners can] understand why innocent bystanders are indignant if the informants turn out to be wrong or motivated by less lofty impulses than those coming from the conscience. . . . Whistle-blowers who have proven to be both disinterested and correct are commended by society. Except that this tends to happen some time after they lose their jobs, their reputations and their friends."[56]

Thus, claims may be perceived as being more legitimate when evidence of wrongdoing is well documented (for example, filed audit figures that show irregularities) or corroborated by others. Consequently, we could expect whistle-blowers to be more effective under these circumstances. Whistle-blowers "perceived by coworkers as pursuing a legitimate claim by legitimate means" may be more likely to achieve resolution,[57] but no support was found for this hypothesis, perhaps because of low power due to small sample size. Alternatively, this may depend on the will of the organization's leaders to do the right thing, as noted earlier. Therefore, we propose:

Proposition 4a: In well-managed organizations and those behaviorally committed to maintaining high ethical standards, whistle-blowers will be more effective when the persons besides the authority to whom the wrongdoing is reported agree that the complaint's content is meritorious or valid.

Proposition 4b: In well-managed organizations and those behaviorally committed to maintaining high ethical standards, whistle-blowers will be more effective when they are not the target of the wrongdoing.

Whistle-Blowing Self-Efficacy

Finally, greater felt credibility or legitimacy, and hence, power, may be reflected in self-efficacy for whistle-blowing, that is, whistle-blowers' perceptions that reporting problems will get them resolved. For example, the employee who believes that telling the safety officer about a perceived hazard may not make a difference, whether because she or he is not valued by management or for any other reason, will likely be less effective than the person with higher self-efficacy.[58] Whistle-blowing self-efficacy is more narrow and specific than is general self-efficacy, which is an individual's estimate of the knowledge, skills, abilities, and motivational force that he or she can bring to bear on a specific situation.[59] Thus, we expect that the higher the self-efficacy for whistle-blowing, the more effective the whistle-blower will be in getting it stopped. Preliminary support for this proposition was found in a study of employees at a military base;[60] for reasons noted earlier, we expect this to be more pronounced depending on the will of top management. We would thus propose:

Proposition 5: In well-managed organizations and those behaviorally committed to maintaining high ethical standards, whistle-blowers will be more effective when self-efficacy for whistle-blowing is high.

Whistle-Blower's Leverage

Another basis of situation-specific power is the leverage that whistle-blowers believe they have over the parties who may be able to stop wrongdoing, that is, the complaint recipient and/or the wrongdoer.[61] A whistle-blower's leverage could arise from any number of legitimate or illegitimate sources, and may extend beyond workplace relationships. For example, a wrongdoer may be dependent because the whistle-blower is a close friend, or because she or he is bound by a norm of reciprocity[62] to return a prior favor, and may give up the wrongdoing once the whistle-blower has expressed concerns. Regardless of the source, we expect leverage to be associated with effectiveness, and preliminary evidence supportive of this proposition has been reported.[63] Once again, we would expect the effect to be more pronounced in well-managed, ethical organizations. Therefore, we predict:

Proposition 6: In well-managed organizations and those behaviorally committed to maintaining high ethical standards, whistle-blowers will be more effective when they have greater leverage.

Organizational Dependence on Wrongdoers

As noted earlier, resource dependence theory suggests that whistle-blowers possessing more resources on which the organization depends will be more effective in stopping wrongdoing. By the same token, unethical employees who possess more resources will also be powerful, and will likely have greater opportunities to use organizational resources in important and questionable ways, and to pressure others to remain silent.[64] One general implication is that the more powerful the wrongdoer, the harder it may be for the whistle-blower to get wrongdoing stopped—all other factors being equal.

The organization may depend equally on the whistle-blower and the wrongdoer, or on one more than the other, and these dependencies vary over time and situations.[65] If the organizations depend on wrongdoers, then top management may be less willing to alienate them by forcing the wrongdoing to stop, which could result in the wrongdoers' withdrawing critical resources. Or, high-level wrongdoers could be profiting from the wrongdoing and have the power to continue it. For example, Enron's chairman of the board, Kenneth Lay, seemingly ignored the initial warnings of the whistle-blower, Sherron Watkins, because of the power of the CEO, Jeffrey Skilling, who was allegedly the primary wrongdoer.[66] Perry predicted that "involvement of the dominant coalition in the target incident" would be negatively associated with whistle-blowing issue resolution, but this hypothesis was not supported in his sample.[67] Once again, however, this may have resulted from small sample size or other factors. Therefore:

Proposition 7: Whistle-blowers will be more effective when wrongdoers are exclusively in lower levels of the hierarchy.

Organizational Dependence on the Wrongdoing

In addition, organizations may become dependent on certain processes, activities, or operations.[68] Because the organization depends on resources from the external environment for survival, it may also depend on continuation of the wrongdoing as a way to gain resources from the environment. For example, an organization may use illegal behavior to reduce its dependence on other organizations in its environment.[69] Organizations that depend on continuation of the wrongdoing for their own survival are unlikely to terminate the wrongdoing when confronted with the evidence. If we assume that organizations are rational[70] or "risk averse" in the terms of agency theory,[71] they normally would not engage in risky behavior (for example, serious wrongdoing) that could lead to embarrassment or costly sanctions unless they had a vital need or compelling reason to do so.[72] We expect that organizations would not engage in "material" wrongdoing (that is, costly) or long-term "entrenched" wrongdoing unless top management considered it critical for the organization's survival.

Material Wrongdoing

The term "material" may be defined as "sufficiently important to influence decisions made by reasonable users of financial statements."[73] If an organization chooses to engage in material wrongdoing, then the benefits of engaging in the risky behavior may be perceived by managers to outweigh its costs.[74]

Some research has shown that the organization's dependence on continuation of the wrongdoing itself, as reflected in the perceived materiality of wrongdoing, is negatively related to whistle-blowing effectiveness.[75] This may occur because top management believes that the organization's survival depends upon the wrongdoing, or because the opportunity for wrongdoing and its consequent benefits is too attractive to forgo. Similarly, another study found that when greater change was "required by the whistleblower's claims," the issue was less likely to be resolved.[76] However, in a more recent study, no relationship was found, which could suggest once again that top management leadership is critical.[77] In better-managed organizations whose leadership expects the highest ethical standards, serious or material wrongdoing may occur simply because top management is not aware it is occurring, and there may be zero tolerance for all wrongdoing and hence a willingness to correct it once management learns of it. In organizations where ethical standards are not so high, managers may depend on material wrongdoing and be loath to give it up. In those situations, whistle-blowing is unlikely to be effective. Therefore, we predict that:

Proposition 8: In organizations committed to maintaining high ethical standards, whistle-blowing will be effective regardless of the materiality of the wrongdoing; in other organizations, whistle-blowers will be less effective when wrongdoing is material or serious.

Entrenched Wrongdoing

Resource dependence theory suggests that when organizations (or individuals) become too dependent on a single supplier of important resources, the source gains power over them. When organizations engage in practices that are illegal or unethical, because they benefit the organization in some way, a similar situation occurs. Organizations that tolerate practices that improve profits, at least temporarily, become increasingly dependent upon them (for example, Enron's refusal to discontinue questionable accounting practices because this would hurt its financial performance). Organizational survival sometimes depends on continuing the wrongdoing,[78] and it becomes fully entrenched in the organization culture, and thus it is harder for whistle-blowers to get changes made. In contrast, whistle-blowers were more effective when wrongdoing had occurred for a shorter period of time.[79] Results consistent with this reasoning have been found in one study.[80] We would expect this result to be more pronounced depending on the extent to which organizations are well managed and ethical. Therefore, we predict that:

Proposition 9: In well-managed organizations and those behaviorally committed to maintaining high ethical standards, whistle-blowing effectiveness will not depend on wrongdoing entrenchment; in other organizations, whistle-blowers will be more effective when wrongdoing is less entrenched.

IMPLICATIONS FOR WHISTLE-BLOWERS AND MANAGERS

The basic premise of resource dependence theory is that organizations are dependent on a number of social actors for needed resources. In whistle-blowing cases, we proposed that situation-specific power of the whistle-blower would be positively related to whistle-blowing effectiveness, because a powerful whistle-blower would be better able to persuade an organization to terminate wrongdoing or because the organization's top managers, as good agents, would be concerned with alienating powerful and needed whistle-blowers.

We would hope that top managers, as ethical agents, would also be concerned with wrongdoing reported by less powerful whistle-blowers, but this may not be the case. As agents charged with defending the organization, they may focus first on the most powerful whistle-blowers or wrongdoers, or on continuation of wrongdoing that seems to help the organization more than it harms it; in other words, they may give greater strategic attention to those resources on which they depend most. Unfortunately, there is very little research on whistle-blowing effectiveness, and a primary purpose of this paper is to offer research propositions in the hope that more research will be completed.

One implication of existing research on effectiveness is that prospective whistle-blowers should consider what bases of power they may possess, either over the wrongdoer (if an individual can be identified) or over the potential complaint recipient. Research on random samples of organizational members (as opposed to self-selected, extreme cases that tend to be reported in the media or are better known) shows that the most typical organizational response to the whistle-blower is to ignore him or her.[81] Findings from a recent study suggest that whistle-blowers who have some form of power or leverage, even perhaps something like knowing a family secret that the target does not want revealed, can help the whistle-blower's voice be heard.[82] Future research could explore these bases of power or leverage to determine which are the most valuable and useful to possess.

Research has also shown that the more that wrongdoing is entrenched, the more resistant the organization is to correcting it, once reported. One implication of this finding is that organizational leaders who are sincere about preventing and stopping wrongdoing should take steps to ensure that they are not satisfied with making minor changes to correct small problems. When important problems are identified, more resources must be devoted to taking the whistle-blowers' concerns seriously and finding ethical and managerially sound alternatives to the current operations.

IMPLICATIONS FOR PUBLIC POLICY

To encourage organizations to be more responsive, policy-makers may want to consider more incentives for correction. They should consider enforcing greater penalties for noncompliance or nonresponsiveness when problems are serious or of a greater magnitude.

Another implication for public policy is that laws should be designed to enhance whistle-blower power in cases where allegations of wrongdoing seem to be valid. State and federal legislators have generally assumed that potential whistle-blowers could be encouraged to speak out if they were protected from retaliation, by law. In fact, changes in the law have not necessarily increased the incidence of whistle-blowing.[83] Many factors, including the lack of "teeth" in the laws protecting whistle-blowers, have been identified.[84] Legal changes should be focused on these factors, including providing incentives to organizations to respond quickly to whistle-blowers and imposing penalties on those who continue wrongdoing after being alerted.

A major change in U.S. law was made by the Sarbanes-Oxley corporate reform law, which provided federal statutory protection to some private sector whistle-blowers. However, as of this writing, only three whistle-blowers have received a favorable judge's ruling since the Sarbanes-Oxley Act took effect in 2002, according to one plaintiff's lawyer.[85] Whether this act will help whistle-blowers be more effective should be examined empirically.

Future research should consider other bases of whistle-blowers' situational power and organizational dependence on the wrongdoers and wrongdoing. Further, causal directions could be explored, but it is very difficult to establish causality in research of this type. For example, when whistle-blowers report that they have suffered retaliation (for example, demotion) because of the whistle-blowing, it is difficult to know whether they are correct or whether the negative action occurred because of poor performance. Often it is difficult to apply the most rigorous research methods to the study of whistle-blowing, but we believe that the importance of the topic requires that researchers strive to study it, as rigorously as is feasible.

CONCLUSION

Researchers have focused considerable attention on two issues: What causes employees who observed organizational wrongdoing to blow the whistle, and what causes organizations to retaliate against the whistle-blower? Less empirical attention has been paid to an equally important question: Under what conditions is whistle-blowing most likely to be effective? As seen with the prison scandal in Iraq, whistle-blowers who somehow get the message out effectively have much greater impact on the organization than those who do not. When the "message" is "heard," organizations often respond quickly to terminate their wrongdoing. When the message is buried, and the whistle-blower discredited, the wrongdoing may continue unabated. Research directed toward examining the role of power relationships—and especially the organization's dependence on the whistle-blower, the wrongdoer, and continuation of the wrongdoing—may help elucidate the conditions that increase whistle-blowing effectiveness. Finally, we strongly urge policy-makers to consider how to encourage organizations to be more responsive to valid whistle-blowing complaints—to fix the problem rather than focus on the whistle-blower. We hope this review will help with that process.

NOTES

This chapter's writing was supported in part by the Robert H. Steers Faculty Research Fellowship at the McDonough School of Business, Georgetown University, and by the

Coleman Chair Fund at the Kelley School of Business, Indiana University. We thank the editors for their helpful comments on an earlier version of this chapter.

1. Hanna Rosin (2004, May 17), When Joseph comes marching home, *Washington Post*.

2. Seymour M. Hersh (2004, May 10), Torture at Abu Ghraib, *New Yorker*, 42.

3. Ibid.

4. Seymour M. Hersh (2004, May 17), Chain of command, *New Yorker;* Seymour M. Hersh (2004, May 24), The gray zone, *New Yorker*.

5. Mike Allen (2004), *Ex-US military chief blasts Pentagon* (*The Age*, cited May 25), available from http://www.theage.com.au/articles/2004/05/24/1085389332276.html; Stephanie Armour (2004), *Women say Wal-Mart execs knew of sex bias* (*USA Today*, cited June 25), available from http://news.yahoo.com/news?tmpl=story&cid=677&u=/usa today/20040625/bs_usatoday/womensaywalmartexecsknewofsexbias&printer=1; Mat thew Barakat (2004, May 6), Whistle-blower wins claim against Atlantic Coast Airlines, *Washington Post,* (transportation); D. Bash and T. Frieden (2002), *FBI agent blows whistle on Moussaoui probe* (cited May 23), available from www.CNN.com/US; Paula Dwyer et al. (2002, December 16), Year of the whistleblower: The personal costs are high, but a new law protects truth-tellers as never before, *Business Week,* (tobacco); Charles Haddad and Amy Barrett (2002, June 24), A whistle-blower rocks an industry, *Business Week,* (pharmaceuticals); Paul Krugman (2004, June 15), Travesty of Justice, *New York Times;* Richard Lacayo and Amanda Ripley (2002, December 22), Persons of the Year, 2002: Cynthia Cooper, Coleen Rowley, and Sherron Watkins, *Time,* (telecommunications).

6. T. D. Miethe (1999), *Whistle-blowing at work: Tough choices in exposing fraud, waste, and abuse on the job*, Boulder, CO: Westview Press; T. D. Miethe and J. Rothschild (1994), Whistleblowing and the control of organizational misconduct, *Sociological Inquiry, 64*.

7. Marcia P. Miceli and Janet P. Near (1992), *Blowing the whistle: The organiza- tional and legal implications for companies and employees*, ed. Arthur P. Brief and Benjamin Schneider, *Issues in organization and management*, New York: Lexington; Marcia P. Miceli et al. (1999), Can laws protect whistle-blowers? Results of a naturally occurring field experiment, *Work and Occupations, 26* (1); Miethe, *Whistle-blowing at work*, cited above.

8. U.S. Merit Systems Protection Board (1981), Whistle-blowing and the federal employee, Washington, DC: U.S. Government Printing Office.

9. James R. Van Scotter et al. (2004), What difference can one person make? Organizational dependence relations as predictors of whistle-blowing effectiveness, *International Journal of Knowledge, Culture and Change Management*.

10. Terry Morehead Dworkin and Elletta Sangrey Callahan (2004), *The mouth of truth*, Bloomington, IN.

11. William De Maria (1997), The British whistleblower protection bill: A shield too small? *Crime, Law, and Social Change, 27* (2); Dworkin and Callahan, *The mouth of Truth*, cited above; Miceli et al., Can laws protect whistle-blowers? See note 7.

12. Miceli and Near, *Blowing the whistle*, see note 7; Marcia P. Miceli et al. (2001), Individual differences and whistle-blowing, paper presented at the 61st Annual Meeting of the Academy of Management, Best Paper Proceedings, Washington, DC.

13. U. S. Merit Systems Protection Board, Whistle-blowing and the federal employee.

14. James L. Perry (1992, August), The consequences of speaking out: Processes of hostility and issue resolution involving federal whistleblowers, paper presented at the Academy of Management, Las Vegas; Van Scotter et al., What difference can one person make? See note 9.

15. Steven Pearlstein (2004, June 23), Fed approval of bank merger ignores record," *Washington Post.*

16. Dwyer et al., Year of the whistleblower; see note 5.

17. Marcia P. Miceli and Janet P. Near (1997), Definition of "whistle-blowing," in *The Blackwell encyclopedic dictionary of human resource management*, ed. Lawrence H. Peters, Charles R. (Bob) Greer, and Stuart A. Youngblood, *The Blackwell encyclopedia of management*, Oxford, UK: Blackwell Publishers; Janet P. Near and Marcia P. Miceli (1985), Organizational dissidence: The case of whistle-blowing, *Journal of Business Ethics, 4, 4.*

18. Granville King, III (1997), The effects of interpersonal closeness and issue seriousness on blowing the whistle, *Journal of Business Communication, 34* (4).

19. Andrew M. Pettigrew, Richard W. Woodman, and Kim S. Cameron (2001), Studying organizational change and development: Challenges for future research, *Academy of Management Journal, 44* (4), 697.

20. Near Miceli, Organizational dissidence, 681.

21. J. P. Near and T. C. Jensen (1983), The whistle-blowing process: Retaliation and perceived effectiveness, *Work and Occupations, 10.*

22. Perry, The consequences of speaking out (note 14), 311.

23. Marcia P. Miceli and Janet P. Near, Stopping organizational wrongdoing: What price do whistle-blowers pay? In *Managing social and ethical issues in organizations*, ed. Stephen W. Gilliland, Dirk D. Steiner, and Daniel P. Skarlicki; *Research in social issues in management*, Greenwich, CT: Information Age Publishing, under review.

24. Perry, The consequences of speaking out; James L. Perry (1993), Whistle-blowing, organizational performance, and organizational control, in *Ethics and public administration,* ed. H. George Frederickson, *Bureaucracies, public administration, and public policy,* Armonk, NY: M. E. Sharpe.

25. Jennifer Frey (2003, October 20), At WAMU, deficits of money and morale; public radio station in turmoil amid changes, *Washington Post.*

26. Ibid.

27. Jennifer Frey (2003, October 31), American U. ousts WAMU director Susan Clampitt, *Washington Post.*

28. S. Clegg and D. Dunkerley (1980), *Organization, class, and control,* London: Routledge and Kegan Paul.

29. R. E. Emerson (1962), Power-dependence relations, *American Sociological Review, 27.*

30. Miceli Near, *Blowing the whistle,* see note 7.

31. Jeffrey Pfeffer and Gerald R. Salancik (1978), *The external control of organizations,* New York: Harper & Row.

32. Ibid.

33. Gerald R. Salancik and Jeffrey Pfeffer (1977), Who gets power and how they hold on to it: A strategic-contingency model of power, *Organizational Dynamics, 5*(3).

34. Emerson, Power-dependence relations, note 29.

35. Pfeffer and Salancik, *External control of organizations,* note 31.

36. Ibid.

37. Jeffrey Pfeffer (1981), *Power in organizations*, Marshfield, MA: Pitman.

38. Pfeffer and Salancik, *External control of organizations*.

39. M. C. Jensen and W. H. Meckling (1976), Theory of the firm: Managerial behavior, agency costs, and ownership structure, *Journal of Financial Economics, 3*.

40. Kathleen M. Eisenhardt (1989), Agency theory: An assessment and review, *Academy of Management Review, 14*.

41. Marcia P. Miceli and Janet P. Near (2002), What makes whistle-blowers effective? Three field studies, *Human Relations, 55*(4); James L. Perry (1991), *The organizational consequences of whistleblowing*, Bloomington: Indiana University Press; Van Scotter et al., What difference can one person make? Note 9.

42. G. Salancik and J. Pfeffer (1978), A social information processing approach to job attitudes and task design, *Administrative Science Quarterly, 23*.

43. Clegg Dunkerley, *Organization, class, and control*, note 28; and ibid.

44. Perry, The consequences of speaking out, note 14.

45. Miceli and Near, What makes whistle-blowers effective? See note 41.

46. Van Scotter et al., What difference can one person make? See note 9.

47. Perry, The organizational consequences of whistleblowing (note 41), 12.

48. J. Figg (2000), Whistleblowing, *Internal Auditor, 57*.

49. A. A. Tavakoli, John P. Keenan, and B. Crnjak-Karanovic (2003), Culture and whistleblowing: An empirical study of Croatian and United States managers utilizing Hofstede's cultural dimensions, *Journal of Business Ethics, 43, 62*.

50. Lilanthi Ravishankar (2004), *Encouraging internal whistleblowing in organizations*, website, cited October 1, available at http://www.scu.edu/ethics/publications/submitted/whistleblowing.html

51. Albert R. Karr (1998, December 15), New EEOC chairwoman Ida Castro's first meeting, *Wall Street Journal*.

52. Kirstin Downey Grimsley (2000, June 14), Office wrongdoing common, *Washington Post*.

53. Miceli et al., Can laws protect whistle-blowers? See note 7.

54. Miethe, *Whistle-blowing at work*, note 6.

55. Perry, The consequences of speaking out, note 14.

56. Judith Martin (2004, June 27), Let's hear it for the rats, *Washington Post*, D6.

57. Perry, The consequences of speaking out, 313.

58. Van Scotter et al., What difference can one person make? Note 9.

59. A. Bandura (1989), Human agency in social cognitive theory, *American Psychologist, 44*.

60. Van Scotter et al., What difference can one person make?

61. Ibid.

62. Alvin W. Gouldner (1960), The norm of reciprocity, *American Sociological Review, 25*.

63. Van Scotter et al., What difference can one person make? Note 9.

64. Janet P. Near and Marcia P. Miceli (1995), Effective whistle-blowing, *Academy of Management Review, 20*.

65. Van Scotter et al., What difference can one person make?

66. Jennifer Frey (2002, January 25), The woman who saw red: Enron whistle-blower Sherron Watkins warned of the trouble to come, *Washington Post*.

67. Perry, The consequences of speaking out (note 14), 311–312.

68. Pfeffer and Salancik, *external control of organizations*, note 31.

69. Ibid.

70. J. D. Thompson (1967), *Organizations in action*, New York: McGraw-Hill.

71. Jensen and Meckling, Theory of the firm, note 39.

72. Van Scotter et al., What difference can one person make?

73. O. Ray Whittington et al. (1992), *Principles of auditing*, 10th ed., Homewood, IL: Irwin, 47.

74. Near and Miceli, Effective whistle-blowing, note 64.

75. Miceli and Near, What makes whistle-blowers effective? Note 41.

76. Perry, The consequences of speaking out, 311–312.

77. Van Scotter et al., What difference can one person make?

78. Melissa S. Baucus and David A. Baucus (1997), Paying the piper: An empirical examination of longer-term financial consequences of illegal corporate behavior, *Academy of Management Journal, 40*; Melissa S. Baucus and Janet P. Near (1991), Can illegal corporate behavior be predicted? An event history analysis, *Academy of Management Journal, 34.*

79. Miceli and Near, What makes whistle-blowers effective?

80. Van Scotter et al., What difference can one person make?

81. Miceli and Near, *Blowing the whistle*, see note 7.

82. Van Scotter et al., What difference can one person make?

83. Terry Morehead Dworkin and Janet P. Near (1997), A better statutory approach to whistle-blowing, *Business Ethics Quarterly, 7*(1); Terry Morehead Dworkin and Janet P. Near (1987), Whistle-blowing statutes: Are they working? *American Business Law Journal, 25*(2); Miceli et al., Can laws protect whistle-blowers?

84. Dworkin and Callahan, The mouth of truth.

85. Barakat, Whistle-blower wins claim against Atlantic Coast Airlines.

REFERENCES

Allen, M. (2004). Ex-U.S. military chief blasts Pentagon. http://www.theage.com.au/articles/2004/05/24/1085389332276.html (accessed May 25).

Armour, S. (2004). Women say Wal-Mart execs knew of sex bias. http://news.yahoo.com/news?tmpl=story&cid=677&u=/usatoday/20040625/bs_usatoday/womensaywalmartexecsknewofsexbias&printer=1 (accessed June 25).

Bandura, A. (1989). Human agency in social cognitive theory. *American Psychologist, 44*, 1175–1184.

Barakat, M. (2004, May 6). Whistle-blower wins claim against Atlantic Coast Airlines. *Washington Post*, 04.

Bash, D., and Frieden, T. (2002). FBI agent blows whistle on Moussaoui probe. www.CNN.com/US (accessed May 23).

Baucus, M. S., and Baucus, D. A. (1997). Paying the piper: An empirical examination of longer-term financial consequences of illegal corporate behavior. *Academy of Management Journal, 40*, 129–151.

Baucus, M. S., and Near, J. P. (1991). Can illegal corporate behavior be predicted? An event history analysis. *Academy of Management Journal, 34*, 9–36.

Clegg, S., and Dunkerley, D. (1980). *Organization, class, and control.* London: Routledge & Kegan Paul.

De Maria, W. (1997). The British whistleblower protection bill: A shield too small? *Crime, Law, and Social Change, 27* (2), 139–163.

Dworkin, T. M., and Callahan, E. S. (2004). *The mouth of truth.* Bloomington, IN.

Dworkin, T. M., and Near, J. P. (1997). A better statutory approach to whistle-blowing. *Business Ethics Quarterly, 7* (1), 1–16.

Dworkin, T. M., and Near, J. P. (1987). Whistle-blowing statutes: Are they working? *American Business Law Journal, 25* (2), 241–264.

Dwyer, P., Carney, D., Borrus, A., Woellert, L., and Palmeri, C. (2002, December 16). Year of the whistleblower: The personal costs are high, but a new law protects truth-tellers as never before. *Business Week,* 106.

Eisenhardt, K. M. (1989). Agency theory: An assessment and review. *Academy of Management Review, 14,* 57–74.

Emerson, R. E. (1962). Power-dependence relations. *American Sociological Review, 27,* 31–41.

Figg, J. (2000). Whistleblowing. *Internal Auditor, 57,* 30–37.

Frey, J. (2003, October 31). American U. ousts WAMU director Susan Clampitt. *Washington Post,* C.01.

Frey, J. (2003, October 20). At WAMU, deficits of money and morale; Public radio station in turmoil amid changes. *Washington Post,* A.01.

Frey, J. (2002, January 25). The woman who saw red: Enron whistle-blower Sherron Watkins warned of the trouble to come. *Washington Post,* C1, C8.

Gouldner, A. W. (1960). The norm of reciprocity. *American Sociological Review, 25,* 161–178.

Grimsley, K. D. (2000, June 14). Office wrongdoing common. *Washington Post,* E02.

Haddad, C., and Barrett, A. (2002, June 24). A whistle-blower rocks an industry. *Business Week,* 126–130.

Hersh, S. M. (2004, May 17). Chain of command. *New Yorker,* 38.

Hersh, S. M. (2004, May 24). The Gray Zone. *New Yorker,* 38.

Hersh, S. M. (2004, May 10). Torture at Abu Ghraib. *New Yorker,* 42.

Jensen, M. C., and Meckling, W. H. (1976). Theory of the firm: Managerial behavior, agency costs, and ownership structure. *Journal of Financial Economics, 3,* 305–360.

Karr, A. R. (1998, December 15). New EEOC chairwoman Ida Castro's first meeting. *Wall Street Journal,* 1.

King, G., III. (1997). The effects of interpersonal closeness and issue seriousness on blowing the whistle. *Journal of Business Communication, 34* (4), 419–436.

Krugman, P. (2004, June 15). Travesty of justice. *New York Times,* A23.

Lacayo, R., and Ripley, A. (2002, December 22). Persons of the year, 2002: Cynthia Cooper, Coleen Rowley, and Sherron Watkins. *Time* (online).

Martin, J. (2004, June 27). Let's hear it for the rats. *Washington Post,* D06.

Miceli, M. P., and Near, J. P. (1992). *Blowing the whistle: The organizational and legal implications for companies and employees.* Ed. Arthur P. Brief and Benjamin Schneider, *Issues in organization and management.* New York: Lexington.

Miceli, M. P., and Near, J. P. (1997). Definition of "whistle-blowing." In *The Blackwell encyclopedic dictionary of human resource management.* Ed. Lawrence H. Peters, Charles R. (Bob) Greer, and Stuart A. Youngblood. Oxford, UK: Blackwell.

Miceli, M. P., and Near, J. P. (Under review). Stopping organizational wrongdoing: What price do whistle-blowers pay? In *Managing social and ethical issues in organizations.* Ed. Stephen W. Gilliland, Dirk D. Steiner, and Daniel P. Skarlicki. Greenwich, CT: Information Age Publishing.

Miceli, M. P., and Near, J. P. (2002). What makes whistle-blowers effective? Three field studies. *Human Relations,* 55 (4), 455–479.

Miceli, M. P., Rehg, M., Near, J. P., and Ryan, K. (1999). Can laws protect whistle-blowers? Results of a naturally occurring field experiment. *Work and Occupations,* 26 (1), 129–151.

Miceli, M. P., Van Scotter, J. R., Near, J. P., and Rehg, M. T. (2001). Individual differences and whistle-blowing. Paper presented at the 61st Annual Meeting of the Academy of Management, Best Paper Proceedings, Washington, DC.

Miethe, T. D. (1999). *Whistle-blowing at work: Tough choices in exposing fraud, waste and abuse on the job.* Boulder, CO: Westview Press.

Miethe, T. D., and Rothschild, J. (1994). Whistleblowing and the control of organizational misconduct. *Sociological Inquiry,* 64, 322–347.

Near, J. P., and Jensen, T. C. (1983). The whistle-blowing process: Retaliation and perceived effectiveness. *Work and Occupations,* 10, 3–28.

Near, J. P., and Miceli, M. P. (1995). Effective whistle-blowing. *Academy of Management Review,* 20, 679–708.

Near, J. P., and Miceli, M. P. (1985). Organizational dissidence: The case of whistle-blowing. *Journal of Business Ethics,* 4, 1–16.

Pearlstein, S. (2004, June 23). Fed approval of bank merger ignores record. *Washington Post,* E01.

Perry, J. L. (1992, August). The consequences of speaking out: Processes of hostility and issue resolution involving federal whistleblowers. Paper presented at the Academy of Management, Las Vegas.

Perry, J. L. (1991). *The organizational consequences of whistleblowing.* Bloomington: Indiana University Press.

Perry, J. L. (1993). Whistleblowing, organizational performance, and organizational control. In *Ethics and public administration.* Ed. H. George Frederickson. Armonk, NY: M. E. Sharpe, 79–99.

Pettigrew, A. M., Woodman, R. W., and Cameron, K. S. (2001). Studying organizational change and development: Challenges for future research. *Academy of Management Journal,* 44 (4), 697.

Pfeffer, J. (1981). *Power in organizations.* Marshfield, MA: Pitman.

Pfeffer, J. and Salancik, G. R. (1978). *The external control of organizations.* New York: Harper & Row.

Ravishankar, L. (2004). Encouraging internal whistleblowing in organizations. http://www.scu.edu/ethics/publications/submitted/whistleblowing.html (accessed October 1).

Rosin, H. (2004, May 17). When Joseph comes marching home. *Washington Post,* 01.

Salancik, G., and Pfeffer, J. (1978). A social information processing approach to job attitudes and task design. *Administrative Science Quarterly,* 23, 224–253.

Salancik, G. R., and Pfeffer, J. (1977). Who gets power and how they hold on to it: A strategic-contingency model of power. *Organizational Dynamics,* 5 (3), 3–21.

Tavakoli, A. A., Keenan, J. P., and Crnjak-Karanovic, B. (2003). Culture and whistleblowing: An empirical study of Croatian and United States managers utilizing Hofstede's cultural dimensions. *Journal of Business Ethics, 43,* 49–64.

Thompson, J. D. (1967). *Organizations in action.* New York: McGraw-Hill.

U.S. Merit Systems Protection Board. (1981). *Whistle-blowing and the federal employee.* Washington, DC: U.S. Government Printing Office.

Van Scotter, J. R., Miceli, M. P., Near, J. P., and Rehg, M. T. (2004). What difference can one person make? Organizational dependence relations as predictors of whistle-blowing effectiveness. *International Journal of Knowledge, Culture and Change Management.*

Whittington, O. R., Pany, K., Meigs, W. B., and Meigs, R. F. (1992). *Principles of auditing.* 10th ed. Homewood, IL: Irwin.

Managing Conflicts of Interest

MANUEL VELASQUEZ and KIRK O. HANSON

Concern with the concept of conflict of interest—in business, government, and other sectors of American life—has increased dramatically in recent years. One cause is a series of business scandals that emerged in 2001 and 2002, and the resulting passage on July 30, 2002, of the Sarbanes-Oxley Act. This law, designed to address several of the perceived causes of the scandals, includes a number of rules explicitly addressing conflicts of interest among analysts, auditors, and issuers of financial statements. Critics of business and government regularly criticize the web of conflict of interest that they believe contaminate governance and decision-making. The concept of "conflict of interest" has become widely used in business, government, and in the media in recent years. So familiar and well known is the concept that when it is used in newspapers and other popular media, it is assumed there is no need for explanation or definition (for example, Bogdanich, 2002). This chapter examines the concept of conflict of interest, which we believe will so strongly influence our understanding of ethics in all aspects of American life in coming years.

Codes of ethics of virtually every professional society—including those of physicians, lawyers, accountants, and engineers—have long included provisions that address conflicts of interest, as have almost all business or corporate codes of conduct (Boatright, 2000). In spite of its wide currency, however, the term "conflict of interest" is of very recent coinage, having first been used in a legal case only in 1949. It did not appear in English dictionaries until 1971, nor in *Black's Law Dictionary* until 1979 (Davis, 1998).

Because the term is so new, it is not surprising that there is no standard or widely accepted definition. *Black's Law Dictionary*, for example, defines conflict of interest as "a real or seeming incompatibility between one's private interests and one's public or fiduciary duties" (Garner, 2001), while the AICPA Code of Professional Conduct states that "a conflict of interest may occur if a member performs a professional service for a client or employer and the member or his or her firm has a relationship with another person, entity, product, or service that could, in the member's professional judgment, be viewed by the client, employer, or other appropriate parties as impairing the member's objectivity" (Wells, Jones and Davis, 1986). Analytical discussions of the term conflict of interest have also failed to come to an agreement regarding its proper definition (Aronson, 1977; Boatright, 1992, 1993, 2000; Carson, 1994; Davis, 1982, 1993; Luebke, 1987, 1993; Margolis, 1979). Contributors to this discussion have agreed that "perhaps no other ethical concept in business is so elusive and subject to dispute" (Boatright, 2000, p. 142; Luebke, 1993, p. 47).

Because of its presence in virtually all corporate codes of conduct being written today, and because of its rising importance in recently adopted legislation governing business, it is important that managers have a clear understanding of the nature of conflicts of interest and the primary methods of managing conflicts when they arise.

After briefly citing trends that make conflict of interest such a concern in 2005, we chronicle the development to date the concept of a conflict of interest, distill a definition of conflict of interest that, we believe, is useful to managers and to those who want to incorporate the notion into their company codes of conduct. We conclude with a discussion of various ways of managing conflicts of interest, some of which are regularly cited in the literature and others we have encountered and implemented in our work as consultants.

WHY THE INCREASED CONCERN ABOUT CONFLICT OF INTEREST?

This examination of the concept of conflict of interest begs the question why conflict of interest is such a preoccupation in the first decade of the twenty-first century. We believe there are several explanations.

First, the sheer size of the conflicting interests that agents have in the modern economy and in modern government dwarf the interests encountered in earlier decades. Agents manage million and even billion-dollar pools of assets. Purchasing agents buy goods by the millions and even billions of dollars. The personal wealth to be skimmed off by minor manipulations for one's own interest exceed anything seen before. Because the stakes are higher, we certainly ought to be more concerned about conflict of interest.

Second, agents in the modern economy are often distant from the principals they serve. The typical American in 2005 deals with financial institutions in distant cities rather than their local bank. Retirement funds are managed by big

New York financial institutions for Midwest workers. Small corporations are represented by agents in distant and even global markets. As distance grows, loyalty and oversight decline. A focus on conflicts of interest serves as a prophylactic measure.

Third, a growing contemporary distrust of institutions has created demands for transparency where none existed before. There is much greater pressure for disclosure of federal government processes, Wall Street fee structures, and even how Little League teams are formed. As transparency uncovers many heretofore unknown conflicts of interest, there is greater pressure to control them. This has led to a growing intolerance for conflicts and "old boy" relationships that might have been tolerated before.

Fourth, an American culture that devalues loyalty and encourages a "me-first" mentality, we believe, has caused agents to exploit their conflicts of interest more frequently. If you aren't taking a bit on the side for yourself, some cynics argue, you are a fool. If the board and shareholders are so lax in their oversight, then the management is foolish if it does not line its own pockets a bit. This trend is exacerbated by the weakening of the traditional pillars of American loyalty and morality—church, family, community, and government leadership. Pastors abuse their parishioners. Children abuse their parents. Elected officials abuse the public trust. In this environment, one can feel a fool for not putting me first.

A BRIEF HISTORY OF CONFLICT OF INTEREST

The concept of a conflict of interest is relatively modern (Luebke, 1987). The term itself does not appear in standard English dictionaries until the late 1960s and early 1970s, and those first early entries limit conflicts of interest to government contexts. *Blacks's Law Dictionary*, which contained no reference to the term until 1979, asserted at that time that the term is "used in connection with public officials and fiduciaries" and that the term "refers to a clash between public interest and the private pecuniary interest of the individual concerned" (1979; cited in Luebke, 1987). If the authority of *Black's Law Dictionary* is accepted, then at least as recently as 1979, conflicts of interest were restricted to "public officials and fiduciaries" and required the presence of a "pecuniary" or financial interest. Doctors, then, who are neither public officials nor fiduciaries, could not have a conflict of interest in relation to their patients, nor could a nonfinancial interest (such as a friendship) provide the basis for a conflict of interest.

Neil Luebke, who has reviewed and studied American court decisions in his study of this term, was unable to find any use of the term "conflict of interest" in any court decision prior to 1949 (Luebke, 1987). In these early uses of the term, as *Black's Law Dictionary* confirms, the only kind of "interest" that could give rise to a conflict of interest was what is now called an "objective" interest, that is, a financial interest or ownership of a business or other property

(Manning, 1964). What was specifically excluded is a so-called "subjective" interest, that is, a feeling such as friendship or affection toward a person that might bias the judgment of a decision-maker.

Today, of course, the term conflict of interest is no longer limited to the field of government—nor to just pecuniary interests. Use of the term has gradually expanded to apply not only to government figures and legal fiduciaries, but also to members of the legal profession, and then to members of the other professions—and finally to anyone who serves as an agent for another party including, of course, managers and officers of corporations. What has remained unchanged throughout this history of expansion, however, is the underlying idea that the term conflict of interest was developed to point to the potential for harm that arises from misuses of the power with which certain socially constructed—and so voluntarily assumable—roles are endowed.

Moreover, the definition of the kind of interest that can give rise to a conflict of interest has also seen a gradual expansion. From being limited to the purely pecuniary or material gains that arise from equity or financial interests, the concept of a conflict of interest has been expanded so that today any kind of familial relationship—by blood or marriage—and any type of subjective interest—such as affection, friendship, love, hatred, and ideology—can be seen as giving rise to a conflict of interest. A judge, for example, who is a friend to one of the parties to a dispute will today be said to have a conflict of interest that disqualifies her from serving as judge in that dispute. A recent hunting trip by U.S. vice president Richard Cheney with Supreme Court justice Antonin Scalia gave rise to an active debate over whether their long-standing friendship—or the recent hunting trip—created a conflict of interest for Scalia, who was scheduled to rule on matters involving the vice president.

DEFINING CONFLICTS OF INTEREST

Roughly speaking, conflicts of interest occur when a person who has agreed to serve the best interests of another party has an interest that he can affect—favorably or unfavorably—by the decisions he makes on behalf of the party he has agreed to serve. Conflicts of interest occur, that is, when one person, who has voluntarily assumed an obligation to serve another party, has another interest related to the service he is obligated to provide that may conflict with the interests of the party he has agreed to serve. Not all conflicts that may arise between the interests of two individuals, however, are considered conflicts of interest. We do not usually consider it a conflict of interest when a parent, for example, has an interest in saving his money for retirement, but must also make decisions about how much to spend on the education of his child. So what is a conflict of interest?

Although it is easy to characterize a conflict of interest in the very general terms we used in the preceding paragraph, it is nevertheless not as easy to provide an exact definition of the concept. A fairly recent, and widely quoted definition of the term, is provided by Michael Davis who writes: "A person has a conflict of interest if a) he is in a relationship with another requiring him to exercise judgment in that other's service, and b) he has an interest tending to interfere with the proper exercise of judgment in that relationship" (Davis, 1993).

The key terms in Davis's definition are "relationship," "judgment," "interest," "interfere," and "proper exercise." By *relationship,* here Davis means a fiduciary relationship, that is, a relationship in which one person trusts another to serve him in some manner. By *judgment* Davis is referring to decision-making that requires the use of one's "knowledge, skill, and insight" in a manner that is not routine or mechanical. The *interest* that can *interfere* with a person's *proper* exercise of judgment can be financial, psychological, or familial and so can include spousal relationships, ownership, friendship, love, hatred, gratitude, or any other influence that can bias a person's judgment.

According to Davis, whether an exercise of judgment under conditions of a conflict of interest is proper or not depends on what people or a specific group of people ordinarily expect, or what certain laws, regulations, or rules require. Finally, Davis argues that the interest must have a "tendency to interfere," which suggests it is strong enough to tempt the agent to use his judgment so as to favor his own interest.

For Davis, conflicts of interest are prohibited mainly because they have a "tendency" to lead to decisions that are of a lower quality than decisions made without a conflict of interest. In his words, when I am under a conflict of interest, "I may not be as good a judge of such things as I would otherwise be" and so my decision is "less reliable than it would otherwise be" (Davis, 1982) and there is "an unusual risk of error." For Davis a conflict of interest is not a situation in which the decision-maker falls short on some sort of moral scale, but one in which the decision-maker's judgment falls short on some scale of "correctness." A person with a conflict of interest is more likely to make an incorrect judgment than one without such a conflict.

This analysis, we believe, is flawed to the extent that it rests on the idea that a conflict of interest requires that the agent actually make incorrect judgments. We and other observers have come to believe there can be a conflict of interest even if the agent manages to make correct judgments. A purchasing agent has a conflict of interest if he decides to purchase supplies from a company that he personally owns and does so because he wants to profit from the purchase. But if the company he owns in fact is one of several that offer the best product at the best price, then his judgments on behalf of his employer may not fall short on any scale of correctness or harm to his employer. Nonetheless, he is still encumbered by a clear and blatant conflict of interest. Though his judgments are "correct" in one sense, his evaluation of the quality of his is that product, and his judgment about the correctness of his decisions may be significantly skewed by his perspective and interest. Carl Kotchian, Lockheed's president in the 1970s, who made payments to Japanese officials to ensure sale of the L1011, argued his actions were not morally flawed because the L1011 was indeed the superior plane.

Decisions made while subject to a conflict of interest are, we believe, wrongful decisions in themselves, but they are not necessarily "incorrect." We will argue below, and we believe public attitudes toward conflict of interest reinforce, that conflicts of interest are wrong because they involve a moral failure of trust. In a conflict of interest, one party places his trust on another party, and the person who has a conflict of interest violates that trust even if he makes decisions that are "correct."

Neil Luebke attempts to improve on Davis by offering a definition of conflict of interest that, unlike Davis's, is focused on the notion of trust and not on the issue of the correctness of particular decisions. He argues that more than mere judgment can be affected by a conflict of interest. According to Luebke, a conflict of interest "exists when the existence or quality of a voluntary fiduciary relationship is threatened" because "the fiduciary party has an interest which is adverse or likely to become adverse to that matter or cause for which reliance was initially placed" (Luebke, 1987). By a "fiduciary party" Luebke means "any party in whom trust or reliance is reposed for the purpose of advising, aiding, acting on behalf of, or protecting the interest of another party" and who "voluntarily" agreed to accept that trust. An interest is "adverse" when it "might bias advice given, might influence efforts to aid or protect, or might lead to still other results contrary to the purpose of the relationship" (ibid.). Correcting Davis, Luebke notes that "it is not necessary for there to be an actual clash of two opposed interests. It is necessary that the direct or indirect interest of the fiduciary actually or potentially threatens the fiduciary relationship" (ibid.).

For Luebke, the essential element in a conflict of interest is not an impaired judgment, but the violation of a trust relationship. A conflict of interest is a situation in which a relationship of trust is threatened, and to so threaten a fiduciary relationship is wrong. Like the definition found in early editions of *Black's Law Dictionary*, Luebke's definition fails to include situations in which a person has a conflict of interest with respect to a client with whom he does not have a fiduciary relationship (a doctor, for example, is not the fiduciary of his patients, but can nevertheless have a conflict of interest if, say, the doctor owns stock in a company that makes a medication he may consider prescribing for patients).

We believe Luebke is correct, however, in stressing that conflicts of interest arise only where an agent has voluntarily assumed an obligation to serve his client. As we noted above, it seems to us that evolution of the concept of conflict of interest shows that it was developed to deal with those socially constructed and voluntarily assumable roles in which the person assuming the role has the power to harm the parties he or she is supposed to serve. These socially constructed roles—including those of judge, lawyer, physician, accountant, manager, and so on—are distinguishable from what we might call "natural" roles, such as the role of "father" or "daughter."

John Boatright provides yet another, and broader, definition of conflict of interest that improves on Luebke in several ways. He writes:

> A conflict of interest may be described as a conflict that occurs when a personal interest interferes with a person's acting so as to promote the interest of another, when the person has an obligation to act in that other person's interest. This is equivalent to asserting that a conflict of interest arises when a personal interest interferes in the performance of an agent's obligation to a principal.

Rejecting Luebke's attempt to confine conflict of interest to fiduciary relationships, Boatright claims conflicts of interest can arise in any agent-principal relationship in which the agent has an obligation to act in the principal is interests. Boatright argues, correctly in our view, that fiduciary relationships are too "narrowly defined" to be able to cover all the kinds of relationships in which real conflicts of interest can arise. A person can have a conflict of interest if the person has an obligation to act on behalf of another party, even if the person is not a fiduciary of that other party. We believe, also, that Boatright is correct in his claim that a conflict of interest can arise in any relationship in which one person serves as an agent for another. Boatright's analysis also differs from Davis's insofar as he focuses not just on judgments but on all actions undertaken on behalf of another person's interests.

Boatright's analysis, however, repeats a mistake that is made by the other definitions we have examined. Boatright claims that the conflicting interest of the agent has to "interfere" with the agent's pursuit of the principal's interests. But this need not be the case, since, as we've seen, conflicts of interest can exist when an agent is intent on pursuing his own interest, even if in doing so he manages to also secure the client's interests. Boatright, like Davis, implies that a conflict of interest requires actual harm to the interests of his principal, and this, we believe, is too narrow a concern. We believe that a person can have a conflict of interest even if there is no likelihood whatsoever that the person will harm the interests of her client. There is no necessary connection between the infliction of actual harm and the existence of a conflict of interest. It is our view that a conflict of interest exists when there exists a certain constellation or structure of relationships, whether or not the structure results in any harm.

Boatright and others provide a useful definition of a potential conflict of interest in a way that includes situations that have not yet necessarily risen to the level of actual conflicts. Suppose a person is the purchasing agent for a company and that person has an ownership interest in a vendor. If the company is currently not purchasing the type of material produced by the company owned by the purchasing agent, and if it is not known when, if ever, the company will begin purchasing such materials again, there is no current conflict of interest. The agent is not currently making any of the kinds of decisions that can actualize the conflict he potentially faces. Such an agent does not yet have a conflict of interest: There is only the potential for the occurrence of a conflict. Under such situations of potential conflict of interest, it is clearly prudent to be aware of the financial and familial interests of a business's agents, but no conflict of interest exists until the agents' roles and responsibilities intersect and conflict with their own interests.

Let us summarize this discussion. First, we have argued that Boatright is correct in his claim that conflicts of interest can arise wherever an agent has an obligation to serve the interests of a principal, and that Luebke is correct in stressing that such obligations are voluntarily assumed. The concept of conflict of interest, we have claimed, suggests that it was developed to deal precisely with such socially constructed roles. Second, we have argued that a conflict of interest does not require that the agent actually do anything that is detrimental to his client. Instead, we have argued, a conflict of interest exists and ought to be of concern when the agent has an interest that he or she can choose to serve, and serving that interest can, but need not, result in harm to the client. Third, we have argued that a conflict of interest requires that the agent actually be involved in making those particular judgments or engaging in those actions in which he is obligated to seek the interests of the client. Putting these considerations together, we can define a conflict of interest as a situation in which:

(A) An agent has an obligation voluntarily undertaken to act in the interests of a principal by performing certain actions and judgments on behalf of the principal (a "role").

(B) The agent has an interest such that the actions or judgments he performs for the principal can be based on whether they serve the agent's interest, instead of whether they serve the best interests of the principal (an "interest").

(C) The agent carries out some of the actions or judgments noted in (A), and he does so while having the interest noted in (B); (an "action").

We hope this definition makes the following points clear. First, conflicts of interest can arise in any agent-principal relationship in which the agent has voluntarily assumed an obligation to serve the interests of his principal. The concept helps us examine whether socially constructed roles with power are protected from risks to those the role was constructed to benefit. Second, the interests that can give rise to a conflict of interest situation can be of many types, including monetary interests, relational interests based on familial or friendship ties, or ideological interests based on commitments to particular ideas or judgments. Third, what makes an interest rise to a conflict of interest is its *potential* role in the agent's decision-making, not the existence of any actual harm to the principal's interests. If an agent can base his decisions on whether they serve his own interest instead of on whether they serve the principal's interest, then the agent has a conflict of interest, even if he does not in fact substitute his own interest for that of his principal's and even if he does not actually harm the principal's interests.

Our definition, then, characterizes a conflict of interest as a structure of relationships: A conflict of interest is a situation in which those relationships identified in (A), (B), and (C) exist together. And the key element of a conflict of interest is the potential substitution of one interest—the agent's—for another—the principal's.

DIFFERENT KINDS OF CONFLICTS OF INTEREST

There are a number of important distinctions that discussions of conflict of interest policies have developed and that are important to our understanding of the concept. We have expanded on those mentioned in the existing literature to identify the following distinctive types:

Impersonal Conflicts and Personal Interests

In the typical conflict of interest situation, a conflict exists between the obligation of an agent to serve the interests of his client and the agent's own interests. However, in some conflict of interest situations, the conflict is not between the interests of the agent and those of his client; instead the conflict is between the interests of two of the agent's clients when the agent is obligated to serve both. For example, a financial services firm may have an investment banking arm retained to sell a new stock issue for a client company. The same firm may also have a brokerage arm that recommends investments in the interest of private investors. The firm can serve the interests of the client company by pushing inappropriate investments on its private investors. These conflicts between the interests of two principals, both of whom the agent is obligated to serve, are sometimes called "impersonal conflicts" in the literature, to distinguish them from the typical cases in which the conflict is between the interests of the agent and those of the principal, which are called "personal conflicts."

It is helpful to keep in mind that conflicts can also arise between two personal interests of the same person. We each have obligations to our spouses to save money for retirement, but may also have obligations to our children to give them the best education we can, and we have obligations to our aging parents at the same time that we have obligations to ourselves and our children. There can even be conflicts among the competing moral obligations of a single individual. We can be said to have a moral obligation to our own families' welfare as well as to the poor of the world. Such moral conflicts are often called "competing claims" and are not generally included in definitions of conflict of interest.

Actual and Potential Conflicts of Interest

An actual conflict of interest exists when all three elements of our definition of a conflict of interest are present: (1) a person is serving as an agent for a party whose interests the agent has an obligation to serve, (2) the agent has an interest that can lead him to base his decisions for the principal on that interest, (3) the agent is actually involved in making decisions that bring this conflict into play.

In a potential conflict of interest, the first two of these elements are present, but the third is not: The agent is not yet involved in actually making decisions on behalf of the principal. The concept of potential conflict of interest is important because it can aid in the selection of agents and encourage for timely disclosure of new conflicts. If one is hiring a purchasing agent for office supplies, it may be irrelevant that the individual has many investments in medical device companies. However, if one is hiring a hospital purchasing agent for medical devices, even though at the moment the hospital is not purchasing the specific type of medical devices made by the companies he has invested in, it may be wise to require divestiture or to select another agent. The broader the official's responsibilities, the higher the potential for conflict of interest. Presidents of the United States may influence almost any investment, and therefore, usually put their investments in a blind trust or entirely in government bonds.

Real and Apparent Conflicts of Interest

In a real conflict of interest, all three of the elements required for a conflict of interest are present. In an "apparent" conflict of interest, one or more of the three elements are absent, and so there is no real conflict of interest. Nevertheless, some observers have a reason for believing (wrongly) that all three elements are present.

The concept of apparent conflicts of interest is important because the ultimate purpose of conflict of interest provisions is to both protect the interests of the principals or the public and to establish a substantial degree of trust between the agent and the principals or other parties affected. If the clients of a company perceive the company or its agents to have a conflict of interest, this is an important issue whether the conflict is real or apparent. If the public perceives the officials in a presidential administration to have conflicts due to their long-standing involvement in the defense industry, for example, the trust necessary for the conduct of government may be undermined.

Sometimes information may lessen the perception of a conflict. Sometimes the perception exists only among a fringe group known to believe that no businessperson, Republican, or clergyman can be trusted. When a perception is either widely held or is held by a constituency important to the organization, it may require action.

Strong and Weak Conflicts of Interest

Not all conflicts are as significant or strong as others. To manage conflicts effectively, it is important to distinguish between strong and weak conflicts of interest. Generally, the greater the monetary benefit an individual may derive from exploiting a conflict of interest, the stronger a conflict is considered to be. And generally, the closer the relationship or the greater the impact on a family member or close friend, the greater the conflict is considered to be. Some observers suggest measuring the level of motivation or temptation to exploit the conflict of interest. If a purchasing agent can earn hundreds of thousands of dollars in kickbacks for picking a particular vendor, the motivation is obviously strong. If a CFO has a high salary, a weeklong vacation with an investment banker seeking his business may not constitute a strong motivation to pick that bank. If a purchasing agent has a much lower salary, then a weeklong vacation may constitute a substantial motivation. The problem with measuring motivation, of course, is that some organizations have used the argument to permit top executives to accept lavish gifts prohibited to lower-level employees.

Conflicts of Interests Involving a Public Trust, a Private Trust, and a Personal Trust

Concern for conflicts of interest is generally heightened in government or quasi-government settings. Public conflicts of interest involve roles or activities in which the agent is a government official and so is supposed to make decisions that serve the *public trust*. Private conflicts of interest are those in which the agent is making decisions on behalf of a business corporation or private organization, and so is serving a *private trust*. Some would argue that conflicts of interest in public charities that benefit from tax exemptions, or even "public companies" owned by thousands of shareholders, are hybrid cases. The agent is acting on behalf of so many, and there is limited opportunity for the public or those shareholders to influence the acts of the company. We believe there is a third category in which an individual takes on a role to act as agent for a single individual, for example, as guardian of his children or executor of his estate. Actions by the agent here serve a *personal trust*.

Individual, Organizational, and Systemic Conflicts of Interest

It is useful to distinguish between conflicts of interest that exist at different levels of aggregation. In an *individual conflict of interest*, the conflict is between the personal interests of an individual agent and the interests of that agent's client.

In an *organizational conflict of interest*, the conflict is between the interests of a company for whom the employee works and the interests of the parties the company serves. The individual agent cannot resolve such a conflict by disclosure or resignation of his role.

In a *systemic conflict of interest*, the conflict arises out of a feature that is part of the structure of an industry, and so the conflicts afflict all companies in the industry to a greater or lesser degree. Until recently, a significant conflict of interest existed in the health care industry because doctors were permitted to own medical laboratories and could refer their own patients to those labs for more and more tests. Legislation now prohibits this type of ownership. Another systematic conflict of interest in health care exists because the doctor and patient determine their treatment, whereas the insurance companies pay the bills. The doctor has had conflicting obligations to serve the patient and her wishes, but also to hold down the cost of medical care in the interests of all.

Pecuniary, Relationship, and Ideological Conflicts of Interest

As noted earlier in this chapter, there are significant differences between the types of interests that may conflict with an agent's role. The differences among them may lead to different managerial responses to them. Among the types of interests are:

1. *Pecuniary.* Monetary interests and material incentives are always easier to identify and measure, and so have traditionally been called "objective interests."

2. *Relationship.* Familial obligations or friendship ties create conflicts and pressures that can be significant. However, these interests can be difficult to identify and measure, and of course may change with marriages, divorces, and estrangements. These have traditionally been called "subjective interests."

3. *Ideological.* When agents are called upon to make decisions on behalf of principals, they are expected to make balanced judgments based on the facts of the particular case. If an agent has an unalterable preference for a particular type of solution, a tendency to rely solely on a particular type of data (for example, to always believe the policeman over the criminal), or a commitment to one particular ideological approach to a problem, they have an ideological conflict of interest that will interfere with their role.

HOW CONFLICTS OF INTEREST ARE MANAGED

Given our understanding of the structure and types of conflicts of interest, what conclusions can we draw about how they might be managed? The literature on conflicts of interest identifies several ways of managing these situations (Stark, 2000). We have expanded significantly on prior formulations in our list of remedies that follows.

To understand how conflicts of interest can be managed, recall that a conflict of interest consists of three elements: (A) an agent who has voluntarily undertaken an obligation to act in the interests of a principal by performing certain actions and judgments on behalf of the principal ("a role"); (B) the agent has an interest such that the actions or judgments he performs for the principal can be based on whether they serve the agent's interest instead of whether they serve the best interests of the principal ("an interest"); and (C) the agent carries out some of the actions or judgments noted in (A), and he does so while having the interest noted in (B) ("an action"). If our theory is correct, then we can predict that conflicts of interest can be avoided or extinguished in three ways: (A) by eliminating or adjusting the role, (B) by eliminating or adjusting the interest, or (C) by eliminating or adjusting the action. It turns out that all of the standard ways of avoiding or extinguishing conflicts of interest fall into one of these three categories:

(A) Methods of managing conflicts of interest by eliminating or adjusting the role that is involved.

1. Avoidance of the role/resignation from the role. If conflicts of interest are wrong, then, above all, they should be avoided. A conflict of interest is avoided when an agent perceives that a role he is about to take on conflicts with a personal interest, and he simply decides not to take on the role. It is also possible that a new personal interest may arise, for example, wherein his spouse now works for a company, which creates a conflict for him. In cases where a new interest arises or is discovered, he may resign from the role to eliminate the conflict.

2. Compartmentalizing conflicting roles. A company that has taken on roles that are inherently conflicting, such as financial services firms that manage IPOs and also advise private investors, may wish to continue in both roles. In such cases, some firms have attempted to create what are known as Chinese walls, separating the company employees engaged in the two activities. Under such an arrangement, employees engaged in one activity are not permitted to share information with another group in the same company. Similarly, the compensation systems for the two groups are kept separate and focused on their specific obligations to their principals.

3. Redesigning the agent's role. In some organizations the decision-making authority of the agent is redesigned to make conflicts of interest less likely or to weaken the conflict of interest by having it influence only one of several votes on a particular matter. Some matters are "bumped upstairs" to be made by a higher official. Other matters are referred for decision to existing or newly created committees where the official with the conflict of interest has only one vote among many or is there solely in an advisory role. In decisions involving millions of dollars or significant impacts, multiple decision-makers or committees are often used. The purchase of aircraft or other big-ticket items are generally not left to a single decision-maker, given the potential for bribery or conflicting interest. The launch of nuclear missiles has always required the concurrence of at least two independent decision-makers pressing separate buttons.

(B) Methods of managing conflicts of interest by eliminating or adjusting the interest involved:

1. Avoidance of the interest/divestiture of the interest. An individual may also divest herself of the personal interest that creates the conflict. She may also have the opportunity to refuse the interest by avoiding particular investments or concurrent offices offered. Her spouse may choose to turn down or resign from a post that creates a conflict for her. Certain interests, however, cannot be divested. It may not be possible to deal with a familial relationship, an ideological commitment, or a significant emotional attachment by divestiture of the interest.

2. **Forfeiture of benefits from the personal interest.** In some extraordinary cases, the interests held by the agent cannot be divested and cannot effectively be placed in a blind trust. In such cases, special arrangements have been made to forfeit any benefits deriving from the interest during the term of the official. David Packard, one of the two cofounders of the Hewlett-Packard Company, served as deputy secretary of state during the Nixon administration. He owned so much of HP's stock that it could not be divested without harming the other shareholders. Congress permitted him to keep the stock, provided that he agreed to forfeit all dividends and all increases in the value of his stock during his government service.

3. **Permitting limited conflicts of interest.** In some cases, conflicts of interest are simply tolerated as long as the interest is limited. Some organizations permit employees to hold investments that constitute conflicts of interest as long as no investment is greater than $1,000. Purchasing agents are allowed to take gifts up to $100 or entertainment up to certain limits from vendors. These limits are established to strike a balance between the legitimate purpose of permitting employees to make whatever investments they wish or encouraging interaction between vendors and purchasing agents, and the dangers of conflicts of interest that exist.

4. **Permitting limited benefit from conflict of interest.** In a certain type of case, organizations have authorized employees to "take advantage" of the agent's interest, as long as the personal benefit is limited. Modest entertainment on a business trip may often be charged to an expense account as a reward for making the trip. Companies may permit personal use of office computers, copiers, and other equipment as long as it does not become "excessive." In one interesting case, a university, recognizing the conflicting roles of maintaining fair admissions but also courting potential donors, authorized the university president to fill a small number of places in the freshman class, no questions asked. This arrangement persisted for many years, but was then abandoned.

5. **Blind trust.** In place of full divestiture, the agent may decide instead to place his pecuniary interests in a trust that is managed in a manner that is not disclosed to him. While the agent may retain the interests, he is blind as to how his decisions will affect those interests and so cannot be influenced by those interests. In a blind financial trust, common for senior government officials, trustees make investment decisions during the time the official serves in office, and the official is blind to what investments are being held in his account.

(C) Methods of managing conflicts of interest by eliminating or adjusting the action involved:

1. **Recusal from judgments affected by the conflict of interest.** In some cases the conflict of interest arises in one type of judgment, but not in others. If the husband of a college professor is being considered for tenure in her de-

partment, she may resolve the conflict of interest by not participating in meetings or votes discussing her husband's case. Recusal, however, is not always possible. A conflict of interest may exist for a majority of the decisions to be made by the agent, but there is no one else to make the decision. In such a case, other measures may be called for. It should also be noted that one form of recusal used by some officials, that is, letting a subordinate make the decision, is generally indequate. The hierarchical relationship makes it impossible for the subordinate to be completely objective in making the decision.

2. **Watchdog review of decisions.** In some cases it may be adequate to have a higher or independent authority review some or all of the decisions of an official to assure that an existing conflict interest has not tainted those decisions. In some companies the decisions of midlevel officials who have a conflict of interest are routinely reviewed and approved by one or more levels of management above them.

There is one important method of managing conflicts of interest that does not appear in the list above: the method of disclosure. In some conflict of interest situations it is not possible for the agent to step out of the role in which the conflict of interest arises, nor is it possible for the agent to eliminate the interest through divestiture, and the principal is forced to continue to rely on the services of the agent. In such cases it is sometimes asserted that the conflict of interest can be eliminated by having the agent disclose the existence of the conflict to the principal. We disagree. According to our theory, a conflict of interest exists so long as the three elements of role, interest, and action are present, and since disclosure does not eliminate any of these three, then disclosure cannot eliminate a conflict of interest. How, then, does disclosure work? To understand how disclosure serves to ameliorate a conflict of interest, we must first understand the ethics of conflicts of interest. We contend that disclosure does ameliorate a conflict of interest, but it does so by addressing the ethical objections to a conflict of interest, not by eliminating it.

THE ETHICS OF CONFLICTS OF INTEREST

From an ethical point of view, the concept of conflict of interest is a puzzling one. Ethical norms generally prohibit conduct that inflicts injuries or harms on others. But as we have noted above, conflicts of interest may inflict harms or injuries on no one—but simply have the potential to do so. In a typical conflict of interest situation, an agent has an obligation to make decisions for the benefit of another party, but that agent can benefit personally if he makes one decision rather than another. A purchasing agent who has an obligation to evaluate and purchase those supplies that best meet the needs of his employer may fulfill that ethical obligation by ignoring his own interest as part owner of a potential supplier. He may buy the products of another vendor, or he may buy the products of the company he owns because he is convinced his company's products provide better value.

In these cases the agent is in a conflict of interest situation, yet he arguably inflicts no harm on the party he is obligated to serve. Why is it still unethical simply to enter into a conflict of interest situation?

We believe (as lawyers have long claimed) that the prohibition on conflict of interest is primarily a prophylactic measure. Seen as a prophylactic or preventive matter, it is unethical to enter conflict of interest situations, not because conflicts of interest inflict injuries, but because an agent is knowingly embracing an incentive to inflict injury on the party he is obligated to serve. The aim of conflict of interest prohibitions, then, is to prevent all situations in which the agent will have this incentive to do something that could injure the party he is supposed to serve. This agent may be able to set aside his personal interest, at least for the moment, but the "typical" agent will not.

But this merely pushes the issue one step backward. Now we may ask: Why prohibit entering the conflict situation (thereby indirectly avoiding the potential injury) instead of more directly and proximately prohibiting the agent from inflicting the injury? What is the ethical justification for prohibiting the person from entering a situation in which he may be tempted to harm the party he is supposed to serve?

There are, we believe, two main kinds of rationales for elevating the prophylactic prohibition to an ethical obligation. The first is a utilitarian justification, and the second a deontological justification (Velasquez, 2003). The utilitarian justification is based on the idea that over the long run, less harm is likely to be produced if agents are prohibited from entering conflict of interest situations than if they are merely prohibited from pursuing their self-interests once they are in a conflict of interest situation. First, if agents are allowed to enter into conflict of interest situations, then it is likely that they will frequently give in to the incentive to pursue their own interests. Such harms will be eliminated if agents are simply never allowed to enter into such at-risk situations.

Second, if agents are allowed to enter into such situations, then the institution of agency will itself be undermined since it would always be possible that one's agent was subject to an incentive to harm one's interests. This would lead to a lack of trust in the agency relationship that would lead to its disuse, and subsequently to a loss of the utility from the institution. Third, while it is possible to effectively prohibit agents from entering conflict of interest situations, it is virtually impossible to effectively prohibit agents from basing their decision on whether they benefit themselves rather than by basing them on whether they benefit the best interests of the party one is supposed to serve. It is virtually impossible for others, or even the agent himself, to *know* whether or not his decision is actually based on the incentive or on his obligation to serve his principal, or whether it has been influenced by selective and unconscious bias toward his personal interest. Consequently, more harm will be avoided by a rule that prohibits what can effectively be prohibited than by a rule that attempts to prohibit something that even the agent himself cannot be cognizant of.

The other major rationale for prohibiting agents from entering conflict of interest situations is a deontological rationale that derives from the expectations of the party that the agent undertakes to serve. A person who retains an agent to act on his behalf does so with the expectation that there is no reason to suspect that the agent he retains has an interest that can conflict with the interests of the principal. An agent who is in a conflict of interest situation is therefore involved in a deception. By agreeing to serve as the agent of that person, the agent has led the other party to trust him to make his decisions on the basis of whether those decisions are in the principal's best interests and so has led that party to think that the agent can serve him fully and objectively and is not influenced by an interest that can potentially become the basis for the decisions the agent is supposed to be making for the principal. Indeed, the principal would certainly not have retained the agent if that principal thought that the agent had an interest that could become the basis of the decisions the agent makes.

A conflict of interest, then, involves three deontological wrongs. First, it involves a deception insofar as the principal is led to believe that the agent is not encumbered by a conflicting interest. Second, it involves a betrayal of trust because the agent led the principal to trust him to conduct himself in a certain manner—that is, unencumbered with any conflicting interests—and the agent knowingly failed to maintain that trust. And, third, it involves a dereliction of duty because the agent has a duty to base his decisions solely on the interests of the principal and to have no other interests that can serve as the basis for his decisions. Because deception, betrayal, and dereliction of duty are wrong, it is also wrong for the agent to enter a conflict of interest situation with respect to a party he is obligated to serve.

We noted above that although disclosure is sometimes proposed as a way of eliminating conflicts of interest, it is our view that disclosure is better understood as a way of dealing with the ethical concerns that underlie the prohibitions of conflicts of interest. Disclosure is sometimes recommended as a way of managing a conflict of interest because it is assumed that if the agent discloses the conflict to the principal, and the informed principal then freely consents to have the agent continue to serve as his or her agent, then the conflict of interest no longer exists. But in reality, the conflict continues to exist because the three elements—role, interest, and action—continue to exist. Disclosure does, however, eliminate the potential deception and betrayal of trust that generally accompany conflicts of interest and that underlie the ethical objections to conflicts of interest. By eliminating the potential for deception and betrayal, the conflict of interest—which disclosure does not eliminate—is tamed. If the conflict is weak or insoluble, then disclosure may be the most practical—and the only effective remedy. In such cases, disclosure can assure that an agent will not be influenced by a conflicting interest because the vigilance of the principal will be heightened. In some other cases, however, the principal may have no choice but to rely on the services of the agent because of the agent's unique competence. In these cases, disclosure may not be inadequate because the consent of the principal, being forced, may not be real.

Conflict of interest regulations have often not only prohibited real conflicts of interest, but have also prohibited the mere appearance of a conflict of interest. If it is difficult to understand why real conflicts of interest situations are wrong, it is even more difficult to understand why it should be wrong for a person to enter an apparent but not real conflict of interest. How can it be justified to prohibit something that is merely apparently wrong and so not really wrong? How can it be wrong for a person to do something that is merely apparently wrong and not really wrong?

Again, the history of conflict of interest rules in politics are revealing. Political officials are prohibited from entering situations in which they would appear to the public to be subject to a conflict of interest because such appearances have the effect of undermining the trust the public has in their office. Because officials have a duty to serve and protect the legitimacy of the office they serve, they have an obligation to avoid those actions that might undermine that legitimacy, and so they have an obligation to avoid the mere appearance of a conflict of interest.

Does this rationale apply also to business managers? Clearly, the officials of a corporation have a fiduciary duty to serve the interests of stockholders. But do they have an obligation to serve and protect the legitimacy of the office they hold? We believe there are some situations in which they certainly do have such an obligation. The trustee of a bank, for example, has an obligation to preserve the trust of the bank's clients, since the bank relies on the trust of its clients and such trust, in turn, rests in part on the trust they place on the officers of the corporation and the role they play in overseeing the safety of the assets of the bank. In these and other similar cases, the officers of a corporation clearly have an obligation to avoid even the appearance of a conflict of interest, since even the appearance of a conflict of interest can undermine the trust that the corporation requires to survive.

CONCLUSION

We believe the identification and management of conflicts of interest will remain a significant concern in business, government, medicine, and all other areas of American life for the foreseeable future. The challenge is to identify the specific type and severity of a conflict and the most effective remedy for it.

There are dangers in both overreacting and underreacting to concerns over conflicts of interest. An overreaction can produce significant regulatory costs and constraints on the efficient workings of all our institutions. Not taking the issue seriously enough can contribute to the declining confidence in all our institutions—a future that will involve even greater costs.

REFERENCES

Aronson, R. H. (1977). Conflict of interest. *Washington Law Review, 58,* 807–858.

Boatright, J. (1992). Conflict of interest: An agency analysis. In *Ethics and agency theory: An introduction.* Ed. Norman E. Bowie and R. Edward Freeman. New York: Oxford University Press, 187–203.

Boatright, J. (1993, winter). Conflict of interest: A response to Michael Davis. *Business and Professional Ethics Journal, 12,* 43–46.

Boatright, J. (2000). *Ethics and the conduct of business.* 3rd ed. Upper Saddle River, NJ: Prentice-Hall.

Carson, T. L. (1994). Conflict of interest. *Journal of Business Ethics, 13,* 387–404.

Davis, M. (1982, summer). Conflict of interest. *Business and Professional Ethics Journal, 1,* 17–27.

Davis, M. (1993, winter). Conflict of interest revisited. *Business and Professional Ethics Journal, 12,* 21–41.

Davis, M. (1998). Conflict of interest. *Encyclopedia of applied ethics.* Vol. 1. Academic Press, 589–595.

Garner, B. A., ed. (2001). Conflict of interest. *Black's Law Dictionary.* 2nd pocket ed. St. Paul, MN: West Group.

Hanson, K. (2003). Discussions and conversations conducted during 2003.

Luebke, N. R. (1987, spring). Conflict of interest as a moral category. *Business and Professional Ethics Journal, 6,* 66–81.

Luebke, N. R. (1993, winter). Response to Michael Davis. *Business and Professional Ethics Journal, 12,* 47–50.

Manning, B. (1964). *Federal conflict of interest law.* Cambridge, MA: Harvard University Press.

Margolis, J. (1979). Conflict of interest and conflicting interests. In *Ethical theory and business.* Ed. Tom L. Beauchamp and Norman B. Bowie. Englewood Cliffs, NJ: Prentice-Hall.

Stark, A. (2000). *Conflict of interest in American political life.* Cambridge, MA: Harvard University Press.

Wells, P., Jones, H., and Davis, M. (1986). *Conflicts of interest in engineering.* Dubuque: Kendall/Hunt Publishing.

Index

About the Editors and Contributors

Marc J. Epstein is Distinguished Research Professor of Management, Jones Graduate School of Management, Rice University, and was recently Visiting Professor and Hansjoerg Wyss Visiting Scholar in Social Enterprise at the Harvard Business School. Previously, he held positions at Stanford Business School and INSEAD (the European Institute of Business Administration). A specialist in corporate strategy, governance, performance management, and corporate social responsibility, he is the author or co-author of over 100 academic and professional papers and a dozen books, including *Implementing E-Commerce Strategies* (Praeger, 2004); *Counting What Counts: Turning Corporate Accountability to Competitive Advantage*; and *Measuring Corporate Environmental Performance: Best Practices for Costing and Managing an Effective Environmental Strategy*, recipient of the AAA/AICPA Notable Contributions to Accounting Literature Award. A senior consultant to leading corporations and governments for over 25 years, he currently serves as Editor-in-Chief of the journal *Advances in Management Accounting*.

Kirk O. Hanson is Executive Director of the Markkula Center for Applied Ethics and University Professor of Organizations and Society at Santa Clara University. In 2001, he retired from the Stanford University Graduate School of Business, where he served in a variety of teaching, research, and administrative capacities over 23 years. A specialist in ethical behavior of corporations, he writes and presents regularly on the subject. He was the founding president of the Business Enterprise Trust, a national organization created by leaders in business, labor, media, and academia to promote exemplary behavior in business; the first chairman of the Santa Clara County Political Ethics Commission; and has written a weekly column for the *San Jose Mercury News*. He has served on the boards of a variety of organizations, including the Social Venture Network, the Entrepreneurs' Foundation, and American Leadership Forum Silicon Valley.

Seb Beloe is the Director of Research and Advocacy at SustainAbility. He co-founded SustainAbility's U.S. practice and has consulted to a wide range of companies (Nike, Pfizer, Shell), NGOs (Greenpeace, WWF-UK) and multi-laterals (IFC, UNEP) on corporate responsibility issues. He also writes regularly for a variety of publications, including *Environmental Finance* and *Humanitarian Affairs Review*, and speaks at major international conferences on corporate responsibility issues. His most recent publication was *Influencing Power: Reviewing the Conduct and Content of Corporate Lobbying*, co-authored with Jodie Thorpe.

Jean J. Boddewyn is Professor of Marketing and International Business, and Coordinator of the International Business Program, in the Zicklin School of Business of Baruch College, City University of New York. His current research interests center on business political behavior, public affairs, the regulation and self-regulation of advertising around the world, international business strategy, and competitive dynamics. He received the 2002 Academy of Management's Distinguished Service Award in recognition of his service as Editor of *International Studies of Management & Organization* since 1971; his pioneering research on comparative management, foreign divestment, and international business government relations; and his leadership roles as an early Chair (1974) of the AOM's International Management Division, and as Vice President (1975–1976) and President (1993–1994) of the Academy of International Business. He is a Fellow of the Academy of International Business, the Academy of Management and the International Academy of Management.

Steven N. Brenner is Professor Emeritus at the School of Business Administration at Portland State University. His areas of expertise are in business ethics, corporate social responsibility, government relations, stakeholder theory, and corporate strategy.

Aron Cramer is President and CEO of Business for Social Responsibility (BSR). Prior to assuming this post, he was based in Paris, where he launched BSR's European office in 2002. He also led the establishment of BSR's Hong Kong office in 2001. Mr. Cramer joined BSR in 1995, and served as the founding director of its Business and Human Rights Program. He has worked closely with dozens of BSR's member companies in numerous industry sectors, providing advice and counsel on the full spectrum of CSR issues, including Ford Motor Co., ChevronTexaco, Nike, Unilever, Royal Dutch/Shell, Novartis, Novo Nordisk and Rio Tinto. Cramer also has provided support and counsel to many of the leading CSR initiatives in recent years, including the UN Global Compact, the Global Reporting Initiative, the Voluntary Principles on Security and Human Rights, and the Fair Labor Association. He has worked extensively with the World Bank, the U.S. Agency for International Development, and other public institutions. He speaks frequently before industry audiences and in other fora, and has been widely quoted in media outlets, including the *New York Times*, *Los Angeles Times*, National Public Radio and others. In 2004, he co-edited *Raising the Bar,* a publication providing guidance on implementation of the UN Global Compact principles.

John Elkington A co-founder and Chair of SustainAbility, based in London, San Francisco, Washington, D.C., and Zurich, John Elkington is a leading authority on sustainable development and triple bottom line business strategy. His latest book was *The Chrysalis Economy: How Citizen CEOs and Corporations Can Fuse Values and Value Creation.* Recent reports that he has co-authored include *Gearing Up: From Corporate Responsibility to Good Governance and Scalable Solutions* and *Risk & Opportunity: Best Practice in Non-Financial Reporting.* He is also Chair of The Environment Foundation, Chair of the Environmental and Social Committee of the Association for Chartered and Certified Accountants (ACCA), a member of the Board of Trustees of the Business & Human Rights Resource Centre, a member of the Advisory Board of an ING sustainability investment fund, and a member of the Advisory Council of the UK Export Credit Guarantees Department. In 1989, he was elected to the UN Global 500 Roll of Honour for his "outstanding environmental achievements."

Nathan Greidanus is a Ph.D. candidate and research associate in the Strategy and Global Management area at the Haskayne School of Business, University of Calgary. He also holds an MBA in entrepreneurship, and Bachelor degrees in Finance and Psychology. His research interests center on international business, sustainable development, and entrepreneurship, with his dissertation research focusing on the interface between large multinational enterprises and small entrepreneurial firms. Nathan has both presented and submitted papers on such topics as "The Multinational's Role in Sustainable Development," "Sustainable Development Innovation in the Canadian and Brazilian Biotechnology Industries," and "Internal Corporate Venturing in Family Firms."

Jennifer J. Griffin is Associate Professor of Strategic Management and Public Policy at The George Washington University, School of Business in Washington, DC. She teaches courses in business and public policy, corporate social responsibility, managing strategic issues and corporate strategy. A "Faculty of the Year" MBA teaching award winner, she was also designated a GW Institute of Public Policy (GWIPP) Research Scholar in 2002. Her research interests are in corporate public affairs, stakeholder relations, and corporate social impact. She has published numerous management journal articles and has been an invited speaker at the U.S. Public Affairs Council, the Canadian Conference Board, the Australian Centre for Corporate Public Affairs (ACCPA), and the

Washington Campus, among others. Jennifer has served as a Trustee of the Board for the Foundation for Public Affairs and as a board member of the International Association for Business and Society.

Fruzsina M. Harsanyi has been Vice President Global Public Affairs for Tyco International since September 2003. Previously she served as Senior Vice President, Public Affairs and Communications for ABB Inc., Vice President for Government Affairs for Combustion Engineering, Director of Government Affairs for The Continental Group, and Special Assistant in the Office of Legislative and Intergovernmental Affairs at the Department of Housing and Urban Development. She serves as a faculty member of the Corporate Public Affairs Institute in Melbourne, Australia.

John F. Mahon is Professor of Management and the first John M. Murphy Chair of International Business Policy and Strategy at the Maine Business School, University of Maine. Prior to his appointment at Maine, Professor Mahon held the positions of Professor of Strategy and Policy, and Chair of the Strategy and Policy Department, at the School of Management at Boston University. He has authored or co-authored over 85 papers and book chapters. He is also the co-author of an introductory text in management, and the author or co-author of over 70 cases in strategy, general management, and public policy/public affairs. Professor Mahon was awarded the Issue Management Council's Intellectual Leadership Award, the first ever given to an academic for the impact his research and executive education has had on the discipline and practice of issues management, and he and his colleagues received an "Outstanding Achievement in Leadership Preparation by Colleges and Universities" from the American Association of School Administrators for the Boston Leadership Academy. Professor Mahon has served as the Chair of the Social Issues in Management Division of the National Academy of Management and as President (and co-founder) of the International Association for Business and Society, and has co-founded another group—Business Issues and Society. Professor Mahon is Associate Editor of *Business and Society* and serves on several editorial boards.

Marcia P. Miceli is Professor of Management at the McDonough School of Business at Georgetown University, where she teaches in the area of human resource management. One stream of her research focuses on whistleblowing in organizations; together with Dr. Janet P. Near at Indiana University, she has published many articles in leading refereed journals, chapters, and a book on the topic of whistleblowing. A second stream of published work focuses on organizational compensation systems.

Janet P. Near holds the Coleman Chair of Management in the Kelley School of Business at Indiana University. Her research concerns whistleblowing in organizations and the relationship between work and nonwork domains of life, focusing on job and life satisfaction. She teaches in the area of organization theory and design.

Douglas G. Pinkham is president of the Public Affairs Council, the leading international association for public affairs professionals. The Council is a non-partisan, non-political organization that provides training, "best practice" information, and benchmarking services to the profession. Pinkham was elected to head the Council in 1997. He serves on the boards of the Boston College Center for Corporate Citizenship, the Center for Ethics in Government, and the European Centre for Public Affairs.

Peder Michael Pruzan-Jørgensen is a manager with PricewaterhouseCoopers' Sustainable Business Solutions in Copenhagen, Denmark. He specializes in corporate sustainable management, responsible supply chain management, labor market policy, and sustainability assurance and reporting. He is editor of *Sustainability Quarterly*, a quarterly newsletter on sustainability and corporate social responsibility published by PricewaterhouseCoopers. Prior to joining PricewaterhouseCoopers he worked for several years with the Danish Foreign Service, during which time he served as the Danish representative in the United Nations General Assembly's 3rd Committee, as well as on the board of the UN Commission on the Status of Women. Mr. Pruzan-Jørgensen regularly contributes as a writer and speaker on issues related to sustainability management.

Alan Rugman holds the L. Leslie Waters Chair of International Business at the Kelley School of Business at Indiana University, where he is also Director of the IU CIBER. He is also an Associate Fellow at Templeton College, University of Oxford. Dr. Rugman has published widely, appearing in leading refereed journals that deal with economic, managerial, and strategic aspects of multinational enterprises and with trade and investment policy. His recent books include: *Multinationals as Flagship Firms* (co-author), *International Business* (co-author), *The Oxford Handbook of International Business* (co-ed), and *The Regional Multinationals*. Dr. Rugman is President of the Academy of International Business from 2004 to 2006.

Karen E. Schnietz is Associate Professor of strategy at the Graziadio School of Business and Management at Pepperdine University in California. Her research focuses on the impact of public policies, particularly trade policies, on the competitive and strategic environment of firms. Her research has been published in *Business History Review*, *Business & Politics*, *Corporate Reputation Review*, *International Organization*, and the *Journal of International Business Studies*, among other journals.

Jodie Thorpe is a Senior Advisor with SustainAbility, an international think-tank and consultancy specializing in business strategy and sustainable development. She is the coordinator of SustainAbility's Latin American "Emerging Economies" program, and advises leading companies on corporate responsibility, with a special focus on the finance sector. She is co-author of a number of SustainAbility reports, including *Influencing Power: Reviewing the Conduct and Content of Corporate Lobbying, Gearing Up: From Corporate Responsibility to Good Governance and Scalable Solutions*, and *Developing Value: The Business Case for Sustainability in Emerging Markets*.

Manuel Velasquez is the Charles J. Dirksen Professor of Business Ethics and Professor of Management at Santa Clara University. The author of numerous articles and case studies on business ethics, he is also author of *Business Ethics: Concepts and Cases* (6th edition) and past President of the Society for Business Ethics.

Alain Verbeke holds the McCaig Research Chair in Management at the Haskayne School of Business, University of Calgary in Canada. He is also associated with Templeton College, Oxford University (UK), and the Solvay Business School, Vrije Universiteit Brussel (Belgium). He has extensive managerial and consulting experience in multinational strategic planning.